BIG BROTHER

BIG BROTHER
The Inside Story

Narinder Kaur

First published in Great Britain in 2007 by
Virgin Books Ltd
Thames Wharf Studios
Rainville Road
London
W6 9HA

A catalogue record for this book is available from
the British Library.

ISBN 978 0 7535 1294 4

The paper used in this book is a natural, recyclable product
made from wood grown in sustainable forests. The
manufacturing process conforms to the regulations of the
country of origin.

Typeset by TW Typesetting, Plymouth, Devon

Printed and bound in Great Britain by
Mackays of Chatham PLC

This book is dedicated to my mother, Harbans, who taught me that no matter how bad things got 'kismet koi kho ne sag deh', meaning 'no one can take your destiny from you'.

CONTENTS

FOREWORD

Big Brother is all about quick fame, but not necessarily success. People often think the two go hand in hand but as you will see by reading the ex-contestants' stories in this book, this is often far from the case. If you dare go into the *Big Brother* House, you will probably have overnight notoriety and even some monetary success, but it's not all red carpets and premières.

There's a harsh lesson to be learned from this quick-fix fame – people have been damaged and hurt. Some have had great experiences and some have even managed to forge a career, but more often than not they were people who took part in the earlier series. These days it seems some people take part for the wrong reasons – to get into the papers – but they fail to realise they can't control what the papers print. As *Big Brother* heads into its eighth series, housemates are guaranteed fame (or at least infamy). Some people think fame can bring happiness, but that isn't guaranteed – there is a dark side to fame. Some contestants think their lives will change forever – but they probably won't. They are just as likely to be chewed up and spat out by the post-*Big Brother* media frenzy as achieve lasting success.

Big Brother does do one good thing: it makes you realise what is important in life. I think this book should serve as a warning to all those who are thinking of applying for any reality TV programme – think twice and if you still think you're hard enough, bring it on! I'll always be watching.

Brian Dowling, 2007

INTRODUCTION

'When will I be famous?' asked Bros back in the days, and millions of youngsters sang along with them. Well, nowadays the kids know that all you need to do to be famous is to just be yourself. Gone are the days when you'd hear a child say, 'When I grow up I want to be a doctor.' Now, in our celebrity-obsessed times, you're more likely to hear a child say, 'When I grow up I want to be famous,' and what they really mean is that they want to be famous for being famous. And who's to blame? The education system? Paris Hilton? *OK* and *Heat* magazines? Or reality TV – namely the TV phenomenon that is the godfather of them all – *Big Brother*? All of the above are largely, though not entirely responsible for creating this new kind of celebrity.

The fact is this: *Big Brother* is huge and I mean HUGE. Every episode is watched by five million people and viewing figures rise to ten million on eviction nights. It has redefined the history of television single-handedly and it has created a whole new brand of celebrity – you don't need talent for it, whether you like it or not, all you soap stars!

You don't need to have worked for it: it's microwave fame – just pop yourself into the most famous show in Britain and in less than fifteen minutes you will become a household name. It's easy, it's fast and, just like junk food, it's often not very good for you.

The recent episodes of alleged bullying and racism in *Celebrity Big Brother* caused an international scandal and generated the most complaints to Ofcom in TV history. Tony Blair had an opinion and Gordon Brown called on the nation for a vote of tolerance. Endemol, the makers of *Big Brother*, couldn't have dreamed up publicity like this.

I was not surprised by the events that unfolded within the House in *Celebrity Big Brother* or what happened in the outside world – as an ex-contestant, I knew how powerful this show was. Just by the mere act of walking out of that House and down the street I discovered the devastating effect it could have, and the reaction it could trigger from the public and the media alike. I felt the passion, the anger and the happiness people showed me. I used to be dumbstruck at the sheer volume and mass hysteria that surrounded me – did people really feel this strongly?

TV critic Sharon Marshall told me, 'Back when *Big Brother* began we knew three things sold newspapers for certain: Diana, Jordan and *Big Brother*.' Six years down the line and I cease to be shocked, as it has become a part of my everyday life.

There are now around a hundred former housemates, some drifting around aimlessly, some the walking wounded, some who went back to their old lives as best they could, and some, well . . . who knows? But they are the reason I chose to write this book. They are the contestants, the stars for all their faults, for all their shame and for all the entertainment they gave Britain.

Big Brother is Britain's national obsession: we want to watch them, know them, befriend them, everything them – like stalkers. Rachel Morris, a psychotherapist who has worked for Endemol on the show, told me that, '*Big Brother* was a programme made for popular psychology, for the people to sit at home and analyse. Pop psychology for the layman. Psychology made easy to read for the untrained person.'

There are many other reasons why I decided to write this book – it was a long time coming. For six years now I have seen how it has become fashionable to take the piss out of contestants, to mock them and laugh at them, to love them and leave them. They were never allowed to be cool, they were never allowed to be anything other than desperate wannabes who made fools of themselves time and time again, and it just seemed so unfair. They went from being loved by millions to being the lowest of the low, but still the public wanted to know all about the whole process.

Ever since my release from the *Big Brother* House I've been continually stopped on the street and asked, 'What was it like?', 'Why did you apply?' and 'What are you doing now?' It was obvious that despite all the interviews with housemates, the TV coverage and the headlines, people still felt that they didn't know the whole story. The public appetite was amazing.

I couldn't escape *Big Brother*. It was there all the time and I thought, if you can't beat them, join them. What did I have to lose? That's the beauty of being a laughing stock – you have nothing to lose. I'm not scared.

I was grown up enough and ugly enough to know that I'd never get a book deal to tell just my own saga, so I thought, well, why not put a number of ex-contestants' stories into one book? Even as I thought about it I knew it sounded impossible. What was I thinking? Who'd be interested in that? I put the idea to my agent and she told me to do my research, write up a proposal and a few chapters. I'd never done anything like that before, but hey, what else does a bored mum have to do all day at home?

And that's where the drama began. I knew it would never be easy, but it's funny how desperation works. I wanted this to happen. I started my book and all the dramas that ensued could have made a whole new reality TV programme – no, I'm not fishing for a series (well, maybe a little – once a wannabe always a wannabe).

I did my research, I knew I had the contacts – I was practically a walking address book for *Big Brothers* past. And that's where the adventure began. If I could tell you the stories! Brian Dowling knows them all, because I'd ring him every day and say, 'You're not gonna believe this one!' and he'd reply 'Now what?' and it got to a point where, although my aim was to sympathise with the ex-contestants, I seriously began to understand why some of them had got such a bad name for themselves.

Some that I contacted were quite frankly rude, unprofessional and thought far too much of themselves. I'm not naming any names, but one texted me at four o'clock in the morning demanding an extortionate fee that was considerably more than I was getting paid to put the book together! One would only do the book if it was going to include Halle Berry, because otherwise why would she want to be involved in a book with *Big Brother* people? One wanted their contract to be checked by lawyers in both Scottish and English law and a guarantee of dinner with Brian Dowling. One agreed to give me an interview but then would always be hungry and faint on the other end of the phone when it came to the interview.

One girl is obsessed with the idea that she's going to be the next Michael Parkinson and constantly whinges and whines about how *Big Brother* 'ruined her life'. She told me she would only give me a single quote for my book, but honestly I didn't want this to be a book full of moaning and griping and that's all she would have brought to it. Most former housemates wanted copy approval but you can put that down to lessons they've learned the hard way after leaving the *Big Brother* House.

It's important to emphasise that these were only a handful of *Big Brother* people, but it did make me see why the rest of us all get tarred with the same brush. And that made me sad because on the whole *Big Brother* contestants, especially the ones that are included in this book, are fantastic. They gave me time, professionalism and were basically just lovely people. They don't want to extend their fifteen minutes of fame by giving their stories. They simply wanted to tell their side. Whether it was a happy one, or a sad one, they felt it was time.

But many former housemates just simply couldn't do it. They found life hard enough after the show and wanted to get on with their lives. And I really, really respected that. Often I'd have to sit down after an interview and actually cry; I couldn't believe just how bad a time they had had and how they neither sought sympathy nor expected any.

Not that anyone offered sympathy: 'It was your choice. Deal with it.' But I felt for them, I really did, because I went through it too. Which is why this book had to be written. Let's be honest: everyone and his dog has an opinion on *Big Brother* and that's fine because that's the beauty of the show, but the only person's opinion that matters is that of the person who went through it. Full stop. If you want to know, what *really* happens, then keep reading.

Big Brother began in 2000. Back then virtually nothing was known of 'reality TV' and the contestants of the very first series had no idea what a phenomenon it would become. Today a British summer isn't a summer without the appearance of *Big Brother* in our living rooms and in our lives. The years since have been a fascinating journey taking us to the edge of our seats and introducing us to people we otherwise would never have met. They become our friends and our enemies, they entertain us for ten weeks and dominate our lives and the headlines.

But is what we see on our telly a true account of what happened? After perhaps the most profound and public experience of their lives, many housemates talk about being 'unfairly edited' and manipulated, and pilloried in the notoriously unforgiving British press. Do they have any right to complain? After all, they know what they are letting themselves in for, as their critics shout back. So it's fair is it? That their lives are now in limbo or even ruined?

When *Big Brother* began it seemed that little was known of life 'after' fast fame and overnight notoriety. What became of these people? What happened to their lives when they went home? Did their dreams come true? And in the immortal words of the *Fame* song, did they live forever? I have always wanted to write a book addressing the profound experience a *Big Brother* person undergoes, by his own choosing. Yet, many articles that I – and probably you too – have read about these contestants concentrated on the salacious, sleazy and glorified aspects. I have tried to create a book that would do justice to the experience of life after fame.

Big Brother is more than just fifteen minutes of fame – its effects are emotional, physical and social and I have never read anything that addresses these aspects. Some of the stories here are not radically new but I have looked at them in a different way than the dreaded and tedious BIG BROTHER RUINED MY LIFE view, which is one dimensional. All of these issues I have tried to address in the following interviews.

My name is Narinder and I was the first Asian to enter the most famous house in Britain.

1. WHY DID YOU DO IT?

The stuff that dreams are made of

(The Maltese Falcon, 1941)

You're standing in the queue in Asda and you know that they've clocked you – they keep turning around and having a quick sneaky glance and at first you think you have a crumb on your face or worse, some kind of foul substance on your clothes, and you start to wipe imaginary debris off yourself but there's nothing there, and then it clicks. Oh. They're staring because you were on *Big Brother*, *five years ago*.

Then comes the approach – they march right up to you and demand: 'Why did you do it?' That's the one, the most asked question, and believe you me, it's a question that every one of the hundred-odd ex-contestants have asked themselves, over and over again. It happens first in that fog-like mental haze after entering the House – at some point during our stay we sit and ponder, why did I apply for this and how did I get *here*? and trust me, we have a lot of time on our hands to think it over.

And so we begin retracing the journey that led us to some disposable, makeshift house in the Big Smoke with cameras watching our every move, and the press sharpening their knives – oops, sorry, *pencils* – ready to pounce on us like a lion on its prey.

*   *   *

I was a wannabe. I'd been trying to get into TV since I was 12 when I'd applied to be a presenter on Network 7, and I'd sent out CVs for literally hundreds of TV jobs and attended countless auditions but all to no avail. I was no fool though. I still studied and got a degree in law – I knew I had to have a back-up plan. I got into acting – I did theatre, I went to Bollywood because there was never any work for Asian actors here, but I came back pretty soon when I realised I was expected to sleep with dirty, grotty old men just to get a cameo because I wasn't the daughter of someone famous. When the *Big Brother* advert came up I thought, this could be my last chance, my last stab at making it.

Some of you will laugh at the next bit – the really cruel will roar with laughter, I have no doubt – and some will shake their heads disbelievingly but here goes: seeing that first 'Have you got what it takes to be on *Big Brother*?' advert was almost like, well, love at first sight. There, I said it! OK, not exactly love, but the same shock you get when you see something and you think, wow, and you want it so bad that you can't sleep at night.

It's a challenge, and you just have to have that man, bag, dress, car, house, whatever. Yes, I do have what it takes, you think, my mates tell me I'm funny, bubbly, different and that I'd 'sooo win it'. Then you think, well, what's the harm in trying? What's the worst that could happen? They might just say 'no' and nobody need ever find out.

Of course, not everyone has the same reaction. The vast majority pride themselves on never even contemplating applying for a show as so obviously, *disgustingly* trashy as *Big Brother*, and they would all agree that the kind of people that apply are 'egocentric, fame-seeking prima donnas' who would do anything to achieve that blind, furious, nothing-will-stop-me kind of fame. And they're the ones who ask, 'What on earth possessed you to apply for that thing?'

But you can't just write it off as 'attention seeking' or 'a bad childhood' – the 100,000 would-be *Big Brother* contestants that apply every year can't be the only 100,000 people in Great Britain with those 'issues'.

What would drive an individual with a normal life and nice little job or even a great career to turn it upside down, rip it from its very foundations and throw it up in the air with zero hope of ever catching it again? And why-oh-why would you go on a TV show that exposes your entire being, from your zits to your tits – men and women alike – to your arse, and basically make an 'ass' of yourself in front of God and the whole world? Well, if you put it like that, why indeed? It's a good question.

BOYD HILTON, TV Editor, *Heat*

What is it that separates the 100,000 people that apply for *Big Brother* and the 56,990,000 people that don't apply? Being self-obsessed, attention-seeking, egotistical, fame-seeking people, that's what. But I'm not saying that I think that's immoral. They are deluded in that they think it will make them famous in the long term, and it's that lack of awareness that makes them funny and interesting often. Thank God they exist.

GARY THOMPSON, Senior Associate Editor, *News of the World*

There was quite a bit of hype in the trade press about *Big Brother* and I remember reading it and it struck me as interesting because no one had done anything like this before. The idea of people being locked in a house for nine weeks just seemed really quirky and weird. It seemed to come along at the right time – people were interested in reality TV and it was a nice marriage of ordinary real life people and showbiz.

MELANIE HILL, *Big Brother One*

I happened to watch the Channel 4 documentary on the Dutch *Big Brother*. It showed what happened to the winners and the success that they had afterwards, but what they didn't say on the programme was that this is a kind of monster that takes you over. The key thing about it was that when you were watching the documentary you didn't see that it was tabloid TV or that the Dutch one was twice as long.

The Dutch version was the first and the British the second and at the end of the show they gave out a number to call if you wanted to apply for the British *Big Brother*. I wanted to be involved because I'm a bit of a geeky nerd and technically it looked amazing – cameras everywhere, the programme had to be turned around in 24 hours, live streaming . . .

I honestly found the whole concept fascinating and because in those days Channel 4 was a niche channel – the one for minorities – I thought it would be a kind of docu-soap. I thought they never did stuff like tabloid TV. This programme should have been on ITV. Channel 4 made these honest documentaries and that's what I thought of it, a real learned educational programme about how a group of people live together. A psychological and sociological experiment. I was very naïve.

The winning of the £70,000 was underplayed as far as I was concerned. I just thought it was so organic to bring people to live together, and back then we had to grow our own vegetables, bake our own bread – real basic living – and I wanted the challenge of seeing how I would survive living with these other people.

SHARON MARSHALL, TV Critic, *This Morning*

I think the problem is that a lot of people go into *Big Brother* thinking it's an easy route into a different life and they think that by being on screen and living in a house for a few weeks they will automatically qualify for a career in showbiz. This whole idea of instant celebrity only works in a handful of cases.

AMMA ANTWI, *Big Brother Two*

It was out of boredom, I applied for fun, a laugh, and I thought it would be an easy thing to do. Not many people had done it before me. It's as simple as that; I'd watched a couple of episodes of *Big Brother One* but that was it really. I never thought I'd get chosen.

MAKOSI MUSAMBASI, *Big Brother Six*

Big Brother started the year I came to the UK . . . There are so many reasons why I applied for *Big Brother*, the first and initial honest reason is that I needed to get out of what I was doing. I was a nurse doing the night shift and it was a particularly bad evening. I'd had three cardiac arrests and one patient did a diarrhoea-type poo all down my leg. There I was crying and wiping myself in the staff room and I started thinking of so many different things – I couldn't afford to get my mum's operation done, I couldn't do this job anymore . . . Everything started flashing back at me and then the *Big Brother* advert came on the telly and I thought, you know what? I'm gonna do it. I called the number and decided to go to the Birmingham auditions, but everyone I told kept saying that I would never get on and that just made me more determined to get through. I always want to do the opposite thing.

DEREK LAUD, *Big Brother Six*

Two basic reasons – the first is I've always had an interest in politics and the one thing that I increasingly came to realise was that more and more people were voting in reality TV contest and fewer and fewer people – especially young people – were voting in general elections. I was beginning to ask myself, why is this? And there's something actually odd about it because in reality TV contests people actually pay to vote. You give them the chance to vote for their government for free and they don't exercise that choice.

The other thing was that, given that politics is about people, I was wondering why it was that politicians were appearing less and less like real people and I think that this has something to do with the rise of popular reality TV shows, and the way that TV has changed. Now the viewer can become the centre of the drama from their own living room and affect the outcome. These reality TV shows ask the viewer, 'Who appears most real to you? Who's the most authentic?'

That was essentially the judgement they were making on *Big Brother* and at the same time as they looked at these people on TV and viewed them as 'real' people, they looked at politicians and conversely thought of them as 'unreal' people because they talk about issues through the concept and ideology and not through the prism of ordinary people's experience.

That's why I decided I was going to do something about it, that I was going to use this opportunity, because I'd just been involved in the last General Election and went around the country in search of votes and I began to think, why can't we enthuse people? The people that are involved in politics don't appeal to the voter, so I was going to put myself in a reality TV contest as a political person and see how long I could survive in a contest and I think it's reasonable to conclude that I didn't do too badly – I got more votes than the entire Shadow Cabinet combined in the last General Election.

EUGENE SULLY, *Big Brother Six*

I was never a fan of *Big Brother* and my mates used to watch it and I always used to say, 'God, why you watching this?' and they'd reply, 'Actually you'd be good on *Big Brother*.' I'd been to a *Blind Date* audition in the past, you know, thought I might get on TV. Why? Because I always liked working in that TV environment. I liked being at the forefront and being seen. I was always the outcast at school, I'd go up to people and put a mike in their face and say 'What d'ya think?' but it would never come to anything. So one day, I happened to be in Glasgow and I went to pick up my mate's girlfriend from the *Big Brother* audition and I thought I can either sit here like a tit in my car and wait for her or I can join the queue.

RACHEL MORRIS, Psychotherapist, *Big Brother*

The most common question that I get asked is, 'Why would someone put themselves up for *Big Brother*?' I believe we are a society of people desperate for attention and fame would appear the most direct route to it. As reality television is the most direct route to fame, being a *Big Brother* housemate appears to make perfect sense. The characters selected are almost always the attention-seeking type. Each has found a way to successfully draw attention from within their relatively small worlds and if it feels great to be appreciated by fifty people, the assumption is that it will feel incrementally greater to be appreciated by hundreds of times that number.

ALEX SIBLEY *Big Brother Three*

I thought it would be a stepping stone for me getting the Nobel Peace Prize – only joking. As a model it was just another modelling job, you do it and you get another job from it. If I'm going to be blatantly obvious, everyone likes the idea of getting famous, making loads of money and doing very little for it and that's it. I'd never watched *Big Brother*, because I'd always been abroad modelling, so Endemol told me to watch the DVDs from *Big Brother One* and *Two* but as you know, you don't really learn much from them.

SOPHIE PRITCHARD, *Big Brother Three*

The money, that was it really. You could win £70,000. I didn't really understand the concept of *Big Brother* because I'd been working abroad on cruise ships for the past two years. I didn't really know how big the media interest was . . . They did tell me to watch the tapes of *Big Brother* but I didn't, because it's just one of those things. You never think that you'll get in, so I didn't bother watching the tapes for fear of jinxing myself.

I thought it would be a fun thing to do, but I didn't know or realise the enormity of the show and how many people actually watched it. Even though I went in midway through the series I hadn't been watching it . . . And then one day I was at work and they phoned me and said, 'We're waiting for you outside,' and they took me home and I packed my bags and went into the House on the Sunday.*

KINGA KAROLCZAK, *Big Brother Six*

I'm always loved singing from an early age and wanted to be a singer, but I never seemed to get my break. It was a real struggle. I was working in a call centre; the monotony of working the same old routing nine-to-five every day was getting to me and I wanted desperately to do something different with my life.

---

* Two BB3 housemates, Sandy Cumming and Sunita Sharma, walked out of the House. Sophie therefore joined the House a few weeks into the series as a replacement.

The auditions for *Big Brother* came up and I thought, why not? I could do this. I discussed with my singing manager at the time whether I should go for it and he said it might help with my career. That's how I thought of it. I felt that if I got myself onto *Big Brother* that I'd be able to do my music and it's so hard to get a record deal these days. If I had the publicity behind me and a fan base, after all five million watch *Big Brother* – then someone would buy my single – that's how I thought of it.

EMMA GREENWOOD, *Big Brother Five*

I had always liked being on stage and have been performing since I was five years old, dancing all around the UK and singing in choirs, entering singing competitions. I just loved being on stage. I want to perform in front of thousands of people – the atmosphere, the feeling of everyone clapping and watching you, getting compliments on your performance, you know?

I was at my peak at fourteen but then I started mixing with the wrong crowd. I was brought up in this council estate and I started doing lots of crazy stuff – drinking, smoking twenty joints a day, raving in Canal Street and then wagging off school the next day. As a result I missed all my drama and singing classes and that's what stopped me pursuing my dream. I wanted it back and knew I just had to get away, so I packed my bags and went to work in Spain but it didn't work out either – the manager was awful to me and so I came back home.

I managed to get a job in an office and one day a friend came in and said, 'Emma you just have to go for the *Big Brother* auditions coz you'd be perfect,' and a light bulb went on in my head – 'Oh really?' – and all of a sudden I got really determined and smart. I read up everything I could find on the net about what they were looking for, and it said things like, 'Stand out from the crowd, be different.' And I thought, perfect, this is my way of getting back on track to my dream. I didn't do it to be famous but to get into that media circle and get contacts.

VICTOR EBUWA, *Big Brother Five*

I did it for the money. One hundred per cent. The fame only comes into it if you stay in the house long enough, so obviously I wanted the fame but it's not my choice.

SISSY (JOANNE) ROONEY, *Big Brother Four*

I applied because I was at a point in my life when I wasn't happy in my job and all me mates said I should apply and that I'd be good at it. Having said that I hadn't really watched *Big Brother*. I probably only saw the last two weeks of *Big Brother One* and I hadn't really watched the other series, as in, I never watched live streaming – all I ever saw was thirty minutes on Channel 4 of, 'Oh, isn't this a laugh!' and I had never read any tabloids or *Heat*. I had never read any BIG BROTHER RUINED MY LIFE stories.

So, anyway, my sister emailed me the application form and said, 'Go on, I dare you,' and if someone dares me, then I just have to do it. And I thought, what the hell. I didn't really have major expectations – I just didn't know. I wish I had gone in thinking, I'm gonna win this show and get this and that, but I simply didn't have that head on.

BRIAN DOWLING, Winner, *Big Brother Two*

I had seen the trailer for the first *Big Brother*, and they were looking for ten people to live together during the summer. Me and my friends were watching it and they said, 'Oh my God, Brian, you're a bit of a show off – you should do that.' Bear in mind I was an air steward – this is seven years ago – and for me it was about living in a house with ten people and they made out that this was a chance to do something different instead of travelling for the summer. And that's how I thought of it.

So I rang the number and it was an answering machine. I said, 'Hi, I'm Brian Dowling, I live in Bishops Stortford and I'm an air steward.' The application form arrived and I started reading all the questions and it all seemed like too much – it was so in depth and then my (now ex-) boyfriend and my parents were saying, 'No way are you doing this show, it's ridiculous – cameras in the toilet and showers!' and I went, 'OK.' And then obviously I watched the first one and I was obsessed.

I watched the last three weeks of it when the whole Nasty Nick thing kicked off* – it was on the news. I remember my flight had landed early and we all ran home just to watch it. My mates kept saying I should have done it. Then the auditions came up for *Big Brother Two*. Again I rang for an application form. The boyfriend that had discouraged me from doing *Big Brother One* had just sent me a text breaking up with me, and I was gutted. There were two pineapple Bacardi Breezers in the fridge; I drank them and thought, fuck you, and filled out the forms and sent them off.

KATE LAWLER, Winner, *Big Brother Three*

I was working in investment banking after returning from Tokyo where I'd lived with my ex for three months. I was bored at work and at that point my twin, Karen, who is the biggest TV addict – compared to me who hardly ever watched it – had watched *Big Brother* religiously from Day One but I hadn't. I'd even bought her the *Big Brother* book for Christmas. I knew about everyone in series two because my sis bought *Heat* and she talked about it all, and I knew Brian Dowling had won and my sis decided that she wanted to do *Big Brother*.

There was so much hype surrounding the *Big Brother Three* auditions because *Big Brother Two* had been so fucking great that everybody couldn't wait for the next series. I was, like, 'cool and I'll help you get on,' and because I was at work doing nothing much, I went on the Channel 4 website and printed off the application form and it was like 25 pages long. I'd been standing at the printer for ten minutes and so I rang up my sis and said, 'It's 25-odd pages long – are you having a laugh?' and then I went through some of the questions over the phone

---

* 'Nasty Nick' – Nick Bateman (BB1) tried to influence voting in the House by writing notes on pieces of paper he had smuggled in. It caused a media storm, although the housemates were unaware until late in the series. After a confrontation in the House he was removed by Big Brother for cheating.

with her and they were quite funny and my sis was like, 'Oh, fuck it, I can't be bothered.' So I just chucked it to one side and left it.

Then one day I was bored at work and just started filling it in and I said to my sis, 'Shall I do *Big Brother?*' and she was like, 'Yes, fucking do it – you'd be great. I'd love to watch you,' and I asked her how much money was involved and she told me seventy grand and because I hadn't ever watched it, I thought there would be phones in there!

All I knew at that point was that you lived in a house with ten others and that someone was evicted each week but I didn't know that there was no contact with the outside world and that we'd have to do tasks and things, but my sis explained it all to me and I thought, sweet, it seems easy.

Then I asked my twin, 'Who won last year?' Brian. 'Who won the year before?' Craig Phillips. And I was like, 'Well, it's about time a girl won it, so if I do it this year my chances are high, coz a girl just has to win it soon.' I thought, I'm only gonna do this if I win it, and win seventy grand.

The ultimate reason for doing *Big Brother* at first was for the whole experience of living in this house – how cool would that be? – and secondly winning seventy grand tax free. And thirdly a girl winning. The fame was something I knew but just didn't think about. I loved the idea of doing tasks, being voted off and being in this house with others and have that whole experience of saying, 'I went in this house, got filmed blah blah . . .' What a good story to tell your grandchildren.

My sis said, 'But you'll be on TV. Aren't you bothered everything will be seen and you'll be famous?' and when Karen said that, I replied, 'Yeah but I won't really be famous.' It kind of just went over my head. At that point I just wanted to be in the House and win seventy grand. My elder sister had just got married and bought a house, my twin sis was engaged and had bought a house and I thought, how am I gonna afford to move out? How? On my own? So if I win seventy grand I can afford to buy my own flat. That's what I thought. Sweet. I was pragmatic.

SAMANTHA HEUSTON, *Big Brother Six*

I wasn't really a fan of *Big Brother*. I had watched Kate Lawler's year but I didn't think then that I would ever do it. Then I was at uni, bored with my degree, so I did it.

ANTHONY HUTTON, Winner, *Big Brother Six*

I was a definite, definite *Big Brother* fan. I have watched all of them – the first one I watched because I was intrigued, but then I just got glued to it. I thought, this show is amazing. Then I watched the second one and got hooked again. *Big Brother Five* was quality. I used to watch it with me mates and I remember once when I was driving up to Scotland with my 70s dancing lads and we were all in the car going, 'If I was on *Big Brother* I'd do this and I'd do that.'

Yes, I did want fame, but more than that I was the biggest *Big Brother* fan ever and I thought me mates would think I was a legend if I got on the show.

NADIA ALMADA, Winner, *Big Brother Five*

I did want the fame, yes, I did. When I was younger my mother said I always wanted to be famous – I was always attracting attention. My mother knew I'd be famous – I always stood out from the crowd, but I suffered a lot because of that as well because attention gathers criticism too. But I did want the fame. And fame is also escapism.

I came from a poor family, a working-class family, and I thought that with fame comes money – of course, it doesn't always work out like that – but I wanted the money, the travelling all over the world. I wanted good and better things in my life.

And I had watched it from the start – I thought it was very captivating, it was a novelty and exciting. Just normal people put into a house and suddenly they become household names. Yes, I was a fan. I even watched the Dutch documentary before *Big Brother One* even started and I rang the number afterwards and they sent me an application but it was too big and I never pursued it. Then I applied for the third series and again they sent me an application form and again I didn't pursue it – I was just too lazy.

Subconsciously I think it was because I just wasn't ready in my life and head. I was interested but I was holding back. Then I had my sex-change operation in 2004 and I happened to be at my friend's house. She's Afro-Caribbean and she was sitting on the floor and I was unbraiding her hair with a toothpick, because she wanted a big change, and suddenly the *Big Brother* advert came on with a number, and so I called again. Luckily because it was no longer by application form, but by open auditions, it was easier – all I had to do was turn up and queue.

I went to the London one as I lived in Surrey. I decided to go early morning. Because I'd had my operation I felt free, just free and more confident to go for it. I was always a woman – I was always Nadia, my job was spraying fragrances in Aldos and before that I worked for Barclays Bank. The breasts I'd had done the year before, then the rest, so I felt nothing could hold me back anymore: I was ready to take on the world and explode. I was really sensing that I could face the world. Do you know what I mean? There was nothing to say anymore that I was different. I felt normal at last. So because of that, I went to the audition.

LEA WALKER, *Big Brother Seven*

I watched the first one and didn't really like it, but as the years went by I really started getting into it, then *Big Brother Four* came on and I thought, how boring, I could do better than that, and decided to go for it the next time. So the next year I went for it but got barred because I did a cosmetic surgery programme. I was really upset about that but then they called me the following year and asked me to come down.

You imagine how your life will pan out – I'm a single mother and I'm not afraid to admit I wanted the fame and the money. Of course that was the reason. I was a single mum and wanted to prove that single mums could do it. I wanted notoriety. I wanted to do this for my son, H, to make his life more comfortable. Hopefully it would change both our lives.

RICHARD NEWMAN, *Big Brother Seven*

I was a huge fan of *Big Brother*. I was. I'd been in the UK for ten years and was a fan of both the US version and the British version but both are very different. In the US the housemates decide who goes and it's a game – there is no public voting as there is here – the British version is all about popularity. I knew what *Big Brother* was all about – manipulation and mind games and, ultimately, survival. It's the working class against Big Brother.

The first *Big Brother* was a game as no one knew what it was about. My motivation for auditioning was simple – the £100,000 prize. That was it. I was 34 and waiting tables, I'd fucked up a lot in my life and at that point it was an opportunity to win £100,000. I knew fame came into it, but it was the money I thought of.

2. THE AUDITION

I'm going to make him an offer he can't refuse

(The Godfather, 1972)

I went out the night I saw the advert and thought I'd have a good think about it. I'm married, I'm Asian and I had just managed to land a good job. I'd watched the first series and knew it could all come to nothing in terms of a TV career, and even in those days I knew there was a sexy side to the show – what would my parents think? I came from a strict Indian family. I'd lived my life in chains, escaped into a marriage – a girl should surely have more to her life than just that?

It was a gamble and it might work. Then again, I'd probably not even get onto the show. I had nothing to lose. I was young and unafraid. It was a challenge, let's see how far I get, and knowing my luck I probably wouldn't even get through on the phone line. But I did and I left my details. A week later a huge application form came through the post.

I filled it in and I remember writing that I'd like Marge Simpson to play my mother in the movie of my life. I also exaggerated a lot. I told them that I was married but I was looking for a 'snog', for instance. Then I had to do a video. The first nightmare was that I didn't own a camera. The second was that anyone I knew that did have one was either on holiday or the camcorder was broken. So I had to hire one, which kept breaking, then working.

I was giving up hope. I had one day to post the darn thing before missing the deadline. I had two minutes recording time before the camcorder would pack up and a whole evening to think of what to do in that two minutes. My husband was the cameraman. What should I do? Sit on the toilet? No, that was rubbish. Pretend to cook in the kitchen? No, too noisy and wifey. I was tired and stressed by this point so I just sat in my bed and said, 'I want to entertain Britain for nine weeks.' Sod it, that's it, just post it.

Then I got a call to come to an audition. I was shocked. I dressed up meticulously and went along. Everyone was larger than life and I was just quiet; not until I had my time in front of the camera did I come to life. But still, I felt I'd wasted my time again. They just didn't seem interested and I hadn't got on with anyone in the team games.

A month later I got a call inviting me to meet the producers in London. I couldn't believe it. I was getting closer. I had never been to London or on a tube but somehow I managed to get to the location, the theatre where *Cats* was being shown. It was all so cloak and dagger. Eight o'clock in the morning. I was standing waiting and no one showed up for ages, so I began thinking I'd imagined the whole thing, then a guy turned up and took me round the corner to meet everyone. It was a good fun chat and that was that. I went home after my little adventure. I didn't hear from them again.

Will Young did it in *X Factor*, Lemar did it in *Fame Academy*, Connie Fisher did it most recently in *How Do You Solve a Problem Like Maria?* and the kids from *Fame* did it all the time. That's right – audition. Admittedly those were talent competitions and *Big Brother* is no more than a reality TV show, but you do need to have some sort of appeal to get through – a personality, a larger-than-life persona, or just something plain different about you.

So you've done the easy bit and decided to apply. Now it's the hard bit: you have to put your money where your mouth is, your eggs in one basket and your bread in the toaster. Most will opt out at this stage and slap themselves hard for ever being mad enough to apply – must have got carried away one evening after too much vino – especially when they see all the wannabes in the queues on the local news.

So what does it take to actually get up and join that line of hope and madness? What possesses someone to get up early, get ready and stand in the freezing cold waiting to be noticed and given that 'chance' of fame and fortune?

PHIL EDGAR-JONES, Creative Director, Endemol

(a) Who made the rule that only people with talent can go on TV? and (b) what is wrong with wanting to do something different with your life? Everybody wants something exciting to happen to them. There is no easy route to fame. People come to this show, we don't go about chasing them and we do make a lot of judgements and a lot of people are removed from the process because we don't feel that they are mentally robust enough to deal with it, or because we think they are completely deluded about what *Big Brother* will bring them. Then they won't be going into the House.

KEVIN O'SULLIVAN, TV Critic, *Sunday Mirror*

Well, that's just not good enough, that's pathetic. It's pathetic. They don't go fishing for these people? The whole audition process is a very exploitative process, it preys on the fact there are a lot of people out there that are desperate to be on TV – it's like the working-class kid who dreams of becoming a footballer. Reality TV has become the new escape route. *Big Brother* appeals to working-class people that feel they are in the gutter and it's a bit like football and showbiz – *Big Brother* is the new escapism for them. They see *Big Brother* as one way of hauling themselves into a brighter future.

And you can see it in their eyes, when they enter the House – they truly believe they can be this great next success. And it's how you deal with that desperation that's how you, as a Channel 4 producer, define yourself as a responsible entity. It's no good saying, 'Well everyone wants to be on TV, and we'll let them.' Look at [some of the former housemates – they are] psychologically disturbed ... They have to be a lot more responsible about who they choose . . . The producers have to take much more responsibility.

RACHEL MORRIS, Psychotherapist, *Big Brother*

In *Big Brother Five* I joined the audition process for the last week. The candidates were down to a final one hundred. They were split into groups of ten and attended a team-building type session. They were informed that they would be watched by a psychologist who would be getting a sense of who they were, what motivated them and of how genuine they were.

I've had much to do with groups in my work as a therapist and have studied the way they work, who drives them and what happens to dynamics of a group when people or places are changed, added or switched. It's for this reason I was invited to join the groups as an expert.

Before each group began, I met with the producers who gave me information about each individual in it. I was asked to pay special attention to three or four people who were particularly interesting to the producers. My role was to judge the dynamic workings of the group and to make predictions based on the behaviour of the applicants during the team-building games we played with each set. Whilst it was not my role to vet the housemates, there were occasions when I observed behaviour that made me feel doubtful of a candidates ability to withstand the pressures of *Big Brother*. When I reported these observations, I felt they were taken seriously.

It became obvious what kind of house the producers had in mind because each group was so similar. Each one seemed to include an outspoken working-class woman, a gay man, a beautiful blonde, an older woman with false boobs, a good-looking cheeky boy, an outrageous flirt and a sensible carer type. My job was to make sure that the characters they had selected were genuine and that their egos were strong enough to take the *Big Brother* challenge.

MELANIE HILL, *Big Brother One*

My audition process was very different to everyone else's, because I was working abroad a lot. I got the application form, had a glass of wine with my friends and had a laugh filling it out and sent it off, and they wanted me to come in. They kept wanting me to come in for these interactive sessions, but I was never in the country, so I never did one of those! But I just didn't think of it as a big deal because with the first series we just never knew anything, or what would come of it. We had no idea. Then they said, 'Look, if you can't make it then can you just send in a short video tape of yourself?' So I got one of my friends to film me, and I just spent ten minutes chatting about travelling and that was it. Twenty or thirty thousand had applied for it this first time. Sent the tape in. I spoke to a psychologist for just half an hour before I went in.

AMMA ANTWI, *Big Brother Two*

I didn't really have any presumptions about what the auditions would be like and when I got there I wasn't particularly surprised at the kind of people that were there, but when they started talking and expressing themselves – they were so much larger than life than me and the more O.T.T. they became, the smaller and smaller I became. I left convinced they'd never call me back.

DEREK LAUD, *Big Brother Six*

I didn't want to go. It wasn't my idea and my friends rang me up and said, 'We've just heard on the radio that there are some *Big Brother* auditions,' and I said, 'I can't go, I'm playing tennis,' and they said, 'We really think that you ought to go,' and I replied, 'I can't possibly go – I'm in my tennis whites,' and hung up and continued playing tennis. They then rang again and said, 'We will send you a car and take you up there and the car will wait for you and bring you back,' so I had nothing to lose.

I didn't know what to expect, I was in my tennis whites. I arrived and there was an enormous queue of people in fancy dress, wigs, drinking beer and lying in sleeping bags and I just grimaced at this sight and thought I can't, I just can't, I can't face this and I'm certainly not gonna queue! So I went to the front and accosted somebody and said, 'I haven't got very long, what's going on? I'm not queuing,' and they told me to come back the next day and so I did, I got up terribly early.

By now, it became a bit of a challenge – another hurdle in life – and one wanted to see if one could get through. So I arrived the next day and was ushered into the warehouse and hundreds were already there; people had slept overnight just to get seen. I went through with ten other people and I could see what the producers were saying: 'Say something about yourself in thirty seconds,' and because I was last in the queue of ten I'd heard what they all said in their thirty seconds and thought, well I don't have to do much better than that! So when it came to my turn I said, 'I'm black, I'm conservative, I'm gay, I'm a Master of Foxhounds and I've worked for two British prime ministers and you'd be absolutely stark raving mad not to choose me.' At the end everyone got up and clapped their hands and I got a stamp on my hand to go through to the next round.

EUGENE SULLY, *Big Brother Six*

So I joined the queue to see what all this malarkey was about. There were two gays in front of me that looked like the Scissor Sisters and a girl behind me that was singing like Lisa Stansfield. I felt relaxed and I was just myself. I did a number of impressions but I was told that I hadn't been successful and to go home, and then on the way home I got a phone call.

They ring you up and say, 'Are you on your own?' and invariably you never are and you just answer, 'Yes,' and they said, 'We've decided we'd like you to come back,' and I just replied 'Oh, OK, what time?' Then the next audition we were all put in groups and had to talk about who we thought was fit and who wasn't, religion and politics. They asked me what my favourite cheese was and I answered, 'Either cheddar or blue cheese.' I told them I had only had two girlfriends and they asked me whether I considered myself a geek and I replied 'No, more like an anorak.' (*laughs*) The whole audition process is like a drug: once you've got through one round you think, let's see how far I can get.

SISSY (JOANNE) ROONEY, *Big Brother Four*

It was just like being on this train and you don't really know whether you're going to get to your destination or not – the destination being the *Big Brother* train station – and I just thought, OK, well I'm on this train and if it stops at this station then great, but you never think it will. I'm a carefree 27-year-old and I went along for the ride. And it's such a long process that you never think of the repercussions carefully or seriously because you think you'll never get on . . . and then you get told a few weeks beforehand that you've been chosen and by then you're brought into the whole thing.

VICTOR EBUWA, *Big Brother Five*

It was easy going through the audition process, and let's be frank – it's only easy if you are what they are looking for. Do you know what I mean? But people come and try their hardest year after year. I only auditioned once. I walked straight up to the front and everyone who had been waiting hours started shouting, 'What you doing? What you doing?' so I started arguing with them and that was it. I got through to the next stage. It was a piece of piss.

EMMA GREENWOOD, *Big Brother Five*

I was clever about my audition; I knew I had to play a role. I saw one of the producers scouring the queue and I said, 'I love your boots,' and got her attention straight away. I'm thick as pig shit but I'm streetwise; not academically clever, but streetwise. The others in the queue were flippin' thick – they thought you had to be loud to get noticed and in-yer-face and that's the key, you have to be that. Then I spotted another producer. I knew he looked important and said, ' 'scuse me mate but I need the toilet – Man United's playing,' and he said 'What?' (it basically means you're on your period).

I think he got it. And then I asked him what he did and he said, 'I pick the people,' and I just responded, 'Oh, but I need to go to the toilet,' to get him thinking that this vital piece of info hasn't clicked in my head . . . So I'm playing 'duh-duh

... stupid' to get him thinking, 'She's a bit stupid, her.' I loved the audition, I loved playing this role, my personality but O.T.T.: enhanced, over the hills.

Then we had to go on in the room and we were told not to start till the bell went off but me being me, playing this role of thicko – I kept talking before it went off. You weren't allowed to use your mobile phone in the auditions and I knew that, but I was purposely picking up and making calls, 'Hiya Mum!' I played up big time. I knew what they wanted. I had to create this character. Phil and Shirley followed me around like a fly on shit. I knew what they wanted to hear and see.

Then they'd ring me up and say, 'Emma, you've got through to the next audition,' and I'd reply, 'Oh, really? Thanks. See you soon,' and then I'd put the phone down and scream! So I continued to play this character and they were probably thinking, is she fucking thick or what? And there's me jumping up and down on the bed thinking, you fucking suckers!

KINGA KAROLCZAK, *Big Brother Six*

In my auditions I overplayed myself slightly – I was still me but a much more exaggerated version. At the end of the day I knew so many people wanted to do this show, and that I had to stand out from everyone else.

KATE LAWLER, Winner, *Big Brother Three*

I had to do a video and I just didn't really feel like it, and I left it so late that they had already started showing *How Not to Get on Big Brother* and people's videos on E4. So I was watching it thinking, what can I do in my video? Karen was saying do something crazy and I remember my elder sister saying, 'Run down the high street naked!' and we were all sat there trying to think of all these crazy things to do and it was literally three days before I decided, why do something crazy that isn't me? Why not just put together a video that's just clips of me and what I'm about?

So I got together all these clips of me when I was younger, holidays with the girls, stuff like that and I filmed a bit extra of my dog and me doing kicky uppies, dancing in a little mini skirt up and down on my bed. Then I got a mate to edit and put music over it – the song we chose was 'Starlight'. The only bit of talking I did was 'Hi, I'm Kate and in the next couple of minutes you're gonna learn a little bit about me,' and that was it. I sent it off thinking, it will never get there. And then two weeks later I got a call asking me to come to an audition.

I remember walking down Tottenham Court Road and down this side street and into this building . . . all I could hear was this *noise* and there was all these freaks, twenty Brian Dowling wannabes and everyone was, like, so outrageous and all I could think was, this so isn't me.

Jade Goody was in my audition and I remember thinking: annoying, loud, you'd better not be in the House with me. We all got called into this room and played all these games. Everyone was so over the top. Then at the end they read out a list of who they wanted to stay, and they read Jade's name out and mine. Some of the people that hadn't been chosen were actually crying. I couldn't believe it, they were that desperate. It meant that much to them, and it occurred to me how big this thing really was, that everybody wanted to be on it.

I waited three weeks and was then called, inviting me to meet the producers and it was from that moment that I had a feeling I'd get in. My twin was saying, 'I've got a strong feeling you're gonna get in,' it was like everyone just knew I'd get in. So I met the producers and I was getting excited. I had to go to KFC in West London, Queensway. And a girl with a black umbrella was going to meet me. I didn't know, but they were filming me at that point. I then met the producers and it went really well; I just chatted about myself and then I met the psychotherapist. He couldn't understand why I wanted to do it, because he said I seemed so 'normal'. And because I hadn't watched *Big Brother*, he told me to watch it on DVD, so I did and what I gathered from them was 'If you act like an idiot, then you'll get portrayed as an idiot.'

I know they do a lot of editing but there was one girl from the first one that got naked, covered herself in clay and rubbed herself against the wall . . . She chose to do that and got called names. Nasty Nick cheated and people hated him. So I figured if I didn't get naked or cheat then I won't have any problems. I'll be alright.

BRIAN DOWLING, Winner, *Big Brother Two*

I had to make a video tape and because I'm an air steward, I made it on board an aircraft, showing me at work, talking to passengers and doing safety checks. And then I sent it off to be made and the company sent it back saying they couldn't make it because while I'm talking all you could hear was the sound of the engine! I was gutted, and thought, you know what? This isn't worth the hassle, I'm not bothering.

Then one day, all my flatmates were out and I was on my own, so I got the ironing board out, stacked it with loads of books, put a camcorder on it and just pressed record and then went, 'Hi, my name's Brian,' and I talked about my teddy bears and kept thinking, shit, why am I talking about my stupid teddy bears? After I'd said all I could, I played it back and thought, how boring, not me at all, not my personality. The first tape that couldn't get done was funnier and more me because I'm talking to passengers and just being me. I am so not going to get picked with this boring tape, I thought, but I sent it off anyway. What did I have to lose?

So, I'm back flying and I had forgotten all about it when one day my phone rang and it was a private number and I went, 'Hello?' and they said, 'Is this Brian Dowling?' and I replied, 'Yes – who's this?' and she said 'Shirley Jones from Endemol,' and I remember thinking, who's Endemol? A passenger? Another airline that I hadn't heard of yet and maybe they were headhunting me? And then she said, 'We would like to call you in for an open audition,' and I went, 'For what?' And she said, '*Big Brother*,' and I was like, 'Oh my God.'

So, a few weeks later I had my audition. We were all in a room and everyone had a tragic story to tell – the first woman who spoke had lost her house, a man had lost his mum to cancer and then the woman before me had just lost her cats in a fire. Then it was my turn to speak and the first thing I said was, 'Oh, I don't like cats,' and everyone just went silent and I couldn't talk. I just got so nervous, and one of the producers had to go and get me a glass of water! I was so embarrassed and thought, I've blown it – I'm such an idiot. I went home and just got on with my life.

I really thought I wouldn't get picked, I didn't think I was interesting enough. I was just an air steward.

SAMANTHA HEUSTON, *Big Brother Six*

I was in bed with some guy – with one of my shag buddies. Got out of bed, went back to my uni flat, didn't tell my friends and just left at about eight o'clock in the morning dressed in my orange hot pants. Hot pants always go down a treat, and I thought it would be shocking, being bright orange. I just walked in and everyone was saying, 'WOW – orange hot pants.' The producers were coming up and down the line. I swapped clothes with another guy in the queue and I did it to grab their attention, that was my intention. Prior to that I had gone and danced in the middle with some girls, I had my Walkman on, I didn't really want to talk to people in the queue, I just wanted to concentrate on what I was going to say. I had that all pre-planned – about my ten vibrators and the men I had slept with – all that sort of stuff. My intention was to go on the sex angle.

It was a sort of girl power – i.e. the vibrators being outrageous – but I was being myself. Then one of the producers, Phil, was talking to me about my vibrators and how I had broken one of them. I don't use them now, I'm quite bored with them, but they were good at the time at uni just for a release.

Some of the producers did put me off and say 'You're a slag,' I just said, 'You're a wanker, I can tell you're a wanker.' I had a feeling they would be calling me again.

ANTHONY HUTTON, Winner, *Big Brother Six*

So I joined the queue – loads of extroverts. I remember one big Scottish bloke who jumped the queue and he told me he positioned himself in a group of ten that looked boring so that he would definitely get chosen. And a couple auditioned together, I remember.

The first bit – you meet some producers and then do the group thing. We all got into an argument over who was the best looking and I was like, 'I'm the best looking.' I think I was actually (*laughs*). I told them I'm a 70s dancer, which they seemed really interested in. I then did one minute to the camera and I showed them my Superman underpants – I had them on. I dressed like that on purpose. My main line was, 'If you put me in that house I will pull.' I wasn't worried about my family, because I'm really close to me Mam and Gran and me Gran was like, 'Get on that show and have some fun.' At the end of the day, they will be dead proud of me.

Then I got an invite to come back the next day. Again, one minute to camera. Then for the next stage we had to fill in a huge application form. All me mates came with me, they all went to the bar. The audition was quite a hostile environment; I walked into a group and as I was walking over, a producer went, 'What do you think of him?' immediately, and people started giving opinions of us. One guy said, 'His hair is like a Lego man.' Everyone was competing to get on the show – it was an audition at the end of the day. I had a feeling I would get on, because I was a 70s dancer.

Then I got to meet the producers and basically I just got ridiculed, just to see if I bit. They kind of want to see how you deal with situations, how witty you are . . . I'd written on my application that I wished I was taller so they kept calling me 'shortarse'. I just saw it as me mates ripping it out of me. I knew it went well, but then I didn't hear for ages.

NADIA ALMADA, Winner, *Big Brother Five*

I went along. I didn't go naked and I didn't wear a carrot as a costume – I was just me and normal. It was cold anyway, so I had my coat on and there were naked people all over. They were filming people in the queue and I was hiding away because I didn't want to be seen. Because if I didn't get through then I didn't want the embarrassment of being seen as one of the rejects or 'here's all the desperadoes applying' (*laughs*). So I saved myself. Then I had to describe myself in one minute and I said that I was a transsexual woman. It's a big deal, I suppose, because it's new and people don't know too much about it and I accept that. It's just my niche. I lost count of the amount of times I was called back again and again for auditions and I even had an extra psych interview compared to everyone else. The closer I got the more excited I got, the more I started believing in it. But all the same I was realistic that I may never get in. I always say never throw fireworks unless you have a reason to celebrate. Fireworks come after the party.

LEA WALKER, *Big Brother Seven*

Well, I wasn't gonna bother going for starters. I'd been to the auditions the year before and got through – I was supposed to go on *Big Brother Six*. I planned my whole life – you imagine how your life will span out as a result of going in the House and then they rang me at the last minute and barred me from going on because I'd done the programme on cosmetic surgery. I was so pissed off. I was really, really upset. So when they called me the following year, I thought, bugger off, but then I thought, you know what? I'm a single mum and I want to show everyone that single mums can do this. So I agreed. My son said, 'Mum, you've always wanted to do this, just go for it.' If he'd said, 'Mum don't do it,' I'd never, ever, ever have done it.

What was very apparent was that the audition process seemed to be different from the year before. What was weird was that everyone else was being assessed but it was like I wasn't being asked to do as much compared to the others. It was clear they wanted me by hook or by crook – I hadn't even been asked to do any guinea pig runs* like all the others had, I did none of that.

---

* 'Guinea Pig run' – in recent years BB producers have placed some people who have auditioned but not been chosen for the House into a 'trial House' for a few weeks before the series begins.

RICHARD NEWMAN, *Big Brother Seven*

They don't have open auditions anymore, it's a casting call. If you look at most of the contestants in *Big Brother Seven*, most of them have done the guinea pig run from previous years. If you're a known face then chances are that you will get in one day. I've been auditioning for *Big Brother* since *Big Brother Five*! I did well and so went back for *Big Brother Six*, where I was chosen to do the guinea pig run, so by series seven they well and truly knew me and I had by now got an understanding of exactly what they were looking for. Each year I had learned more and more about what I had to do – be real, be genuine and be able to hold your own in an argument. I think they choose people from the dummy runs because they need to be sure that the people they put in the House are what they say they are – they are constantly checking and verifying and it also gives them a chance to see who you would and would not get on with. So I was a pro at this.

MAKOSI MUSAMBASI, *Big Brother Six*

I auditioned from 4 a.m. in the morning – you go through so much in the audition process, audition after audition, psychologists, producers . . . I almost felt like I was being interviewed for some job with the CIA. It was only a game show, but you really have to work for it. You are asked so much, so many forms, so many tasks, passwords to continue phone conversations! But I have a very high endurance level, and the further I got the more challenged I felt. I'd achieve one level and then that gave you a sense of satisfaction. All the way through I was confident I would get in, they called and asked me to go into the guinea pig house and I said, 'Absolutely not, you get me for the real thing or not at all. I am not a guinea pig, Makosi is not a guinea pig person.'

ALEX SIBLEY *Big Brother Three*

I went along to these group auditions and there were all sorts there – 'I'm 46 and I can still do the splits', people dancing – it was funny. I got invited back again but I was living and working in Hamburg so I couldn't always make it and I remember they wanted me to come back to do a VT [video treatment] with my parents, but I couldn't coz I had a life in Germany. I wasn't that desperate for it, and they decided to come to Germany to see me. They must have wanted it but I didn't want to get too excited – it was like any other modelling casting I went for, some you get some you don't.

3. THE TALK OF DOOM

You want the truth? You can't handle the truth

(*A Few Good Men*, 1992)

F ame! I want to live forever! Fat chance. You'll be lucky if you're remembered by your own family once you're evicted. Loved by all? Not even Princess Diana pulled that off. A pot of gold at the end of the rainbow? You're more likely to find a pot to piss in by the end of it all.

So why-oh-why do hundreds of thousands of people apply each year? Even when the papers are saturated with BIG BROTHER RUINED MY LIFE stories rather than TOP TEN BIG BROTHER EARNERS? Or is it just that you subconsciously skip over those articles whilst your eyes widen like a wolf's who's just seen dinner at the JADE WORTH EIGHT MILLION headlines? Even when you audition, the producers insist that they deliver the 'Talk of Doom' – how it may not lead to the life you expected. So what's it all about? What is this 'Talk of Doom' and why doesn't it work?

I have a very clear memory of the 'Talk of Doom'. Even though it was only the second series, the producers did, to be fair, give me warnings: 'The Asian community may go against you, have you thought about that? The press may dig up stories.' They grilled me for a good half hour and to be fair to myself too, I did take it seriously and I took it hard.

My husband and I sat and discussed everything that could possibly go wrong in terms of my family and the community.

Big Brother had, after all, been a risqué show the year before when the contestants got naked and rolled around in clay! What was a young, married Asian woman like myself thinking of by going on a show like that?

I was risking throwing away my career as a medical rep., but then again, I was taking exams that meant that theoretically I could still go back to that industry if I so wished, couldn't I? No one had said that I wouldn't be able to. What if I didn't win and made no money? Or if my family disowned me?

The fears and doubts were endless, and we would-be housemates couldn't win either way, because in those days nothing was written in stone – simply not enough people had done *Big Brother* for us to be able to predict what would happen when we were out of the House. Besides, I still thought I'd never get in, so what was the point in the what ifs? I went to bed and vowed just to get it out of my head.

These days it's very different, there are so many more BIG BROTHER RUINED MY LIFE stories and the catastrophe that faced Jade Goody, Danielle Lloyd, Jo O'Mera and Shilpa Shetty in the 2007 *Celebrity Big Brother* would and should have been enough to put off the most hardened of wannabes, but thousands still turned up for the *Big Brother* auditions that were held that same month. Not even an international race row and the spectacle of Jade and co. being hit with death threats could deter these people with stars in their eyes – why is *Big Brother* a no-brainer?

PHIL EDGAR-JONES, Creative Director, Endemol

We do make a lot of judgements and a lot of people are removed from the process because we don't feel they are mentally robust enough to deal with it. They need to have that coping mechanism to deal with the world outside afterwards. If we don't think a person has that coping mechanism or is totally deluded about what *Big Brother* will bring them, then they won't go in the House. It's transient fame, but we do tell everyone this and we say, 'You won't be the next Brian Dowling, and the chances are you won't make any money.' So

I sleep well in my bed at night because we warn everybody until we are blue in the bloody face.

KEVIN O'SULLIVAN, TV Critic, *Sunday Mirror*

They always say, 'Yes, but we have psychologists on hand to help these people and we warn them.' Even psychologists have quit because they say 'Endemol don't care'. It's not good enough because it's obviously not working – every year we have at least six contestants who say, 'It's fucked up my life,' and look back on it as the most traumatic and negative experiences of their lives. And probably most of them will in the end. It just means that the producers have an answer when people like me say, 'You are exploiting these people.'

RACHEL MORRIS, Psychotherapist, *Big Brother*

I think people go on *Big Brother* because they want their lives to change. The assumption is that it will change for the better as we do not usually knowingly make decisions to worsen our lives. *Big Brother* may change your life in one direction or another but the real disappointment is when it doesn't change anything – that your fifteen minutes only actually last fifteen minutes and you're left back where you started.

One of the things I witnessed was the 'Talk of Doom' as it was known (at least on *Big Brother Five*). It lasted an hour and a half and was given by a producer at the beginning of each group. The talk seemed to challenge every hope or assumption a candidate might have made about appearing as a housemate. It warned of the potential invasion into their privacy and the privacy of their family and loved ones. It asked them to consider the impact it could have on their family, work, social and love life and all the complications and worst-case scenarios were described and listed. Then come the success stories: Kate Lawler, Brian Dowling, Jade Goody and the point is made that while *Big Brother* can be a platform for a media career, it's not a guarantee of one. I was only privy to this very small part of the selection process but the 'Talk of Doom' in my opinion was a very fair and realistic warning. It clearly laid out the possible outcomes of becoming a house-mate, both negative and positive, using past *Big Brother* experience.

However, while you can force an applicant to listen as part of a captive audience, you can't make them hear! It's very human to listen selectively. The issue here is that the hope outweighs the risk and sometimes I wonder if that's not because the candidates feel they don't have that much to lose. Maybe they are the more vulnerable of us but that doesn't mean that vulnerable personalities shouldn't be represented on TV. To be honest, if we ban vulnerable people from telly, we'd have very few presenters or actors to entertain us. It's the act of being vulnerable that forces us to create interesting person-alities in order to distract people from seeing the real us. The problem with being a housemate is that there's nowhere to hide, so eventually your cover will fail and your vulnerability will be revealed for all to see. For some that can be devastating, for others it's an incredible freedom.

BOYD HILTON, TV Editor, *Heat*

These people are told of the risks, or they should be given this mantra: a) it's not long lasting fame, your fame will only last as long as you're in the House and b) you won't be the next Jade and c) you are selling your soul to the devil.

But they still want to do it. By *Big Brother Four*, *Five*, *Six* and *Seven* the contestants must have known what they were letting themselves in for, and I don't mean that they will know what the experience will be like in that incredibly intense situation 24/7. I mean that you know that the media will obsessively follow this thing and will pick heroes, villains and embarrassing people, and if they don't know that then they really need to have a strong word with themselves.

MELANIE HILL, *Big Brother One*

The only Talk of Doom we got was that there might be a bit of press interest but maybe not. And that was fine to me. No big deal. No one was aware what a phenomenon it would become – even Endemol didn't – when the whole Nasty Nick thing happened. They then realised that they had something on their hands that they couldn't cope with. People inside couldn't cope with the interest that they had and they had to get an external agency – John Noel – in to deal with it all.

AMMA ANTWI, *Big Brother Two*

The Talk of Doom was rubbish. They didn't tell me anything that I hadn't already thought of, for example, 'the press may talk to your family'. But in hindsight, it's what they didn't tell me. I know people may think, 'Well it was only *Big Brother Two*, what could they warn us about?' But Nasty Nick had had death threats – they didn't tell me I could have death threats and they knew that by our *Big Brother* series.

They didn't tell me all the things Mel Hill had been through. They didn't warn me that people will make up stories about you. That people will judge me when they don't even know me, that I could potentially be the victim of verbal and physical abuse by the public . . . The one thing I wish they had told me was, 'Once we are finished with you we are going to have nothing to do with you,' and at least then I would have been aware – forewarned is forearmed, so to speak.

I always thought, Endemol will look after me, because that's the impression they gave me. If they had told me that I was going to be on my own after it all finished, then I wouldn't have been so willing to have listened to everything they told me and trust everything they said! Having said that, yes of course, I still would have done *Big Brother*. Sometimes I have more balls than brains.

BRIAN DOWLING, Winner, *Big Brother Two*

The Talk of Doom? That was a weird one for me because I'd told the producers that my family knew that I was gay and that it wasn't a problem, coz they tell you that the press will find out your secrets. And I was like, 'Oh I don't have any,' but the truth of the matter was my family didn't know I was gay and I was shitting it in case it did come to that. But I figured what was the point in telling my family I was gay if I didn't get chosen? If I got chosen – and that seemed very unlikely – then I'd face that hurdle, but I wasn't going to tell my family a huge thing like that on the pretext that *I may* go in. So I left it.

KATE LAWLER, Winner, *Big Brother Three*

Yes, the psychologist said, 'What if everyone hates you?' and I said, 'They won't. I know because I'm not a nasty person,' and he said, 'They could edit you badly – I'm still counselling people from the first series that are still mentally screwed up.' I just wanted to prove him wrong and by this stage I was so bored by the whole process I was like, 'Just choose me or don't . . . if I'm hated then I'll just leave the country and go to Spain.' I wasn't aware of any BIG BROTHER RUINED MY LIFE story. I knew one thing – I'm sane and down to earth.

VICTOR EBUWA, *Big Brother Five*

Only a moron would go on that show if they weren't prepared and I was one of the most prepared housemates in the history of the show. It's common sense isn't it? To think of what could go wrong if it all goes tits up? You don't need to have a 'Talk of Doom' – think for yourself, man.

EMMA GREENWOOD, *Big Brother Five*

I was given the Talk of Doom from Day One. The producers would try to knock me off my perch all the time. They would belittle me and take the piss out of me just to see how much I could take, and I gave as good as I got. My expectations were, well nothing comes on a plate with silver cutlery. I knew I'd have to work for anything I wanted afterwards. And also my friends and family did warn me – 'Emma, think about this, you want to be an actress and you won't be able to do acting for a while after *Big Brother* because you won't be taken seriously,' and I thought yeah, they are right but I'll take the risk anyway. I needed them contacts – I'd let myself down in the past five years and I thought, shit, this is my only chance to grab it back, quick. Maybe I did wrong?

EUGENE SULLY, *Big Brother Six*

Because my entry into the House was so quick and last minute, I only got to talk to the psychologist over the phone, and he did try to talk me out of doing it by saying things like, 'How would you like it if the headlines in the papers said "BIG BROTHER VIRGIN BOY!"' I replied, 'Well, I don't think the Archbishop of Canterbury will be waving his fist in rage at a virgin.' (*laughs*) But seriously, the psychologist was trying to get me to think about the situation and he did make me think hard. But at the end of the day I'm reasonably intelligent enough to know the score – I mean, this is *Big Brother*, after all.

KINGA KAROLCZAK, *Big Brother Six*

I was given the Talk of Doom all the time. I remember in one audition the producers sat us all down and said very seriously, 'This could affect your family, your loved ones, your kids. The press may vilify you, your life will never be the same again . . . If you want none of that, walk out now,' and no one walked out, they all wanted it that much.

DEREK LAUD, *Big Brother Six*

Yes, of course I had my fears. I was given the Talk of Doom and I took it seriously. If you're younger, which a lot of these applicants are, then the Talk of Doom isn't really going to put you off, because when you're terribly young then you have very little in the way of a past and very little to lose. In my case, I was older with a very substantial past.

Saying to a young kid, 'Oh they're going to dig up stories about you and your past,' well, what are those stories going to amount to? Not really very much! But if you're older and you have an established career, especially in the field I was in, well then there was a great deal to lose. I thought, if this goes wrong I'll never be chairman of a company again and my face wouldn't be welcome back at Downing Street. I could be regarded as something of a public joke – I'd built up a reputation in business and politics, so for me there was actually a lot riding on it.

ANTHONY HUTTON, Winner, *Big Brother Six*

Yes, I went to meet a psychologist before I met the executives. Basically I had to talk about me upbringing, me family, me dad not being around. Girls I'd slept with. He gave us all the 'what are your ambitions from this show?' question.

But me uncle did have a good word with me after I told him that I was going on. He said, 'Have you really had a good think about this? You think about this. You maybe could be known forever-after as the arsehole from *Big Brother*. That's what you could be known as.' It did make me think for a bit but then I thought, you only live once – I'm gonna go for it.

NADIA ALMADA, Winner, *Big Brother Five*

The night before, one of the producers came to see me in my hotel room and I'll always remember this for the rest of my life, I said to him, 'Thank you so much for choosing me and giving me this opportunity,' and he replied, 'Don't thank me yet; you could be selling your soul to the devil.' I just thought, fuck it. But obviously, nothing he could have said at that point would have put me off – you just don't want to listen. You just want to be in there, in that house. The only thing he could have said to put me off was if he had told me I was going to die!

LEA WALKER, *Big Brother Seven*

We were given the Talk of Doom all the time – in fact that's pretty much all I remember from the auditions. All the warnings I got – your family will be brought into this, the press may tear you to pieces, your friends may sell stories. I have to say, it's the one thing I'll give Endemol – they proper warned us of the pitfalls. But nothing they could have said would have put me off.

RICHARD NEWMAN, *Big Brother Seven*

God yeah, we were constantly warned. But hey, I'm a grown man and by *Big Brother Seven* I knew what I was getting into and what might or might not come out of it. It's interesting because I was the one contestant that knew why I was there –

because there was an opportunity to win one hundred grand. It's all about expectation. I was old enough and wise enough not to expect anything other than a chance to win that money. I had no desire to go in there and be famous. At that point in my life I had nothing to lose really. Regardless of Talks of Doom, I had made lots of mistakes in my life, I was 34 years old and I was waiting tables and had just split with my partner. It was Russian roulette.

MAKOSI MUSAMBASI, *Big Brother Six*

Yes, we were given the Talk of Doom or whatever you want to call it. I have no time for such a stupid so-called 'warning'. I really resent it when people say, 'Well you should have known the pitfalls, you were warned and you watched previous series.' My answer to that is that there had never been a Makosi *Big Brother*. I am the first Makosi on *Big Brother*. What I've gone through could only have happened to me. So Jade being called a pig could only have happened to Jade and not me, because I don't look like a pig.

We are all different people and we experience different things as a result of being on *Big Brother*. I am unique to me, no one from my culture has ever gone on *Big Brother* and so when they give you the Talk of Doom how could they warn me about how Zimbabwe would take it if I wore a bikini? And besides, they didn't warn me that going on would have the potential to make people hate me – send death threats – so I wouldn't be able to go back to my own country. If I had been warned that, then that would have stopped me.

4. THE CALL

You had me at hello

(Jerry Maguire, 1996)

It was about a week before *Big Brother Two* began and I had given up hope. I'd thrown my heart and soul into getting my new qualifications and was content with a future in the medical industry. I'd just finished my last exam and was at the hairdresser's and my phone rang. It was a private number; I answered and it was Deborah, one of the producers. She asked me where I was and I said, 'At the hairdresser's,' and she asked me if I could step outside for a moment so I ran out onto the street, my hair dripping wet and shampoo in my eyes and she told me I was in, and I screamed and she started laughing. I put the phone down and texted my husband, 'IM IN'.

They dried my hair and I ran home, and my hubby was in the kitchen yelling, 'Oh my God! I never thought you'd get in! I can't believe it.' And I said, 'What the hell am I going to tell my family? Please will you call my brother and break it to him?' I knew in my heart of hearts that if my family had said no, I would never have done it – couldn't have.

So my husband rang my brother and I had to go out to the garden because I was dying with suspense. I was convinced my brother would say no. What he did say was '*Big Brother*'s that rude programme, isn't it?' and my husband replied, 'Only some of the housemates were.' Then my brother said, 'If she wants to, she should do it,' and I collapsed. I literally fell against the wall – that's how important it was to get my family's blessing.

Then I rang and told my mum who really didn't have a clue and I laugh now when I remember that she said, 'Well, what's the phone number in this house you'll be staying at? So I can call you?' and I had to break it to her, 'No, Mum, you won't be able to talk to me for maybe weeks,' and she just didn't get it.

Next I had to pack my whole life away. I had to give up work. I called up my boss and asked if I could have an extended leave of nine weeks and then come back, but she told me they couldn't take me back after such a long time. 'Why do you want to? Where are you going? On holiday?' And I said, 'Sort of, but I can't tell you the real reason,' and she got very frustrated. 'You're not going to prison are you?' and I said, 'Sort of.'

It was awful because I couldn't tell them – *Big Brother* had warned me not to – so I had to give up my job, and do you know what? I was actually really sad about it, really sad. I even kissed the bonnet of my company car when I had to give it back. But that was it. I had already changed my life overnight. I was told things can change in the wink of an eye and they had. I felt lost but excited.

I could compare it to being told you've just won the lottery. But that's not true, is it? For starters you probably won't get millions at the end of it. I could compare it to landing your dream job but then being told you haven't quite got it yet. It's a weird one, when you get the call you're over the moon – my God they picked me from thousands and thousands! I must be so special . . . So why would I even contemplate whether to do it or not? I've got this far after the military style auditions, I'll be damned if I say no now, am I daft? Well . . . actually . . . just maybe . . . What are you supposed to think when you get 'that call'?

MELANIE HILL, *Big Brother One*

I was at work and I vaguely remember them calling me and telling me that I'd got in. You have to remember that it just wasn't a big deal then. I was shocked, yes, but I immediately thought, well, I've been accepted, I've got this far – I can't turn my back on it now, but what do I do about work? How do I tell them? And in those days there wasn't all the big secrecy so I told my boss all about this new TV show and asked if I would have a job when I got back. It could have been eight weeks or one week, and he said yes.

It was never, 'Yes! I've got in,' we just didn't know then. It was more, 'Oh, this is a bit of a problem re. work and logistics.' So basically I went home and discussed it with my mates and they all said, 'Well, you might as well do it. You've got the time off work.'

I was just umming and ahhing the whole time. I wasn't sure if I should do it. It was just this weird thing. I told loads of people about it and no one knew what it was, they all said, 'Oh, that sounds a bit weird. Living in a house with strangers, no contact. Weird.' And I'd say, 'Yeah,' and they would say, 'But if you wanna do it, do it.'

In retrospect you would think, do I really want this kind of attention? If I'd known there would have been that amount of attention I would never have done it. All I knew was that one guy from the Dutch version had launched his own clothing line afterwards. That was it.

EMMA GREENWOOD, *Big Brother Five*

A little part of me was thinking, 'Are they going to call? Will I get in? Yeah I will. No, I won't!'

I had just finished work and I was making a microwave curry at home and the phone rang, 'Hi Emma. Congratulations, you're in the House,' and instead of screaming I just went, 'Oh, I forgot all about that.' And then they said, 'This is one thing you can't tell anyone. Promise us you will keep this a secret.' Then I put the phone down and rang all my mates and told them and we all got pissed. Then Endemol shipped me off to France.

SISSY (JOANNE) ROONEY, *Big Brother Four*

I played it really cool but when I put the phone down, I was shaking and I called my mum and she didn't pick up, then phoned my sister and she didn't pick up and finally I phoned my boyfriend and the phone was engaged. I had no one to tell!

AMMA ANTWI, *Big Brother Two*

Getting that call was shocking. I didn't get excited, I was just filled with dread that I'd have to tell my mum the truth – that I took my clothes off for a living. I'd protected her from that because otherwise she would have just worried endlessly, and I enjoyed what I did for a living – it was easy money. So anyway I went round and told her I'd been chosen to go on *Big Brother* and she was delighted for me. Then I told her about the table dancing and it was the most heartbreaking thing I'd ever had to do.

She broke down in a flood of tears; she couldn't understand why I did it. She just cried, but I didn't want her to find it out from the newspapers – that would have been worse. We talked some more and the next day she gave me her blessing and told me she loved me. I told her that when I came out of the House, I'd give up stripping and look for a normal job. Something I'd live to regret.

KATE LAWLER, Winner, *Big Brother Three*

I remember. It was my birthday – 7 May – when I got the call saying I'd been chosen and it was the best birthday present ever. I told my mum, dad and sisters and Karen was screaming, 'Fucking hell, fucking hell!' and my dad kept saying, 'You're gonna win it, you're gonna win it!' My best mate was saying, 'You're gonna win it.' And I kept saying, 'No, I won't,' and they were saying, 'Girls like you and guys like you and it's time a girl won.'

That's when I started thinking about the aftermath and what would happen. 'So, now I'm in it, what's gonna happen when I come out?' I said to my dad. 'Can't I go back to my normal job afterwards?' And he was like, 'Yeah, you probably can because you don't know what's gonna happen then.' Karen said, 'Aren't you bothered everything will be seen and you'll be famous?' and when Karen said that I replied, 'Yeah, but I won't really be famous.' I just wanted to win seventy grand and get my house and a great story to tell my grandchildren.

BRIAN DOWLING, Winner, *Big Brother Two*

I was in the living room of the girls' house I was staying at – because the tenancy was up on my old house and I hadn't got a new place yet – and the phone rang and it was Endemol, and they said, 'We've got some bad news for you,' and I thought, shit, and they said, 'You can't go on your holiday.' I had told them I had a holiday booked, and I just didn't get it and replied, 'Oh, OK, it's not your fault, not to worry,' not even thinking right. All I could think was, oh well, I didn't get in, and then they said, 'Well, Brian, do you want to know why you can't go on holiday? Because you're going into the *Big Brother* House.' I said, 'You're lying?' Then I was quite professional and said, 'That's nice, I'm available and I'll see you in a week. Bye.' Then I put the phone down.

My first thought was, oh my God – I have to tell my parents I'm gay. I was shitting it, sick to my stomach, thinking, in less than a week I'll be going on national TV and I have to tell my parents and my six sisters that I'm gay and I'm their only son. Not only that, I'm from a tiny Catholic village in Ireland, and with the Irish Catholic background if you're gay you go to hell. I'm supposed to get married, have children and go to church and there's me in gay clubs in Soho dancing to Kylie! I thought, they will disown me and I'll have no family when I come out of the House.

So I decided to tell my sister Michelle first as I'm closest to her, and she kind of knew I was gay and she said that she would tell my mum and dad for me. So that night I went out and got pissed on pineapple Bacardi Breezers thinking, my mum's disowned me. I didn't dare phone them. I knew she was telling them at nine but I just drowned it all out. The next morning I knew I had to call my mum and face the music – I was prepared for her to be distraught and say, 'You can't go on *Big Brother* and be out.' And you know what? If she had said that I totally would not have gone on *Big Brother*. I have to respect my family at the end of the day and what would be the point in going?

I said, 'Hi' and she said, 'Hi, are you sure this is what you want to do? I mean you're not just trying to be fashionable are you?' And I said, 'I'm not just trying to be fashionable Mum, I'm gay,' and she said 'OK,' but I think she must have been sick.

Then *Big Brother* called me again and I thought, I knew it was too good to be true, they've made a mistake, but luckily they were warning me about 'paparazzi', that there were paparazzi outside the window. So there I am in Bishops Stortford, frantically closing all the curtains and thinking, what's paparazzi? Is it a bird or something, it sounded like a bird. I just didn't understand, all I knew was that I was to avoid it.

VICTOR EBUWA, *Big Brother Five*

Basically, I was at uni in my student house and I was collecting my washing and I got a phone call – private number – and thought, it's those *Big Brother* wankers. They were calling on a private number all the time saying there was yet another audition process to go through. It was starting to annoy me, because I knew it started in May, so I'm thinking how can it be May and they still haven't decided who's going in?

It was always, 'There's another audition or another interview process or something else we need to find out or a home visit,' and it was getting tiring. Why was it taking so long, man?

So anyway, I pick up the phone and I'm like, 'Hello' and it's Shirley Jones, the executive producer. 'Hi Shirley, what do you want now?' and Shirley says, 'Oh, ha ha ha ha, you're a ray of sunshine. Victor there's one thing we want from you.' I was like, 'Why is it taking so long Shirley?' And she said, 'We want to invite you to the House on 28 May.' This was on 6 May. I was like, 'What house is it now? How many more rings of fire do we jump through before we sort this shit out?' You know what I mean? And she said, 'No, we are inviting you to the House.' 'Where is it?' 'No, I'm inviting you on the show,' and I go, 'Ohhhh, OK. What took you so long?'

In my head I knew I was going to get in and even when I told a couple of mates they said, 'Oh, OK. Cool.' They just expected it to happen – if I didn't get in it would have been silly. It was really like that. And I was saying that along the way. I said I'd seen the rest of the contestants that were auditioning, most – ninety per cent – of them were garbage.

'You're quite confident, aren't you?' 'Well Shirley, you always knew you were gonna put me in. I knew you were gonna put me in. Is there anything I need to know?' She said, 'Yeah, get your passport.' But it did make me think, if they've chosen me then what other psychopaths have they chosen? And judging by the monumental disaster of *Big Brother Four*, when Channel 4 lost sponsors, and had endorsements scrapped, I knew there would be nutters in there.

DEREK LAUD, *Big Brother Six*

I was in the back of a car with Michael Howard and the telephone rang. It was Endemol and I said, 'I can't possibly speak to you now, I'm busy.' So they called me later in the day and said, 'You're through,' and I said, 'Well, now I'd like some time to think about this and whether I should really do this,' and it took me three days to make up my mind.

EUGENE SULLY, *Big Brother Six*

Big Brother Six began and obviously I hadn't been chosen. I didn't mind as I was told I was on the reserve list and I thought, 'Oh, it's never gonna happen.' And as the series went on, I began to feel relieved that I hadn't been chosen because most of the people that year were pretty ghastly, in fact a particularly ghastly lot. They were all so O.T.T. and trying to kill each other mentally and I kept thinking, thank God I didn't get chosen, it would have been hell, I would have been eaten for breakfast!

Then I got another phone call saying, 'You haven't given us your medical form back,' and a feeling of dread crept over me. Then I didn't hear from them again till the following week and they said, 'You will be on *Big Brother* but you won't be a housemate, but you *will* be in a house and may be given the chance to become a housemate.'

So I discussed it with my friends and they all said, 'You have to do it,' but going in would mean I'd miss the XTRAX party, which is always very entertaining and my mate said, 'If you do *Big Brother*, then next year you'll be *hosting* the XTRAX party.' So I thought about it some more and had the go-ahead from work. I told my boss, 'It's a house on TV where people don't really get on very well.' And then I told my mum and she said, 'Alright, but be careful. The people in there can be quite difficult.' So then I rang Endemol back to tell them I'd decided to do it and they said, 'By the way, you'll be expected to wear a fig leaf on your private parts as you walk in,' and I thought, oh, for God's sake.

SAMANTHA HEUSTON, *Big Brother Six*

I got the call in May about a couple of weeks before the show began and I told my mum and she was like, 'Oh my God!' and then I told my brother and he went mental, he just didn't want me to do it. He said he was going to tell people and I took a fit and started crying uncontrollably. My family just didn't want me to do it. They thought it was just a psychological experiment that fucked people's lives up. But I was going to do it no matter what they said.

NADIA ALMADA, Winner, *Big Brother Five*

I was at work and I remember I got a couple of missed calls from a private number. I couldn't take them because I was at work. So I had to ask to go to the toilet when the next one came, but my manager followed me because she thought that I was having a sneaky cigarette – it was terrible and stupid. I took the call in the toilet and they said, 'Hi, we would like you to be a housemate.' I think I fainted onto the toilet and thought, oh my fucking world. So shocked that I almost had no reaction. My body went into shock and obviously I couldn't work for the rest of the day. And I never went back to work again.

RICHARD NEWMAN, *Big Brother Seven*

I was at a gay club called The Edge with some girlfriends and it was a private number call, so I quickly ran out and took it and the producer said, 'Congratulations, Rich, you will be going into the House this year. You have three days to get ready. And you will be going abroad.'

It was strange, because I had been on dummy runs and then not got in. I didn't want to get ahead of myself just in case in the end they would change their mind again. So I was calm.

MAKOSI MUSAMBASI, *Big Brother Six*

I was at home and I'd already walked out of my job because I'd had enough. Then my phone rang and they told me. I was very excited, I called my sister and she couldn't believe it: 'Oh my God, you're gonna be on TV!' I started planning already; I knew from watching previous series that not the most intelligent people went in ... And so I started playing dumb and daft as soon as I was told I was on the show.

KINGA KAROLCZAK, *Big Brother Six*

I was at work at the call centre and *Big Brother* rang, so I ran and took the phone into the toilet and my manager ran after me and started banging on the door: 'You are not supposed to be taking calls, get out!' The producer was saying, 'Congratulations, you'll be going into the House.' I got out of the toilet and told my boss I had to go to the hospital and as soon as I got out of the building I rang my mum and told her. She couldn't believe it; I was talking two to a dozen, all in Polish, and by the time I got home the car to take me away was already waiting and the *Big Brother* person was at my door.

She ran in with me and helped me pack. All sorts was going through my mind; I was excited. I'd dreamed of this for so long but they told me that I may not become a real housemate and because it was at such short notice, to be honest I couldn't think straight: not a real housemate? Shit! And then, oh my God, I'm gonna be famous, but then I thought, hold your horses, Kinga. I didn't know what to think, I couldn't even sit and discuss it with my family because it all happened so quickly. All I knew was that my dream was about to come true.

ALEX SIBLEY, *Big Brother Three*

I remember I was on my little balcony in Hamburg looking over the city and I got the call, and my girlfriend at the time was with me and I put the phone down and said, 'Oh, I'll have to pack. They want me to go on *Big Brother*.' I had all my stuff there, I had to get a ferry straight over and to tell my modelling agency I couldn't do any work till I was out of the House. *Big Brother* had told me not to tell anyone but I did in Hamburg; the only people I told in London were my parents, they didn't really know much about it and I told them, 'Well, I suppose you'll be able to see me on TV.'

LEA WALKER, *Big Brother Seven*

On a Friday. I had just landed a job presenting on a motoring channel – just what I'd been working to get and then the phone goes. 'Lea, where are you?' Home. 'We've got news. How long would it take to sort out things with your son because you've got four days. You're going in the House.' When she said I was in the House I felt physically sick. My heart jumped so much that I thought it was going to burst through my chest.

I was like, 'Oh my God they have picked me.' I phoned them back and said, 'You have just told me I am in, haven't you?' She said, 'Yeah!' and she was laughing. I said, 'Oh my God I can't believe it.' She said, 'You'd better get all your stuff sorted.' I have never felt so special in my life as I did that night. Out of all these thousands of people they had picked me.

5. GOING INTO THE HOUSE

Fasten your seatbelts, it's going to be a bumpy ride

(All About Eve, 1950)

The day I left Leicester for London was the saddest day for me, because my husband couldn't come with me – he had to go to a company conference. It's weird but even then I knew things had changed so much already. I wrote letters to my loved ones explaining why I couldn't tell them, and I wrote a letter to my husband – it was sad and I was tearing up as I wrote it, this was an enormous life change. I was walking out the door, onto a train and into the most famous house in Britain and leaving behind everything I knew and loved – my safety, the whole life that I'd just walked out of . . . I remember getting into the taxi and looking back at my house and just crying.

When I got to London, I was sparked up and thought I'd go shopping for clothes as I hadn't had a chance in Leicester, but when I got there the chaperone was at the platform and she bundled me into a car and straight into hiding. I didn't get it and kept saying, 'Can I go to Covent Garden?' and she'd say, 'We can't do that,' so she had to go and get me what I needed.

Then she took my phone away from me and then I began to get scared and said I wanted to phone my husband. She allowed me one phone call and that was supervised and my husband couldn't talk properly either because he was at his conference and had two nosey parkers following him around all day. I asked if they would post the letter to him, and they actually ripped it out of the envelope and read it in front of me. I felt I was losing him already – I was in one world and he was in another. Then we had the so-called 'last supper'. My brother and niece came down to London – my hubby couldn't – and it was lovely to see them. That made me feel much better, and stronger about things.

The psychologists' theory is that only people desperate for attention would go into the House and, well, if entering the House is anything to go by, then they are without a doubt, unequivocally, one-hundred-per-cent correct. It feels like one of the most attention-grabbing moments in the history of television, bar Judy Finnigan and her bra at the National Television Awards! All eyes are on you and at that moment you most probably are bigger than Britney. It's your entrance into the most famous house in Britain and it will never come again.

But you don't just get a call and then the next moment you're walking into the House. No, you could have been told weeks or days before – these days housemates are even taken into hiding. But what's going through your head? These are your last moments of being an unknown, just another face in the crowd, being able to come and go and do as you please. Enjoy it, enjoy your last supper.

MELANIE HILL, *Big Brother One*

It was nothing like it is today, when you go into hiding. I was at home packing – I just packed for cold and hot weather – and then a car came to pick me up and we went to a hotel the day before, a horrible hotel. I just hung around the whole day. It was no big deal. They took a few pictures for the press. I didn't have any fears, none.

Actually, my biggest *biggest* fear was that they would take my conditioner bottle away. I'd filled up a whole cider bottle of conditioner because the rules were that you could only take one bottle of it. They had a Dutch woman there who came over to help them do all the vetting and I remember her saying in a really thick Dutch accent, 'I have never seen a hair conditioner this big! I'm not sure about this!'

Then they take everything you're not allowed away from you and that was it. And I put little bits of makeup on the dresser on some toilet roll – bit of blusher, lipstick – as the runner had suggested and got ready.

Then I got in the car to go the House. We all arrived at the same time, in the morning, and we all got out of the cars together and stood with our families and waited to go in. No crowds and no paparazzi. In fact, as I remember it, there was a bit of a queue as we went in because we all got searched. So I went back to where the friends and families were and chatted to my mate till the queue went down. Then we all finally got in.

VICTOR EBUWA, *Big Brother Five*

I tell you what, there are a couple of things I remember. How can I say it? Nothing really phases me up to a point. The only time I remember thinking, shit, what's going on? is when they put me in a room at 11 a.m. in the morning and left me sitting there waiting and waiting. Then I had a meeting with the producers and I said, 'Just get me in the fucking House now.'

I'd been sitting around for ages and was proper pumped for the event. I was wired up. I said to them, 'Let me get in there and start eating these housemates alive!' That's literally how I was. I was like an animal that you tease and throw meat to. They had to calm me down.

Then they wheeled in my suitcase and it had my name on it with the *Big Brother* logo and I was like, 'Shit!' and my chaperone said, 'What?' and I said, 'This is really happening, isn't it?' and he replied, 'Victor, this is the first time in three weeks that I've seen you crack.' You see, up to that point it had all seemed like a dream. It had all been too easy.

I know it's some people's life-long dream to get on *Big Brother* but I literally got up one morning, washed my arse and rolled up there and here I was about to enter the House. So when the suitcase came in I had that moment, but then like a flick of a switch it was all boom! It's almost game time now.

This is what happens before you play football – you get a little adrenaline rush, your heart starts pumping and you're like, *right!* And in football the first thing I do is to run up and tackle someone.

I was then blindfolded – all for effect – and I said to my chaperone, 'What the fuck is this all about?' and then before he could answer the door opened and I stepped outside. People were going crazy and screaming, 'VICTOR! VICTOR!' and I just worked the crowd. I had tunnel vision and I just wanted to get into that house. And there's this moment after you've walked through the crowds when you're in that tunnel bit and you're caught between two worlds. Just for a split second. So there's the door behind you where you have left the world as you know it, and there's the door in front of you and I always, *always* remember thinking, which way shall I go? Shall I turn around and run? 'Sorry guys but I can't do this.' But then I thought, fuck this, LET'S KICK SOME ASS.

DEREK LAUD, *Big Brother Six*

So I was getting into the car and everybody was running around with microphones and it was like the set for a James Bond movie. I thought, gosh, what are they all doing? It all looked rather ridiculous to me. All the other cars were lined up next to me and I could see into the cars. I saw a girl with a PVC outfit on and I remember thinking, oh dear. I was rather hoping it would have been like attending a cocktail party in Chelsea but clearly not! I wasn't nervous of the crowds; well, it takes a lot to unnerve me. I've seen great big set-ups – working for prime ministers – so it wasn't daunting. I went in first. I knew I was something of a catch for them.

SOPHIE PRITCHARD, *Big Brother Three*

When I walked in it was the most nerve-wracking thing of my life, my legs were shaking that much, I thought my legs would break – literally. I was that nervous.

I can't remember ever being more nervous – not even when I got married.

MAKOSI MUSAMBASI, *Big Brother Six*

I remember they wouldn't give me a hairdresser, and my hair was a mess so I said, 'I'm not going in unless you get me a hairdresser,' and I meant it. So they got me a hairdresser and told her that I was going on *EastEnders* as an extra. So she does my hair and finishes it with just ten minutes to go. Even my orange dress was last minute, I was supposed to wear something else but it got ripped!

I wasn't afraid; I knew people were going to love me. I know that sounds arrogant but I knew they would, and as I walked through the crowds I thought, what is my mum going to think? because I hadn't told her I was going in. As I walked through the doors I made a vow to myself that I would last the whole three months and that I wanted to be the last girl standing and the star of the show.

KINGA KAROLCZAK, *Big Brother Six*

I was told I had to wear a fig leaf bikini. I've never ever worn a bikini in my life – I'm chubby and I just didn't want to, but they basically said that if I didn't then I wouldn't go in. I'd got too far just to turn it all down, but I seriously did think, well I can't go in. I'm so not confident in my body but it was either that or not go in. So in the end I put it on, feeling very self-conscious. I had to have a few drinks to give me the courage to wear it.

EUGENE SULLY, *Big Brother Six*

It was all basic routine and protocol. There was a lot of waiting around and they asked me to draw a picture! Then it got to nine o'clock in the evening and by then I was really nervous and to make matters worse they produced the pants! I went into the changing room and they took away all my other clothes and I put the pants on and looked at myself in the mirror and desperately wished I'd toned up. My body looked so flabby.

Then they told me it was time to go and I clearly remember feeling like I was going to my execution – you know the protocol, you know you're going to do it, not that you're literally going to be put to death, but just the uncertainty of the outcome. All these people are holding your hand and as soon as that car door opens you're on your own. They told me to walk down the centre and get on the round thing – a diagram before would have been nice, because I messed it up. The geography wasn't that clear. The crowds were screaming and it really boosted my ego and I started doing thumbs up signs – I'm not very creative when it comes to striking poses. I got to the door and thought, here goes nothing.

KATE LAWLER, Winner, *Big Brother Three*

My mum and dad wrote me a letter and I read it and cried. It was just telling me how much they loved me and would enjoy watching me and that's all I thought about – my family and mates watching me, not the whole of Britain. It was weird. I remember saying to my chaperone, 'What will they put me in as? I know they have a slaggy girl every year, a pretty girl, a geeky girl. Am I gonna be the sporty girl?'

Ours was the first year that they had the big crowds and it was night-time and it was live and we weren't told anything. I could hear all the crowds and Davina McCall [the presenter], and suddenly they said, 'It's your turn.' I was well nervous; they were searching me and I was thinking, shit . . . is this really happening to me? Am I gonna be on the telly?

I just wanted to get in the House and meet all these people I'd be living with – just get in. I had my little suitcase ready and the car pulled up and I opened the door and just stepped out. There were lots of lights and flashes and suddenly I heard all the screaming; I saw my family and I ran over and hugged them. They were saying, 'We love you, we love you,' and I was saying, 'This is fucked up, this is weird,' and now I'm scared, all these people were looking at me and touching me. I didn't like it – it was scary. Then I had my picture taken by paparazzi, walked up the stairs with my heart racing – I didn't turn round – and opened the door and thought, yeah, I'm here.

EMMA GREENWOOD, *Big Brother Five*

I got to the hotel and they told me that I couldn't watch the TV and they'd taken the fuse out of the telly. So when they left me I just took the fuse out of the kettle plug and put it back in the telly plug. They're so stupid.

So I sat and watched TV all night because I just couldn't sleep. Morning seemed so far away. When it finally arrived they came in to check my suitcase so I didn't have something in there that we weren't allowed in the House. So there's this cute guy looking through my knickers and I fancied him – I was so embarrassed, I wouldn't have minded but they were Primark £1 knickers! Then I was dumped into this car, blindfolded.

I was excited, so excited. Not nervous. Armpits like the Lynx advert. I felt like I was tripping . . . 'Oh my God, I'm going into the House with cameras all over the place and I'm gonna love it!' I just couldn't concentrate, I was that excited . . . but we had to wait in this room all day, so I just asked for a tape and music and danced to *Dirty Dancing*.

So finally we had to get ready and we were each put in a car . . . Everyone was screaming . . . it was amazing, that was amazing . . . Then I walked into the House and went, 'Oohhmmphh!'

LEA WALKER, *Big Brother Seven*

It was the morning of going into the House and I was in my hotel room watching *Lorraine Kelly* and Makosi and Lesley Sanderson* were on talking about how *Big Brother* ruined their lives. And it struck me as whingey and I thought, you're the one who's ruined your own life, not *Big Brother*. It didn't put me off going into the House. Maybe it was a warning.

So anyways, I'm in the car and I could hear this guy with Tourette's [Pete Bennett, the eventual winner]. I've never been so scared in my life. They were booing me as soon as the car door opened. My boos were the worst. I said to my driver, 'I

* Lesley Sanderson, a housemate in BB6, was allegedly raped in a hotel in Leeds a few months after the end of the series.

can't get out, my legs won't move.' My chaperone had to drag me out the car. I was too scared to look at the crowds of people and when I finally glanced over I saw this girl and she locked eyes with me and shouted, 'You fucking slag!'

I was petrified, I couldn't understand what I'd done wrong. They promised me it was all a pantomime and not to worry about the boos. I was walking up the stairs and kept thinking of my son, H. My immediate thought was, I have to get out of this now, because I didn't want my son bullied at school. They swore to me it was all pantomime but I couldn't understand why I was getting booed before entering the House.

In all the series of *Big Brother* no one had ever been booed before entering the House. But then I thought, I've come too far now to go back. And so I walked down the stairs and opened the door.

SAMANTHA HEUSTON, *Big Brother Six*

I was elated to be walking into the House for one reason only – it would be my ultimate revenge on all those people that had been horrible to me. There was one guy at uni who I was in love with, and he was my shag buddy sort-of-thing and I mentioned *Big Brother* to him and he just laughed and said, 'You're gonna end up the next Jodie Marsh and you've got a crash helmet haircut.'

I was very unconfident at school and got bullied a lot and always singled out. So I really psyched myself up those two weeks that I was in hiding and practised my walk into the House, and when I got out the car I thought, take that, mate, and knew they'd all be watching.

NADIA ALMADA, Winner, *Big Brother Five*

On the day I was stuck in this one small room; it was awful, there was smoke everywhere because I kept smoking and I couldn't breathe. I was hot, then I had to do my makeup and I put on my white suit, and I was stressed about getting any mark on it. Then I told them that I wanted to be last one in. And I was the last one in! And last out!

As I was blindfolded, I kept saying, 'Don't get my suit dirty! Don't get it dirty!' It was raining hard. Then they opened the doors and the crowd went ballistic. And if you watch the clip you can see my lips moving and I kept saying, 'Where are my friends? Where are my friends?' because we were given the assurance that they were there. And then the moment I was about to go through the door, I saw my friend and waved. Then the doors suddenly closed behind me.

ANTHONY HUTTON, Winner, *Big Brother Six*

I was dead paranoid in case anyone had seen us, because they kept scaring us by saying that if we got spotted then we wouldn't get into the House. The excitement was all building up. I had to wear a mask to go to the studio, like a Halloween mask. Then I was put in a changing room to wait and I could hear all the producers on their phones. I put on me best suit and thought, right it's time to get it in.

I wasn't nervous about the crowds because of being a 70s dancer. I was used to being on stage and getting loads of attention – I liked that kind of feeling it gave me, the adrenaline, the attention. I can't understand anyone who goes on *Big Brother* and then says, 'I don't like the attention.'

I got out the car and it was just absolute carnage, and all that was going through me mind was, all me mates are watching me back home. I didn't think, oh the whole of Britain is watching me, just me mates, and so I overdid it and ended up getting booed! I look back and think how stupid I looked. If I'd been watching me I'd have thought, what a twat! but I knew me mates would find it funny.

And then when I was getting booed I thought, fuck!, but I kept a good face and just thought it was standard procedure for everyone to get booed! And then as I was walking into the House I looked back and I saw some lad going (*mimes action*), 'Wanker!' And I thought, oh God.

AMMA ANTWI, *Big Brother Two*

I wasn't deadly nervous or overly excited. I'd had some weed in the morning at the hotel to relax a bit and my biggest concern was where I would dump the weed that I had hidden in my bra. I managed to get rid of it, but looking back I so wish I had smuggled it in, it would have been so easy (*laughs*).

BRIAN DOWLING, Winner, *Big Brother Two*

We got put into the hotel the night before and I felt scared because when we went into the hotel they were making us put coats over our heads, and were using all these terms I didn't understand like, 'We need to do a VT,' and all I kept thinking was, I'm an air steward – tea or coffee? Talk about something I can understand like taking off or someone fainting, something I can handle!

And then we got taken to a studio to have press photos taken and do interviews for *Big Brother's Little Brother*,* which wasn't around for *Big Brother*, so again it was all bizarre to me. I'm just an air steward! You know when you're a kid and you have a day out and you don't quite understand what's going on but it's all exciting and different? Well, that's how I felt. And I kept thinking, why all this interest in me? Then later that evening we had what is called the 'last supper' and they filmed me and my best friend Kris having dinner, which was weird. Then they took me to my hotel and Kris went off to a different hotel. I couldn't sleep of course, and all I kept thinking was, what am I doing? They took my phone off me and so I couldn't talk to anyone. I kept thinking, just say no. Part of me thought that if I stopped it then, I would have upset so many people, so I went with, 'just do it'. I'm normally very good at judging situations but I couldn't think straight with this.

The morning for me is now a blur. It was morning in those days to enter and it wasn't live, and we were allowed a friend or a family member to wave us in.† Then I put on that stupid orange T-shirt – I should never have worn that orange T-shirt,

---

* 'Big Brother's Little Brother' – a companion show hosted by Russell Brand featuring humorous daily commentary on events in the House and interviews with the evicted housemates.
† In the first two series of *Big Brother* the housemates entered the House in the morning, with no live audience. Now the entrance to the House is almost as big an event as the evictions.

it made me look like I was wearing lipstick, which I wasn't. We were in the holding area and they told us not to look at or even talk to the other contestants as we all walked in, in groups of three or four back then.

I thought, how stupid, we will all begin talking straightaway, but no one spoke to me. I couldn't believe it. I thought, right your cards are marked. And then you walk out of the holding area and there is just a small crowd of family and friends cheering us all in and photographers taking pictures and it was just the weirdest feeling ever.

I was speechless; you almost can't hear anything and I felt my whole life was passing me by. Very dramatic I know, but I couldn't comprehend how filling in an application form had led to this. They say it will change your life and it's at that moment that you realise what they are talking about. And then I thought, shit, this could be the worst mistake of my life.

ALEX SIBLEY, *Big Brother Three*

They had kept me locked up in a room for hours and it just makes you more anxious, but I suppose they do that on purpose. I wasn't nervous of the crowd because of the work I'd done – I'd worked in the Royal Albert Hall to huge crowds. I thought it was funny that they were all cheering me – they didn't even know me – and I remember thinking, hold on, I haven't even started yet.

RICHARD NEWMAN, *Big Brother Seven*

I came back from Belgium where I'd been hiding in a hotel, and it was such a palaver having to wear a mask when I was being driven into Elstree. Actually I was feeling very car sick! Then I was out in a room for a good eight hours. I was nervous, started thinking, am I doing the right thing? I think you start thinking that at that point because you're in this room and you have all this time to reflect and it all starts dawning on you – God this is really going to happen, in eight hours you will be on that red carpet, walk up the stairs and, boof, you're dropped right into it, and it's like getting on a rollercoaster at the funfair and the only way you're going to get off is when it stops. And that's how it is.

I had a lot to contend with – my mum back in Canada was having chemo. My mum and dad insisted I carry on and *Big Brother* assured me they would let me know if anything happened. I know people might say, 'Oh, you shouldn't have gone in,' but my family are on the other side of the world and my life is here. It's not as simple as getting on a plane and going home: you don't have to be sat on top of your mum and dad to show you care.

So then it was time to get in the car and I was sat in there trembling, and my chaperone is saying, 'It's OK, it's OK,' and by now I have taken the blindfold off and can see the crowds, the flashes, the House, the big screen. 'Oh my God, this is it,' and my chaperone said, 'Don't worry, you'll be fine, Richard,' and those were the last words I heard from the outside world.

She got out, opened the door for me and there it was: BOOF! I didn't get booed, I seized the moment and had fun with my entry. Going into the House wasn't a big deal for me or sensational, because remember I had done it all in the dummy runs, so I sort of knew what to expect. It's all secretive then as well. The anticipation for me was seeing who my housemates were going to be! So I go down the stairs and open the door and was pounced on by Shahbaz.

6. LIFE IN THE HOUSE

Toto, I've got a feeling we're not in Kansas anymore
(The Wizard of Oz, 1939)

My biggest fear about going into the House was the other housemates – what would they be like? Would I get on with them? Would they be obnoxious? I had good reason to be worried, because I remember being gobsmacked at some of the people in the House when I finally went in. Initially I thought, OK, I can see why they chose some people, but others I just couldn't figure out. Then when I got to know them it was actually worse – they were astonishingly grey people. I did expect characters – *Big Brother One* had some right loonies.

To this day, I will never know why they chose certain people. Some ruined the entire experience for me – being controlling, ignoring those they didn't like. Others hovered around them because they thought they were favourite to win. If it had not been for Brian, I would have walked out, and if Paul Clarke and Helen Adams hadn't fallen in love then it might have been the worst *Big Brother* ever. All the big characters went out first. I have to admit I didn't play most of my housemates too well at all; I didn't like them and they didn't like me, and in retrospect I realise that if I had really wanted to get far in the game I should have bitten my tongue like Brian always advised me to – but then I was never in it to win. I felt some of the other housemates were just not worth the energy – they were rude and arrogant and hell-bent on winning the game, and that made me want to go in the opposite direction. I couldn't believe their desperation. I remember when Josh Rafter walked in,* how delighted I was and how all their faces fell – that was a real spanner in the works! They complained that, 'it wasn't fair of Big Brother'. I remember thinking, Jesus Christ!

I felt aware of the cameras for the first few hours but then I completely forget about them, because there was so much more to be thinking about. The cameras were the least of my worries. Mind you, I couldn't go to the toilet until week three because I just couldn't bear knowing there were cameras and people could see!

Penny was the first to go and I couldn't believe the public had booted her out instead of Helen, who I thought was the most annoying person in the House. The rest of the House didn't like Penny because she threatened them. Not since I left the House have I experienced the feeling of devastation I felt at the moment when Davina announced Penny's name for eviction. I thought, what the hell have they been showing?

You could see it in my face – it just fell. I missed her terribly. And I was starving, because we'd failed the first tedious task, which was all about lighting a fire, and we had only been given basic food rations as a result. I remember we had one tea bag to last us from the Wednesday until Sunday and no sugar, so we used icing sugar as our sugar fix! To be fair, although I didn't like the others, we did pull together when it came to tasks, I suppose because we were hungry. And when people are starving, arguments soon arise – much to the delight of the viewing public and, even more so, the producers.

PHIL EDGAR-JONES, Creative Director, Endemol

I didn't work on *Big Brother One* but I was as obsessed as everyone else. I started on the second series, by which time *Big Brother* had become the first programme ever to become multi-platform – by that I mean it went on a satellite channel,

---

* Josh Rafter was chosen by the public to enter the House in the second week of BB2.

E4, and on the Internet as well as Channel 4 – and that was such a big phenomenon. I also started up *Big Brother's Little Brother*.

The way *Big Brother* comes together is quite a complicated process. The producers have a big say in how it's run but so does the channel. The voices of Big Brother are the producers and they do a shift and sometimes they work in the gallery (a viewing and editing room where producers can watch a live feed of the show). The story producers, they work 24-hour shifts. So one person sits and watches a whole day of *Big Brother* and out of 24 hours of material we have to make a half-hour show.

That is then viewed in the morning by senior producers who make some changes. The only thing the story producers are told to do is, 'Watch this show for a day and pick out that stuff that would make you ring your mates to tell them. That's your story.' Also to pick up threads from the previous day. Then we come in and watch it again.

We've got cameras everywhere but we can't record every-thing, so there is a selection process going on. So it is terribly frustrating because we can't show everything – people are sometimes being incredibly funny but we can't show it because we have half an hour to tell a story. The process is a lot more mundane than you may imagine it is: what we choose is the most engaging and dramatic storyline to the viewer, what somebody would find interesting and it's a soap opera so it has to have a logical narrative.

Sometimes we are sat there and one producer is saying, 'There's this happening with these two,' and another producer is saying, 'But maybe a budding romance over here.' It really isn't as cold cut as 'ratings'. What I'm trying to say is that it is all accidental. What nobody sets out to do – and this is absolutely true – is say, 'Right, that person's a baddy and that person's a hero and we need to make this person look like this and that person like that.' We don't try to get rid of people. It has to be fair, it all has to be fair. We still keep the fairness of the game show – the two core fundamentals remain the same: the housemates decide who leaves, not us, and the viewers choose who goes, not us.

RACHEL MORRIS, Psychotherapist, *Big Brother*

TV is about telling a story, and you can never tell all the story so you choose a thread of that story. So, if you're going to tell a story to your mates down the pub are you going to choose the boring thread or the interesting one? I guarantee you will choose the interesting one: 'One day you went shopping and someone got mugged and then later on in the day you tripped.' What will you tell your mates? You will go home and tell your family and friends the dramatic story – that's what television is. It has a responsibility to tell the interesting story.

BOYD HILTON, TV Editor, *Heat*

I think it's a brilliantly produced piece of TV. It's a great idea in the first place but on top of that year after year, the way *Big Brother* operates – the way Big Brother gets the contestants to do things, the tasks, the conversations in the diary room, and the editing of course – is all amazingly done. It's much better than a soap opera because it's real and because the dialogue isn't being written by some idiot trying to copy how somebody speaks – it's real.

When journalists say there's nothing real about reality TV, what they mean is that it's contrived. Yeah, of course the format is contrived – you know you're going on TV, you know there's cameras everywhere but it's still real. It's a contrived reality. But it's still reality. What you're saying isn't scripted. It's drama with real people that become characters in your mind the more you watch them and that whole experience becomes very enjoyable for millions and millions of people. There are now five million hardcore fans.

GARY THOMPSON, Senior Associate Editor, *News of the World*

Big Brother was a godsend. We decided to put *Big Brother* on the front cover because it was selling so well and it was letting us connect with readers that traditionally papers find it hard to connect with – the 18–34 year olds. They are the hardest people to get to read a newspaper, but if *Big Brother* was on the cover they would pick up the paper.

Big Brother was on TV 24/7 and so you were guaranteed a story. You had ten housemates who were all by definition extrovert people with interesting backgrounds. It was just a completely new phenomenon that we just got excited about. In the earlier series it was a lot more pedestrian and reserved and even the most minor incidents would get picked over – I mean look what Nasty Nick did. He cheated and it was the biggest deal in Britain, and these days the housemates are in bed all but having sex and it's not even making headlines. Every year the boundaries are pushed. You went from Mel flirting in *Big Brother One* to Anthony and Makosi in the pool . . . No one cares anymore.

MELANIE HILL, *Big Brother One*

Everyone was talking a million miles an hour when I first went into the House, and the only one that was quiet was Tom McDermot – it was freaking him out. Everyone else was just loud and chatting away: 'Who are you?', 'What do you think will happen?', 'How will this programme pan out?' The only time we discussed life afterwards it was really, really innocent. And I look back and think, bless.

We discussed things like, 'Imagine if we get an interview afterwards?' Imagine. And we would talk about what we might do when we got out. But we truly believed no one was watching us, we were just boring. We had no idea about those big screens that they put up in Leicester Square and Manchester. No idea. I had friends who were walking through Leicester Square and looked up and saw me making a cup of tea on a massive screen and it freaked them out.

We thought the House was lovely, but by the end it was just this hollow, dirty, nasty TV structure. It was charming, basic but fine, it had a garden, a vegetable patch. In the first two weeks you could really hear them moving the cameras around and we used to joke that after people got evicted, they were killed and that noise was the sound of their bodies being lugged about in the camera run. So it was just surreal. We got to know the cameramen, because we could see through. By the end, we started going slightly mad. Just hearing those four voices.

I was never worried about being naked. I didn't have a problem with my body. We knew they had cameras in the shower and toilet, but I remember Caggy [Caroline O'Shea] and others would shower in their bikinis. They really didn't want to get naked. But that was odd to me because I thought, this is a programme where you know there are cameras everywhere – in the bed, under your bed, in the toilet – why would you be worried about them seeing your bum? Everyone else was fine about it.

I really liked my housemates. Caroline was the funniest thing ever – she always had us in stitches but she was erratic. Very up and down – she couldn't cope with the pressure and stress of being nominated and not being liked ... She couldn't understand why people didn't like her.

We had to do tasks, or else we had no food. Sada Walkington was not a team player – she had a boyfriend and wouldn't mix with the boys at all – and it caused a huge divide between the girls and the boys. If the boys ever wanted to come in the girls' room, Sada would say 'no' and it caused such tension. I had huge arguments with Sada about it. Sada was a big character. She was mental but funny. I was one of those that bridged the two groups. I would love to see them all again. Fundamentally we were all really nice and alright. We had arguments but we sorted it all out. There was pain when people left but we got on with it.

BRIAN DOWLING, Winner, *Big Brother Two*

I remember going in and the door going 'vodoom!' closing behind me and I'm thinking, that's it now. I saw Bubble first and he had been in my audition groups. Then everyone was just saying 'hi' and introducing themselves and it's all 'la la la'. I remember looking at Helen and thinking that she looked like my kind of person because she looked like an air stewardess.

I was really excited that I'd be getting to know other cultures and I remember you [Narinder] and I were in the garden and you said, 'Are you gay?' and I said, 'Yes,' and then you said, 'Well, we'll be the Paki and the Poof.' And I was like,

'Okaaay.' I knew instantly that I wouldn't get on with Stuart – instantly. Also Elizabeth, because she wasn't a girly girl. I knew I wouldn't bond with them.

When you walk in the first thing you look for is the cameras: 'There's one, and, oh, there's another,' but then you just forget within hours. I thought the House was lovely compared to the *Big Brother One* House. We had separate boys' and girls' rooms back in our day.

I remember we were always hungry. These days they give them alcohol to start fights but we were starved. We'd fight over who got the extra chunk of chocolate – they were light-hearted rows, if that makes sense. Quite naïvely I thought everyone was nice and that I was having a good time. It was like a holiday – sunbathing, games, laughter.

But the first eviction came up and it was Penny against Helen and Penny went – I couldn't believe it, she was my mate and I went into the toilets and cried. But then you carry on. I didn't think anything else would come bite me in the ass but then an extra housemate walked in and everything changed for me.

AMMA ANTWI, *Big Brother Two*

I remember thinking how lovely everyone was and how lucky I was. It was only after a couple of days that people's true colours began to show . . . like Penny, she was just too much and she did my head in. Period. She did everything in such an over-the-top way. She was venting about everything – always in your face. And then there was people like Narinder – Narinder who I thought I'd really get on with on the first day – she was bubbly and fun but then started turning into this catty, bitchy person.

I never had a game plan, I couldn't see the point in it – you can't make people like you or force yourself on people. I wasn't smart enough for a game plan. You'd have to be extremely smart or a great actor to have that.

Bubble was my saviour, he was the one person I could chat with and breathe a sigh a relief with. But all in all I enjoyed being in the House, I loved all the tasks, even the fire building task! I know some *Big Brother* people feel they are manipulated through tasks like that – we were sleep deprived, but I don't think that was Endemol being so manipulative, I think it's more simple than that – they had 24-hour streaming and people want something to watch at two o'clock in the morning! Not everything is a conspiracy!

When we were hungry was because we had failed the task, not because Endemol were being evil and wanted to starve us so we'd fight – the fact is we failed tasks and therefore had no money for food. But you have to remember it's TV, so of course they will manipulate to a certain extent but what do you expect? It's a TV show.

I was bored a lot of the time but then I remember it all changed when an extra housemate walked in half way through and I thought, fandabbydozy!

ALEX SIBLEY, *Big Brother Three*

I thought everyone seemed really nice at first, I really liked Alison, didn't think much of Lynn nor Jonny – not with a haircut like his – but basically I liked everyone. It took a few weeks before I realised they were all filthy and if I didn't clean then they never would. Because I'd never watched *Big Brother* I didn't realise that being a pain in the arse would get me nominated. And I was up for eviction the first week. I'd even told my mum and dad, 'Don't worry, I won't be out the first week, I'll be fine.'

SISSY (JOANNE) ROONEY, *Big Brother Four*

Our House was known as being boring and to be honest, things were very mundane and the days very long in the house, so when the ratings weren't very good they needed something to show and I feel I was edited to look like a crier. Whining and crying all day. So they put me in several times crying because not much else was happening. I only cried a few times and certainly less than others. But I'm not sat here whinging about it – I have to accept it.

EMMA GREENWOOD, *Big Brother Five*

I was thinking, am I here or not here? I just wasn't aware, wasn't on the ball ... I'd lost all my senses ... almost like floating in an altered state of consciousness. I thought, oh my God, oh my God ... I'm here. I was over the moon, really happy and I felt I'd achieved something. Something to tick off my list. I knew where I was meant to be in life ... I'd done it. I felt like I was in a spaceship or something, and thought, the psychologists have done well here.

I wasn't nervous. I instantly liked Marco Sabba but felt I wasn't bonding with Victor like I should have. I've got an urban background – been brought up in a black community – and thought, yeah, we'll get on and talk about music. I'm thinking I'd get on with him, I've been brought up in the ghetto, used to me rice and peas. Me curry goat ....

Now I know why we didn't get on. Victor's been bought up in a posh community. His mum's a doctor and his dad's a lawyer. He went to private school. We didn't click because he thought I was thick as pig shit and he was educated. He acted the gangster but he wasn't underneath it all and I thought, who you being? And he was angry at me, thinking, are you really that thick?

When I was younger I was the ghetto girl – I've got big earrings in, hair slicked to the side and tracky bottoms on. I said the 'N' word because that's what we said on the street where I grew up. They'd call me custard because I'm white and I'd say 'N' back.

Victor didn't like it because he didn't like me anyway and was shouting, 'I can't believe you called a black man a nigger!' and I was like, 'No, I don't mean it like that, you're not listening to what I'm saying. I'm explaining.' So then I knew he was causing me problems and I thought, 'You need putting in your place.' I couldn't leave it. Especially a man that's in my face. I've been brought up like that; I used to nick cars and stuff.

I kept thinking, why am I not clicking? I knew Jason and Victor had a game plan but I didn't. I lost all my senses – smell, touch – and felt like I was on another planet. I was disoriented and relaxed. I played up to the cameras big time – the food fights for sure – but I did also forget about them.

The two sides formed. We were the fun lot and the kids, basically, and they were the boring old farts. We'd just do things to get at them.

VICTOR EBUWA, *Big Brother Five*

And I walk into the House and it's just quiet – one second roaring crowds and then just silence. I was dying, chomping, to compete in this game and as soon as I saw everyone I thought, hold on, something's not quite right here, I've been set up. And I realised that there must be some psychopaths in here to deal with. The series before had been just ordinary nice people and the penny dropped looking around – they had definitely upped the anti with the kind of people I saw before me.

I didn't know these people – they could have been eleven dicks! I was also the only black guy in here – that was my instant and immediate thought. It's a big, big issue, when you're an ethnic minority in that show. You never start off on the same level. You never ever, ever start on the same social standing. You have to work and graft for it.

Whatever you do is a hell of a lot more exaggerated. For example, if I have an argument with somebody I'm automatic- ally aggressive and dangerous like an animal. Jason Cowan can get angry and it's OK. So I thought, OK, I'll have to be the white man's friend here, kiss arse a little. That first week I was buying favours all over, I was a true politician.

I knew for me to survive in that House I had to be able to manipulate people, that was my game plan – you can't go into a game without a game plan. *Big Brother* is not a laugh, it's not about pissing about for ten weeks with your mates – it's a flippin' game! There are morons who go on that show who think it's a laugh but it's a clear-cut game and I planned to win that game. The first key is not to get nominated. I could afford for one person not to like me, even two, but not three. You can't leave the House if you haven't been nominated whether the public dislike you or not. It's only a popularity contest in the last week. Secondly, you've got to get on with everybody and not to let them know that you don't like them. Thirdly, don't piss any of the women off. You piss them off and you're leaving.

The first night I remember I had no conversation with anybody, no one threw any conversation my way. I felt segregated. But as it was everyone was talking crap. It was obvious Dan Bryan was playing a game. But Emma was a hard one, she was trying to play the black buddy, 'Oh yeah, I have lots of coloured friends in Oldham, you're my nigger, you're my nigger,' and I couldn't believe what I just heard. You don't drop the 'N' word – I don't care who you are – and I said, 'Shut the fuck up,' and she said, 'What?' They never showed this, ever. But she showed lack of respect too many times and as a result divisions formed in the group.

Me, Jason and Ahmed Aghil were on the one side and the idiots on the other side. It was street politics in that House, like the ghetto. Looks were being exchanged between each group. You could walk innocently into a room and there would be Nadia just grilling you with her eyes. And then Emma and Michelle Bass got evicted; I cannot tell you how happy I was. Two down and two to go.

NADIA ALMADA, Winner, *Big Brother Five*

I immediately saw Emma, who I had met at the auditions, and she came bounding over. I had no initial judgements on anyone, I was open to them. Jason had a thong on and I thought, what the fuck? (*laughs*). Everybody was bonding – Victor and Jason, Shell Jubin and Vanessa Nimmo. I wasn't really at first, everybody was so much louder than me, if you can believe that (*laughs*). And more vivacious. It was so much to take in. I felt a little alienated because of my accent. Everybody was running around naked, boobs out, and Shell ran around with no pants on – I would never have done that!

Big Brother Five was the evil *Big Brother*. The House was designed that way too – low ceilings, sloped walls. And we had communal bedrooms for the first time ever too, but because I come from a very large family and had lived with others in shared accommodation I had no problem with that. I felt very comfortable in myself.

Oh God ... Gradually as time passed I became more friendly with some people until there was a clear division and our group were the children. I became a child, I took on child-like behaviourisms. It's almost like being in a school playground and Big Brother is the headmaster. So you become naughty. I was repressed so much as a child before my sex change, and always trying to conform to what is considered 'normality'. Being in the House allowed me to forget all of that and become the child I never could be. I could be that child! It was like going through puberty again. Like going back in time. I was reliving my childhood.

We were the children – the destroyers of the House and they [the 'Jungle Cats' – Ahmed, Jason and Victor] were the cleaners, the teachers, the philosophers. Boring. I was like, 'Fuck that, let's go mud wrestle or something.'

DEREK LAUD, *Big Brother Six*

When I got into the House what struck me immediately was how young the others were – they would all get excited about things that didn't excite me. Whenever Big Brother spoke they'd all start shrieking, 'Ohhh, what did Big Brother say?' and 'Oh my God, the diary room!' They kept running to the diary room and I thought, what on earth are they going on about? What goes on in the diary room? Because I'd never watched *Big Brother* I just couldn't get into it, and it took me ages before I went into the diary room.

I got used to the cameras straight away. They were very small, it was just the noise that was slightly annoying – like a snake slithering in the grass. I didn't take immediate dislike to anyone. I loved Makosi – I thought she was very beautiful and striking. I thought, wow. What people don't understand is how small the House actually is. The whole place is smaller than my entire apartment.

Then Big Brother would start playing games with the alarms in the morning and then they would regulate the temperature all the time – hot and cold, a lot of it was terribly juvenile.

The pranks played by Big Brother – I found that hard to cope with.

MAKOSI MUSAMBASI, *Big Brother Six*

I had no game plan, I was just playing along with the others. I knew they had game plans so I played them at their own game. When I went to bed at night I was so exhausted from playing the game. I loved, absolutely loved, being in the House. I loved all the different people and I would wake up everyday and think, what shall I do today? As much as I hated Saskia Howard-Clarke I even loved playing the game with her. In any situation I would rather be the head not the tail, and the head hardly ever has a game plan. The only thing I worried about was getting boring. I needed to entertain a little more.

SAMANTHA HEUSTON, *Big Brother Six*

The minute I got in there I begged them to let me have a couple of minutes to myself in the diary room without it being viewed. I just thought, shit, I can't deal with this. I had rehearsed and practised the entrance for two weeks and imagined all those people looking at me, and it was a bit too much. It's a bit pathetic really, the minute I go in. I got in there and I was the third person to go in and I felt lonely, scared.

When I went into the diary room I just started crying. I didn't realise there would be so many cameras in there, they were moving and made a lot of noise. We as housemates thought it was a bit excessive that year compared to previous ones. I suppose I'm a shy girl at heart and I don't know how confident I am at this – you know big personalities can make you unconfident.

The minute I got in there I had this feeling that it was like being back at school. It felt like it was a cleansing for two weeks – I was thinking about school and how it affected me. It's weird, I knew it was going to be like that for some reason. I just kept thinking about how quiet I was at school and that affected me for years because I felt like my personality was being trapped. I would be really mad outside of the classroom with my friends, so I was like a giggly girl who had to stay in her box.

I felt back at school again and like that girl who I used to be ... I thought, my God I could never feel like this again, but it did feel like that. I don't know really ... There was one time I was sitting with Anthony, Maxwell Ward and Saskia and I was trying to talk about my friends but couldn't get a word in and they weren't interested, as if I was talking shit all the time. There was another time we were sat in there and they were saying that there's someone in here that the public might like because she's a bit of an idiot and they might like that. I just thought, my God I think they are talking about me or to me.

No, I bonded with Science [Kieron Harvey] but there was always that limit. They did it with Science as well, the minute he even spoke. I think the producers edited him really badly and the other housemates encouraged him to be like that. They made him react like that because they were bullying him so hard, Science could have got even worse. I was amazed how well he coped. Every morning he would try and speak and I would stick up for him and they would say, 'Shut up,' and Derek would start on me.

It was so claustrophobic – I never thought it would be like that and it was so hot in the House, which is why I didn't wear any clothes. I was sick a lot of the time and had headaches, we were begging for air conditioning. It was quite easy the first few days because most people were having a hard time, like Lesley Sanderson. I was really bubbly the first week and got on with all the boys, and the minute I saw Maxwell Ward I thought, yes, there's a funny person in here and I've got friends.

ANTHONY HUTTON, Winner, *Big Brother Six*

It was unbelievably intense. I can't describe it. My heart was pumping so hard. I saw everyone else and was careful to be polite and introduce meself to everyone. The House was really colourful, I couldn't get me head round the fact that I was in the programme that I had obsessively watched. The first few days I couldn't even sleep.

The cameras didn't bother me, it was more that I still couldn't believe I was in the House and then when I was in the diary room, I was like, 'Fucking hell I'm actually in the diary room.' The emotions I was going through – I just can't describe. The first person I met was Lesley and I came out with the cheesiest line ever. I said, 'Is that a Wonder Bra you're wearing, because it's doing wonders for me,' and Maxwell went, 'Oh my God, that's just cheese.'

I immediately hit it off with Maxwell because we started talking about girls; he really liked Sam and kept going on about her – 'Oh, look at Sam,' – and I thought, sound, he's into girls and seems down to earth. I was expecting some crazy people and there was – what with Kemal Shahin walking in with a sari on – so Maxwell was just normal and a lad.

I was taken aback by Science when he came in because he was so in your face and his name was Science. I thought, fuckin' 'ell, and then Kemal came in. It was like, fuck me, this is gonna be mad. Everyone was just so dominant and just wanted their opinion heard.

The next morning things just kicked off. What we didn't know was that Makosi was given that task* and she wouldn't get out of the bed and that alarm kept going off! I told her diplomatically to get out of bed . . . It was kicking off left right and centre. But I got on with everyone apart from Derek – he didn't like Geordies. He didn't like me . . . He was an amazing character but not a nice bloke.

Sam was in our group to begin with. It was me, Maxwell and Saskia and her but she would just sit there and giggle. She wasn't a bad lass but on the third night she sat in me bed and I got the impression that she fancied me, and then we sat in the living room and she started holding me hand! And I was like, 'It's day three! And you're holding me hand. This is not gonna be another Stuart and Michelle.' It made me so uncomfortable. I said, 'What you doing?' and that made her feel uncomfortable.

---

* Makosi was instructed by Big Brother to make herself unpopular and gain as many votes for eviction as possible. For completing this secret task she would be guaranteed to remain in the House. One of the ways she did this was to stay in bed when Big Brother set off a shrill alarm in the morning – the alarm continued for as long as she stayed under the covers.

EUGENE SULLY, *Big Brother Six*

Got into the House and the first person I see is Kinga, who I had done the guinea pig run with. We were told by the producers not to acknowledge each other as if we knew each other and what's the first thing Kiki shouts? 'Eugene!' Thus destroying the verbal reality of the whole programme. I couldn't ignore her so I said 'Kiki!' and put the kettle on and what's the first thing Big Brother does? Call us three into the diary room and tell us we were not in the House – bastards. We were told we were going into the 'Secret Garden' – a sub-House.* I thought, shit. I thought I would have been in the House for at least a week and suddenly I realised I'd just be in this 'garden' and probably get kicked out after a few days, and all people would remember of me was the fig leaf I was wearing. It dawned on me that this could cost me my job.

LEA WALKER, *Big Brother Seven*

Well Big Brother started playing mind games with us from the minute we walked in, they didn't let us have our clothes and this really stressed everyone out – your clothes are your identity. In a strange and alien environment they're the one thing that would give you that feeling of comfort, but they cleverly didn't let us have our clothes and it threw everyone. It made me feel like shit to be honest.

The first week was all about Shahbaz . . . he just pounced on everyone. He hardly slept and he'd stand on his bed and get his cock out . . . I swear on my life that's what he did and I'd say, 'You dirty fucking bastard,' and he'd go off crying that he was this 'poor Paki poof' and I'd be like, 'What!? It's got bugger all to do with your race or sexuality – you can't just get your thing out and wank in front of us girls!' Then he'd go in the diary room for hours or sit in the bathroom and talk to the cameras.

---

* 'The Secret Garden' – Eugene, Kinga and Orlaith lived in a hidden house decorated as a jungle. They had to steal clothes and food from the main House, and only Makosi knew they were there. She later had to choose two of them to go into the House.

He . . . made out he was the victim; it was so hard living with him – he would flip from one personality to another, if you said anything to him that he didn't like – he'd just flip! And I'd go in the diary room and say to Big Brother, 'I don't feel safe, this man is not right, there's knives in the House and sharp objects. He reminds me of an ex that treated me badly' – Shahbaz had the same traits as him – but Big Brother did nothing. So what I used to do was hide the knives under my bed when I went to sleep – I know it sounds a bit much but . . . I didn't feel safe. Then one day he went in the diary room and never came out.

RICHARD NEWMAN, *Big Brother Seven*

Shahbaz jumped on me, Glyn Wise was dressed as a lifeguard and Lea and her boobs in gingham . . . I thought, oh my God, I've got myself into a fine mess. Mind you, I could hardly talk. I was dressed as a cowboy. But that first night isn't all fun and laughter, you're still traumatised at that point – it's like being shot out of a cannon and the House is where you land, all dishevelled. Not only is it impossible to be thinking of playing a game but it's also pointless – anyone who goes onto *Big Brother* has to realise that it's a popularity contest.

The game belongs to the general public, not you. They ultimately decide who stays and who goes. So there was no point me trying to be clever or manipulative because effectively it wouldn't work, because if the public see that they will vote you out as soon as you come up for eviction.

Grace Adams-Short is a great example of that – she played the game in the House like a pro. She manipulated everyone in the House and was incredibly popular, hence she didn't get nominated, but then Susie Verrico* came in and put her up and – bang! – the public voted her out. I decided I was going to be just me; besides, as soon as I walked in and saw Pete I knew he was the winner.

---

* Susie Verrico – Nestle ran a BB promotion by hiding a 'Golden Ticket' in their products; the ticket holder would be able to enter the BB House. Susie bought her ticket from Ebay and went into the House in week three.

Shahbaz invaded your personal space and I believe that you have to be invited into someone's personal space and within hours he had off-loaded major personal stories about rape and molestation and it really pushes you away because it's only the first few hours!

I immediately loved Lea, Nikki and Pete. Didn't like 'The Plastics'* – Imogen Thomas, Grace – they were conformists and just looked the same and followed each other. I couldn't bear it.

KINGA KAROLCZAK, *Big Brother Six*

I went into the 'Secret Garden' and Makosi could only choose two people and she didn't choose me. I was gutted and felt humiliated – all my dreams had come to nothing and worse still, I was probably going to be a laughing stock for wearing that fig leaf bikini. I hid under the towel and cried my eyes out. All these people that had picked on me all my life and friends I had fallen out with . . . I wanted to show them, 'Look I'm on TV and I've done something with my life,' but instead when I got out, it was worse than I expected.

KINGA THE MINGA were all the headlines. As a woman I felt so ugly, so very ugly. People were shouting, 'Minga!' following the press line, and I lost a stone in weight as a result of this onslaught of criticism – 'Oh, you looked repulsive in that bikini.'

I knew one thing for certain: before *Big Brother* I got lots of attention from guys but all of a sudden I was this ugly girl and the people that I knew didn't want to know me – even friends. They were embarrassed to be associated with me. I was the laughing stock. And yes, I had watched *Big Brother* before but I hadn't read the newspapers ever, just the magazines, and magazines paint a very different picture to the papers.

In magazines it's all sweetness and, 'Isn't this and that *Big Brother* person a success,' so I was in shellshock. I just stayed at home and prayed they'd put me back in; I just needed this one chance to turn it around. I rang the producers and they

---

* Grace, Imogen, George Askew, Lisa Huo and Sezer Yurtseven formed a group in the House and were dubbed 'The Plastics' by Richard.

told me that there was no chance of me going back in. They said, 'Look, love, just buy yourself a nice frock for the finale.'

So I rang my old boss and asked for my job back. Yes, I'd be a joke but at least they knew me already. Then a few weeks afterwards, I remember feeling the most depressed I ever have felt in my life and I couldn't sleep. It was three in the morning and I went downstairs and put the telly on and there was Orlaith McAllister sleeping in her bed. She hadn't walked out like she said she would, so I knew that was my last chance and it was gone.

I felt like shit. I went back to bed and just cried myself to sleep begging God to just change my life somehow if not by getting me back in, then just something to get me out the hell I was in. I'd lost my dignity and my friends, my confidence and felt like the ugliest girl in the world. It was just this dark tunnel and I could see no way out, I cried.

Then at about ten in the morning my mum came into my room going, 'It's the producer, it's the producer on the phone,' and I just thought, oh, it's probably about going on *Big Brother's Little Brother*, so I take the call and it's Sharon. 'Morning Kinga, look outside.' And so I look outside and there's a car there with a Carebear in it standing at the door and I was like, 'What?' And she said, 'We want you back in the House,' and I dropped the phone.

I was shaking. My mum picked it back up and Sharon continued, 'Orlaith walked out this morning so we will put you back in under one condition,' and I was like, 'Anything!' and she said, 'You cannot utter one word about what has been happening in the outside world – the bombings – otherwise we will drag you out.'* So I was like, 'I promise, I promise.'

Then I hung up and before I packed I closed my eyes and said, 'Thank you, God.'

SOPHIE PRITCHARD, *Big Brother Three*

In the beginning I actually enjoyed being in the House. I thought everyone was lovely. I noticed Jade looking at me up

---

* The 7/7 terrorist attacks on the London Transport system occurred during the filming of BB6 in 2005, so the housemates were unaware of what had happened.

and down always, but nothing to worry about. I met Lee Davey and that was very special. But then I really noticed Jade's dislike for me, the night Sandy jumped over the wall and escaped. I could see her talking to Adele Roberts saying, 'She's fake, she's false,' and I could hear her!

I said to Kate, 'I'm sure she was talking about me,' and she said, 'No, no, she wasn't.' Jade never said it to my face, always behind my back. And it started like that and went on and on like that. We never argued because I'm not a controversial person. Looking back, I wish I'd just told her to fuck off, but I approached her nicely and said, 'I think we should talk, I know you've been bitching about me behind my back,' and we sat down and talked.

Her explanation was that I was 'too nice'. She couldn't understand why I was so friendly with people, but I'm like that – I am just nice and it's almost my downfall but what can I do about that? That's how I am. Jade just couldn't get that . . . she thought that because I was being just nice, I must have a hidden agenda, and she felt threatened by that, coupled with how I looked. So she constantly would call me 'fake'.

The last week was the worst, it affected me so badly. Anything I said they'd laugh at and I just withdrew; it was like a witch-hunt against me, and I felt powerless. Jade had this way of just making you feel like poor . . . It broke me. It totally broke me. People said I was quiet in the House but what did they expect? Against that?

I was up against Jonny for eviction and knew I'd be going, but when it came to my eviction and I was walking out of the House, up the stairs Jade was saying, 'Fake, fake fucking fake.' And I'm walking up the stairs to leave . . . I really felt like walking back down the stairs and smacking her one, but I thought, no Sophie, walk out with dignity. I walked out and didn't get one boo, all cheers and I thought, fuck you, Jade.

KATE LAWLER, Winner, *Big Brother Three*

Jonny Regan ran up the stairs and took my suitcase and I thought, a gentleman, I like you, then suddenly I saw Jade and thought, oh my God, the nutcase from my audition is here, and she said, 'Oh my God!' I met everyone and immediately fell in love with Alex – I thought he was the most beautiful man ever – and I loved Alison Hammond, who after a few weeks was my best mate. I knew after the first night Jonny and Alison were the two people I'd always be mates with to this day.

Jade was annoying everyone at this point. And then that week Davina announced that the public had been voting all week to evict someone, and the top two were Jade and Lynn Moncrieff. I didn't mind which went, but it was Lynn, and then the game really began.

At first I kept hearing the cameras but within 24 hours you forget. I always looked a mess because I just didn't care.

Everyone asks me if I had a game plan in the beginning, but, no. I will admit this – looking back now, I know I held back when it came to all the arguing in the House. There were so many times when I could have said, 'Will you just fuck off?' but I didn't. I bit my tongue instead. I don't have time for rude people. When Sandy Cumming was being really nasty to me, I was like, 'What is wrong with you? I haven't done anything to you,' and he just said, 'I don't like you, Kate, and I don't like Jonny.' And I replied, 'You don't like us because we are loud and funny and sometimes I'll try and run up a wall when I'm drunk. You're a grinch.' And Alex was the same – it was only in the last week that he started letting loose and having a laugh.

When Jade was in the *Big Brother* House in my year, she was exactly the same as she was in *Celebrity Big Brother* this year . . . From day one she was aggressive, rude, argumentative. She created a bad karma in the House and I remember [the way she treated] Sophie.

The moment Sophie entered the House the whole House could see Jade was jealous of her – probably because she was pretty. I remember thinking, what has Sophie done to make you behave so horribly to her? Jade then got Tim and Adele involved and as a group they made Sophie feel very awkward and uncomfortable – exactly the same way as Jade, Jo O'Meara and Danielle Lloyd did to Shilpa Shetty in *Celebrity Big Brother*, laughing, piss-taking etc.

I finally had it with Jade the night of the 70s roller disco in the final week. After the disco Jonny and I were in the diary room having a moisturiser fight and talking to Big Brother with our 70s wigs still on! When we came out Jade did her usual, 'You've been lying' rah-rah in-my-face rant to Jonny and me about something that had happened ages ago.

She has – and I noticed it this year with her argument to Shilpa – this weird obsession with creating an argument and calling people liars! Random! But I snapped and finally did what millions of viewers had wanted one of us to do for nine weeks and stood up for myself and said, 'Just stop being such a horrible argumentative bully! Don't shout in my face! Talk to me like an adult like everyone else!' It didn't change anything . . .

Watching it this year shocked me as I thought she may have changed but she hasn't . . . *Celebrity Big Brother* confirmed exactly why I never remained friends with Jade and why she didn't win *Big Brother Three*.

I was amazed with the way Shilpa handled her arguments . . . I would have lost it!

7. CABIN FEVER

I'm not bad, I'm just drawn that way

(*Who Framed Roger Rabbit*, 1988)

After they ask you why on earth you applied to be on the show, the thing that everyone wants to know is, what is it like in the house? I only have one answer for that: it's hard. Come and have a go if you think you're tough enough, and I promise you, you won't be – it's gang warfare in that House, street politics. Just imagine going to sleep one day and waking up in a war zone. That's what life in the *Big Brother* House feels like.

You are cut off from the rest of the world, ripped apart from everything you love, living with people you don't know. You have absolutely no contact with the outside world. What I would have done for just one phone call, just to quickly say, 'Hi Mum,' and everything would have been OK, but that's the whole point, right?

After a while, as mad as this makes me sound, I started looking at photos of my family and husband and wondering if they really existed. My mind started playing games – it was almost as if their faces were fading out of the picture. Everything was turning black and white! Contrast this with Jade's recent *Celebrity Big Brother* – she had her mum and her fiancé in the House with her and even then she behaved the way she did under pressure.

How do you think it feels for the rest of us who don't have our loved ones by our side? I would imagine my life before *Big Brother* and could hardly remember it. My entire life consisted of what happened in the House – Bubble and the other housemates had become my family and the House my home. I'm a strong person, a very strong person, and as Amma pointed out, I don't suffer fools gladly, but I could feel the experience breaking me – what on earth was going on out in the outside world? Were people even watching?

David Wilson, an academic criminologist who briefly worked on the show, commented that, 'The contestants forget within a matter of days that they are being filmed. About ninety eight per cent of their behaviour is when they do not remember the camera is there,' and it's true.

When Endemol gave me the Talk of Doom they had warned me that just because *Big Brother One* had been a success that didn't mean *Big Brother Two* would be one too, and that in fact the opposite usually happened. I truly believed that the only people watching were our families!

PHIL EDGAR-JONES, Creative Director, Endemol

We're under a lot of pressure to make a good programme, and yes, the show is edited but the thing to say about editing is this: however much you are edited your real personality does come through. I think there are things that all of us don't recognise about ourselves that you will watch and not like. We as people edit ourselves; in our own minds we select the things that feed our self esteem and make us feel better about ourselves and we deny the things that don't. We all do it.

Unfortunately, when you're on the telly as much as the *Big Brother* housemates are and all that is streamed, then the bad things that you do, that we all do, will equally come out. I think that when people come out and have a bad experience, they latch onto that as the bad thing that was projected on them.

So, yes, there is a process of editing in the story we choose to tell – for example Kinga with the bottle – she did do that.* We didn't edit her putting the bottle up there, did we? But that's the point I'm trying to make, we also showed her doing other things but the viewer chose to remember that incident – so there's also a process of editing going on in the viewer's mind.

If you look at the web forums you get people supporting, for example, Lea, and they're going, 'They're just trying to make Lea look bad and Richard is getting all the good coverage and being edited really well,' but then you get Richard fans saying, 'Richard's being edited really badly and Lea's getting edited really well' – so we cannot win! Because they have done their own editing in their heads.

You like some people and not others and actually that's not editing – the same edit has been shown and you will like that contestant, and another person will hate that contestant and have completely different views – so where does film editing come into that? What I'm trying to say is that there is a whole load of editing going on everywhere – we edit, the contestants edit and the viewers edit.

RACHEL MORRIS, Psychotherapist, *Big Brother*

TV is entertainment. Nobody is interested in a story that includes all the fine details whether you're down the pub or making a TV programme; we want the salacious stuff. *Big Brother* gets criticised by housemates after the event for 'editing them unfairly' but all this really means is that they have been shown in a less than flattering light. *Big Brother* does not 'make it up'.

Of course the producers have the power to manipulate an audience, but they can only use the material that is actually filmed. A housemate will complain that they were misrepresented – that the whole story hasn't been told – but that doesn't change the facts. If you were mean to someone, even if that person has picked on you all day, you were still mean. It might seem unfair that only your behaviour was edited in and

---

* Kinga was filmed allegedly simulating sex with an empty wine bottle after a night of heavy drinking. Kinga denies that she did anything other than pretend to perform the sex act.

therefore skews the story somewhat but that doesn't make it a lie. We hate to be seen out of context but in a 24-hour-a-day live film, context becomes something in the hands of the editor.

A truism in therapy is that what resists persists. What you try hardest to hide becomes the thing most easily seen. So I would say if a contestant complains about being portrayed as a bully for example, the evidence of bullying will have been retrieved from actual events of bullying. It's not a cartoon manifestation of that contestant – it's really them, really saying and doing those things. What the bully is complaining about is that that's only one aspect of their personality and you didn't show the other sides of them to balance it out.

And yes, it is possible to victimise somebody in *Big Brother* through editing, no doubt about it. If you show somebody as grumpy and that's all you show then you can definitely manipulate the way someone sees that person, but what the producers can't do is directly misrepresent that person. And that's the risk you take when you go on *Big Brother*.

BOYD HILTON, TV Editor, *Heat*

The whole editing process and the fairness of it has kind of been washed away for me because of E4 and live streaming. You can't complain about live coverage – I watched you, and you were like that. It's not the job of *Big Brother* to be scrupulously fair to all the people in it. That's what's so misguided about the contestants who go on *Big Brother* – they need to remember that it is not the job of the show to be fair to them. The job of the show is to entertain the viewers – five million of them – not to be fair to the twelve contestants in the House.

SHARON MARSHALL, TV Critic, *This Morning*

Unfortunately your fate is in the hands of the editors and yes, it is cruel and unfair but that's the risk you take. There is a cruelty about *Big Brother*, there is such pressure for the producer to go bigger and better each year and to have to deliver a different format, and perhaps the producers are now less caring about the people and what they have to go through. I do have huge issues with the psychologists that put these people forward. I question whether a lot of the housemates should be put under that pressure. Early psychologists have walked out of *Big Brother* because they have seen how these contestants are manipulated. Three months of being locked in that house – I mean I do seriously think we will have a suicide.

MELANIE HILL, *Big Brother One*

We were allowed to talk to the psychologist at any time we felt we needed to and one time I was in the diary room and something really bizarre happened, but because it was the first series I just didn't click. He wanted to talk about my 'flirting' and I kind of went, 'Huh?' I didn't get it, I just wasn't flirting – as far as I was concerned, it was nothing – but he felt there wasn't something quite right about it, which I thought was outrageous. I mean, flirting?

I should have seen what was coming, what they were showing and what was going on in the outside world, but it was the first *Big Brother* and I just didn't put two and two together. I went out of the diary room and promptly forgot about the conversation – that's how naïve we were in the first series. That's how innocent. They were editing the programme and making us look a certain way. We were oblivious and focused on our little world of living basically and growing our own vegetables.

I had two lows in the house. The first low was when Andy Davidson went. I just couldn't understand why the public would vote him out. He was the one that held us all together and made people get on with the tasks – we had hard tasks that went on for days. We were really hungry all the time. So Andy was the one that could push us all forward and get on with the tasks.

But what I found out later was that the other girls didn't like this about him and found it patronising and basically he got nominated and evicted. We were so close, we'd been to the same uni. And I just didn't get why he was evicted, but what I didn't know was that he had been doing all this sex talk and got the tag 'Randy Andy', and I hadn't heard him talk like that. And women voters didn't like it.

And then you had Nick making everyone feel paranoid and dithery by showing people names on pieces of paper and at that point I didn't like it – it wasn't funny anymore. I'd sit there and think, where did he get a pencil from? And I don't think Big Brother had a clue what was going on either. Nick was quite clever about it but it was just silly nonsense! But it made you paranoid. Suddenly you were thinking, oh my God, there's a conspiracy, this is weird. How had Andy gone against Caroline, who was going from one extreme to the other, on the edge – she was crazy, she couldn't cope with being in the House. 'Nick is now showing people names?' I just didn't get it. Then I thought, how am I going to cope with all these people in here? I felt alienated from the girls and wanted to walk out. But Andy said, 'You've got to promise me that you won't leave.'

The second low was when I heard Darren Ramsay nominating me – he was a mate. I used to go up to Darren for daily hugs, a little bit of a cultural thing. He missed his kids, I missed my mum and we'd hug. He made me laugh, he was funny. His reason for nominating me was so I could go home and see my mum, because I missed her. I heard him nominating me and the reasons why. And when he came out I asked him why, because I would never have nominated a friend, never a friend. I really cared that Darren nominated me. I couldn't believe he nominated me over Claire Strutton, who had just come into the House [to replace the disgraced Nick in week six]! He came out of the diary room and I just couldn't look at him. We told him that we had just heard him and he didn't believe us at first, then he got really upset and he basically went in to see Big Brother and had a fit with Big Brother.

I got up and went into the bedroom and he followed me and I just burst into tears. He was holding me. I said, 'How could you?' and he just said, 'I want to change my vote now,' and I said, 'It doesn't matter, I've heard you now.' We couldn't believe what had just happened. It was all wrong.

Then we had to re-nominate and I wasn't up for eviction. Craig had said he wanted to take me out after it all ended, and either I said no or made it clear I just wasn't interested in that way, but whichever it was he nominated me for the first time, and it was clear to me that he voted for me because I said I wouldn't go out with him. I just couldn't believe it and then Claire said I'd cried in order to manipulate the whole situation, so that they would have to do the whole new re-vote. I went in the diary room and said that voting for someone just because they missed their mum was pathetic. Just a pathetic reason to vote for someone. So anyway . . . my low was the betrayal.

The Nick thing was also a big low. It was pretty horrid. It was bone-chilling TV, to watch Nick squirming around like that and Craig confronting him. It was the first time that Craig had been so eloquent, because he was hurt, so hurt that Nick had tried to stitch him up. We knew that he had been showing names to people but we just didn't know to what extent and then we found out and it was horrible.

Craig handled it so well, that's why he won. It was working-class boy against public-school boy. Very representative. He handled it beautifully because he spoke from the heart – it was just honest. Nick then went and cried, and he got taken out the back door. It was horrible. They had security at the door because they thought Darren and Craig would do something but Big Brother was very clever – they called them both in the diary room and said, 'Make sure it's OK and there's no trouble.' So that's why I find it shocking that on Fight Night* it took so long for security to get involved – it shows that that's what they wanted. That's what made *Big Brother*. They cut the Internet stream and everything. These days there has to be a full-on fight with blood and everything for that to happen!

We always knew that Nick lied about everything – within a week. In the House it is difficult and you learn tolerance. But it was nice; it was afterwards that it all went to shit and horrible. Everyone just went all mental.

---

* 'Fight Night' – In series 5, Emma and Michelle were subject to a 'fake eviction' and taken from the House and sent to the '*Big Brother* Bed-sit' where they could watch footage of the remaining housemates talking about them. They were then smuggled back into the BB House and hidden under a table bearing food for a party. When the dish covers were lifted, they were revealed. Tensions erupted into a full-blown fight and the show's security staff had to intervene.

BRIAN DOWLING, Winner, *Big Brother Two*

I remember when Josh walked in and I was in the kitchen with Amma and Narinder, and Narinder started screaming, 'Fucking hell!' and Helen was like, 'Oh, he's lovely,' and I thought, shut up, Helen. Then Josh opens his suitcase to give us alcohol and cigarettes and I saw a teddy in his suitcase and I thought, good God, gay! And I thought Big Brother is doing this on purpose for me to get off with him . . . He was not my type.

Then we all sat down with Josh to chat and I felt like the fattest, the ugliest I've felt in my life – I was wearing shorts and T-shirts from Next and he had on Gucci, Diesel. And I thought, I'm so ugly. I had belts from Topman!

When he said he was gay he said, 'I'm on Brian's team,' and he pointed and I couldn't look. I was thinking, please God, please, don't let him be pointing at me, and all of a sudden the cameras all swooshed to me and just stayed on me and everyone just looked at me and Josh and all of a sudden that's when it all began: 'Oh my God, people are thinking we're going to fancy each other. People think we're gonna hang out now just because we're both gay.'

But I did feel he was sometimes patronising towards me. He was eleven years older than me, remember. We just never got on. And then we had a huge fight on my birthday – I was just being petty looking back – I was 22, just a trolley dolly, not that worldly and in comes this older, wiser, gay guy. I felt inferior. The argument was horrible and I have to say the bits that they showed to the public were limited and I came off lightly, because that was the same night that Amma and Stuart had their fight and that got more coverage.

And the great thing about the way I acted with Josh was *Little Britain*'s 'Only gay in the village' sketch. That was inspired by me in the House. I met David Walliams much later and he confirmed that also – they had always had this sketch about a gay guy but they didn't know how to work it, and then they saw me in *Big Brother Two* being all camp and flamboyant, going, 'I'm the only gay in the House,' and then Josh walks in and I say, 'But I'm the only gay in the House!'

and that created one of the most famous sketches ever and I think that in itself is amazing.

KATE LAWLER, Winner, *Big Brother Three*

The lows were when the House got divided into 'poor' and 'rich'* and I remember being on the poor side and Alex was on the rich side, and he got to choose who could go over to the rich side and he chose all the girls but me, and I thought, wanker, thanks a fucking lot. He hated me. I was left with all the boys but it turned out to be great. I played mum and looked after them all – did their washing and drank beer. We had the best time.

The rich side were having such a boring time. And then at the end of that week Spencer Smith got evicted and I looked over at Alex's face and it was all smug and he smirked. I was so angry that my period came on. I broke my glasses and I just went into the diary room and cried and cried. At that point, I think a lot of women in the country thought, we like Kate, because women could relate to me – Spencer had left, I'd got my period and broken my glasses and I'd cried. People were like, 'Oh my God she's so mental.'

Then I spent another week on the poor side. Jade and Adele were both up for eviction and we were all convinced Jade would go, and when Adele's name came up it was so, so confusing. But Jade and I had a love-hate relationship in the House. In the last week we really got on.

The night I got drunk and was falling over in the bedroom, I don't remember that as being a big thing. I remember falling over and thinking, dick! but I thought, who would watch that? because I was in the bedroom on my own and I didn't think they'd show me on my own. Why would they? And that was like the biggest clip. Mad.

I was well worried about what my family would say because I'd snogged Adele and I thought, shame, I snogged a girl on

---

* 'Rich and Poor' – for a few weeks in series 3 the House was divided between rich and poor, with housemates on different sides of the divide being given either luxurious or meagre food rations.

TV, and then thought, bothered?! It's not like I would have had sex on TV!

AMMA ANTWI, *Big Brother Two*

Josh walked in and I was so pleased. He was definitely my kind of person, in that I knew he would be the kind of mate I would have in the outside world, and he still is actually. I didn't immediately notice any problem between him and Brian but then it became apparent how insecure he made Brian feel. All of Brian's insecurities came out when Josh walked into the House – Josh was this confident gay man and Brian was a gay man who wanted to be accepted in the heterosexual world and he also felt sexually threatened by Josh. Brian didn't want to get on with Josh, though he tried a lot. That's an example of positive editing because they hardly ever showed any of that going on between Josh and Brian!

But anyway life went on in the house and it's weird because you do forget that life on the outside actually exists, and the only time I was reminded was when on eviction nights Davina would make her announcement and you'd hear the crowds and only then you would think, bloody hell, I really am on the telly aren't I?

When Stuart and I fought, that was me at my extreme – I went stir crazy. He had been vile and nasty. He had said that he knew what kind of background I came from and that he didn't approve and I just lost it ... Brian and Josh also had their big fight that night and they never showed it – Brian lucked out big time, because he was wrong in the fight, he was a wanker to Josh. But they never showed it – whether it was on purpose or not, I don't know. They showed my fight with Stuart instead. I did ask the producers afterwards why, and they said it was because our fight was more animated and loud – that's why they showed ours and not Brian's. Who knows?

When Bubble got evicted, that was a big low. I was closest to Bubble. I was increasingly finding Paul so annoying ... better contestants were being evicted over him! A part of me thought they must be seeing a very different story to what we were. He just talked shit and it wasn't even comical. If you had tripped, he had fallen off a building. And he was beating everyone in every eviction week after week. I never understood it and still don't understand it – I knew my time was up soon.

ANTHONY HUTTON, Winner, *Big Brother Six*

I'm a free-flowing person. I'm just a party person and I wanna have fun. Both Orlaith and Makosi are gorgeous sexy girls! As soon as Makosi walked into the House I thought, boom! She looked unbelievably striking. We had something going on from the start but there was something that meant I couldn't click with her, I couldn't work her out. And she would start going on about being a couple outside the House and I was like, 'Nah.' There was no way I was being the object of a business deal. I wanted to be a single lad, I'd just come out of a long-term relationship.

Makosi to this day says I slept with her.* I can't believe that lass! I'm not even gonna defend it anymore! The movements she made and putting her head back was because I was poking her. I wouldn't have fucked someone on TV. We'd all had a few to drink. It was a spur of the moment thing. I regretted the whole pool thing because I thought of me family watching and I've got two little cousins and I thought, fucking hell, they had to watch this. Still, loads of man points from the lads.

Afterwards, I watched the footage back and I remember Maxwell said, 'Did you two have sex?' and my reaction is like amazement and shock, 'No!' And even she said immediately afterwards, 'No, we didn't have sex.' I would on the spot do a lie detector. I would do it now.

I didn't know that she'd said she was pregnant in the diary room. If we had had sex I would have told her to take the morning after pill!

---

* During week six Makosi and Anthony allegedly had sex in the House Jacuzzi, although both give different versions of what happened. Makosi later requested a pregnancy test, although she was accused of having fabricated the whole scare, leading to her being branded a liar when she left the House.

MAKOSI MUSAMBASI, *Big Brother Six*

It was something that happened as a result of a number of factors. Firstly, you are locked up in a very confined space. Secondly, you are not thinking straight anyway. Thirdly, I had consumed so much alcohol, and you know when something starts and it just carries on and you somehow can't stop it? I had drank a lot and it was a very, very, very stupid moment that I regret bitterly.

If I could turn back time that moment would not exist in my life. It was the worst mistake I have made in my life, it was so stupid to do 'that' in front of millions. And people feel it contributed to my downfall, or that I then thought I was pregnant. If you have unprotected sex, then for any woman that would be the first worry! Why was it so wrong to voice my worries in the diary room?

If people thought it was a game, and if that helps them sleep at night then so be it. I know what happened, and I know what I went through with the worry of having had unprotected sex. I wasn't the only one in that pool. But I can't help thinking would the story had been different if I'd been a white, blonde and blue-eyed woman? I think race plays a huge part in the *Big Brother* game.

At the end of the day look at what was said to all the ethnic minorities in the house. [One person] said to me, 'You people have chips on your shoulder,' and Big Brother never warned her or reprimanded her. Although I played it very confident underneath it is very hurtful. I was told to go back to my own country – again nothing was done. [Someone else] put a scab in Science's food! And then they said stuff like, 'I'm not racist, I have a black cousin.' I mean, for crying out loud! They are the worst racists!

And the only reason the public liked Derek was because he said he would have voted BNP because of Science! Race was evident in the house daily, the house was divided because of race. You had me, Kemal, Derek and Vanessa on one side and Saskia, Maxwell, Anthony and Craig on the other side. I mean, come on, I don't want to play the race card or go too far with this but the obvious is the obvious. And the reason we never said anything or complained was because then we would have been accused of playing this 'race card' and being 'victims' and I'm certainly no victim. And also you can't accuse people of being racist because you run the risk of pissing a lot of people off ... It's very tricky. But the public did see for themselves what was going on in there, hence why Saskia and co. were evicted.

Bullying is also rife. In an environment like *Big Brother* you can easily become a bully. Yes, Lesley bullied Sam, but bullying is a method of getting people out [of the House] – it's a competition and with Sam, she was this pretty no-cellulite girl and looked fab in a bikini and they picked on her and were basically very nasty to her. They hid her stuff and by the end she was cracking. They thought she could win it and they needed to eliminate her. I stood up for Sam, I stand up against bullies.

DEREK LAUD, *Big Brother Six*

I'd lose it sometimes, I used to listen to the other housemates talking and I was astonished to hear them constantly saying things like, 'I can't wait to do the red carpet when I get out and go to film premières,' and I used to say, 'You're all mad,' and they'd say, 'Oh, and meet J-Lo on the red carpet,' and I'd say, 'None of you have any great talent and why would J-Lo be walking the red carpet with you? She's an extremely talented woman.' But this is the illusion they all had.

LEA WALKER, *Big Brother Seven*

When I used to see all these former contestants come out of the show and start complaining, '*Big Brother* ruined my life,' I used to think what a load of shit – editing can't do that – but I swear it does. I don't care what you say but it does. Until you're in there you just don't know. They made me out to be stalking Pete but we just bonded and had a laugh. They edited it as if I was all upset about him and Nikki and I so wasn't.

I missed my son, H, so much and I used to talk about him all the time but they never showed that and when I cried because I missed him too much they showed me crying, but not *why* I was crying – and it was the night when Susie came in. It's bang out of order. They never showed how bad Shahbaz was, they made out that Richard bullied him but it was so far from the truth. I don't know why they protected Shahbaz so much. Who knows? But he'd cry to the camera one minute then stand up and start laughing!

There was one part in particular that sticks out with the editing, and it was Pete who mentioned this when we came out of the House, and he said, 'Have you looked at the way they have edited you? Have you seen this the way they have portrayed you?' He said, 'It's not fuckin' fair man.' I said, 'Pete, let it go, baby, it doesn't matter,' and he said, 'You were like my mum!' and I said, 'I know.'

Nikki had fallen in love with him within a couple of weeks, and she said, 'Can you keep an eye on him because I think he's falling for Aisleyne [Horgan-Wallace].' So I would ask him questions about Nikki and was sworn to secrecy by her, and he thought it was me and I was trying to be secretive and she didn't want him to know. And one night when he wasn't very well and wanted to talk, and it was the night when Susie came in and we all had the meal. Pete said, 'Can I talk to you?' and I remember it like it was yesterday, and the cameras couldn't see our lips – we were talking closely – it made it look like I was leering over him. And I thought, they know that. They know that that's not what really happened. It's bang out of order.

SAMANTHA HEUSTON, *Big Brother Six*

Anthony would comment that I talked in my sleep, which I do do when I'm stressed or down, but he was making out that I kept him up all night and made a big issue of it. And then Lesley started at me, always at me and going mad at me in group situations and no one would stick up for me. She'd be saying, 'You're this, you're that.' She had my makeup once, and it had my [contraceptive] pills in it and the worst thing I could imagine was bleeding on TV – it freaked me out, but they made it look like I was really vain and just worried about my makeup! And then the others would all laugh at me and talk about me.

But it wasn't even that so much that got to me – it was the cameras, I just couldn't deal with the cameras still. I would go to the toilet for a poo or woman stuff and I would try to do it as quickly as possible because I could hear the cameramen rushing to the toilets and I would then rush even more to quickly wipe myself. One time I got poo all over my hand because I was rushing so much. I mean how embarrassing, a cameraman seeing that!

Then when I was trying to sleep the cameras would follow you and focus on you and you would look up and see the camera on you and you would hear them moving all the time. The only way you could escape was to go in the cupboard and pick your nose and even then you'd be worried and think they might even have cameras there! I know people will say, 'It's *Big Brother* – of course there's cameras everywhere,' but you just don't realise until you're in there just how intense it is.

I thought the public would really like me and I didn't even care if the housemates didn't, and when Lesley went in week one I thought, right, I'm going to go for it, and then Mary O'Leary went – and was a bitch to me too – and I thought, I must be really popular and now I can handle this. But by that time the whole house was against me and I became friends with Science and he was alright, but then again I was even warring with him. He would get really stressed about the chicken and things. And by week three I was up for eviction.

RICHARD NEWMAN, *Big Brother Seven*

The younger ones wanted to scream all the time and the older ones just weren't affected or phased by it. The Plastics were awful. All they talked about all the time was life after *Big Brother* – all the magazine deals they would get, how much money they would make and what clubs and parties they would go to, awful places like Chinawhite. Grace was the worst. She namedropped all the time about all the people she knew that were famous and all the people that would help her. The Plastics were also very calculating, they knew that if they got together with a male in the house that they could have that budding romance story, except they were all but shagging in bed within two days of being in there – hardly Helen and Paul!*

The criticism they threw at me was that I wasn't fun, but we just had very different ideas about what fun was. They would always try to rattle me. We could always hear the Russell Brand crowds going into the studio and we would often hear them shout stuff. Even though we would all be sat in the garden and hear exactly the same, the Plastics would say, 'Gosh Richard, that's awful,' and I'd be like, 'What?' and they'd say, 'Didn't you hear them calling you a wanker?' Stupid games like that. I'd say, 'Really? God, I'm so upset.' They were constantly trying games on me like that. I was victimised as a kid, so I knew what it was like to be very much alone in a big crowd.

My idea of fun didn't entail bullying – [some of the housemates] bullied Susie when she came into the house. Like when Susie came in and had to be the golden girl and got to wear gold? Well, the Plastics hated this and decided to wear gold as well and chant and prance in front of Susie.

I was accused of bullying Shahbaz, but I know I didn't. What I did do was I isolated him. In the outside world it's very easy to walk away from a person that you don't like. And I had to cut Shahbaz off because he was too full-on and I was constantly in the diary room telling the producers he was mentally unstable and should be taken out. He was seriously unstable.

Towards Glyn he was bordering on the perverse! He was himself bullying Glyn, he would get aggressive and turn. But the *Big Brother* producers were looking for a scapegoat. Eventually he was taken out. Bullying may be the wrong word in all of the above; maybe it's more just humans wanting to form a clique and do that thing where you want to be part of that gang in unfamiliar circumstances.

Big Brother would definitely manipulate us though, but through temperature control – that's how they do it. I like my rooms cold, so it was interesting that if a fight erupted and you

---

* Paul Clarke and Helen Adams' burgeoning romance unfolded gradually across series two, and was a big hit with the viewing public.

were at the centre of that row then all of a sudden the room would become the temperature you hated – hot or cold. Also at parties, we were not only plied with alcohol but also sugar. We'd been rationed all week then all of a sudden piles and piles of sweets were there and naturally you get a sugar rush and get hyper. And also placebo alcohol . . . You're being manipulated through food.

I have always been of the mind that *Big Brother*, certainly by series seven, (a) cannot make you out to be someone you're not, (b) they cannot put words in your mouth, and (c) you are responsible for everything that you do. But now having experienced it, I know it's heavily edited to either make you look good or bad. We are all three-dimensional characters but what you see is people being one dimensional. We all have multiple facets to our personalities but because it's edited you won't see that person as a whole.

Conversations – which I remembered clearly – when aired had been chopped up and it changes the entire complexion of the tone. The winner is, in my opinion – and it was certainly true of *Big Brother Seven* – already determined by the producers. Then they will make your bad points worse.

Lea is a classic example. She was edited badly, very badly. In the House she was so funny, she had a great Northern wit about her and yes, a very dry, adult sense of humour, which I, as a gay man, very much appreciated – but they only showed her crying all the time, which yes, she did do, but only five per cent of the time, not all the time!

Susie was also badly edited, made out to be boring and drinking tea all the time . . . I was a classic turnaround case. I wasn't liked too much at the beginning and then they showed the letter from my mum* and the public were touched, so the producers could hardly edit me badly after that! I never talked about my mum and her chemo in the House because firstly it's incredibly private and secondly, I didn't for one second want people thinking I was using the sympathy vote.

---

* Richard received a letter from his mother while he was in the House as she was undergoing chemotherapy.

KINGA KAROLCZAK, *Big Brother Six*

I went back into the House the next day without the fig leaf bikini, and it was my chance to turn this around and make more of an impact. I couldn't wait to show all those people that had taken the piss out of me – ha! I'm back in! I loved Eugene and Derek and disliked Craig who always made it obvious that he didn't like me, and made me feel as if I was lying all the time when I talked about my life. Then the bottle incident happened.

You know what it is? When I drink – and I've quit now – I turn . . . I was very, very young then, I'd just gone through a painful break up where I found out that my ex had cheated on me, so there was a lot of hurt. I don't think I need to go into detail about the bottle incident night but all I will say is that it didn't happen how it looked, it was a silly situation that got out of hand and it was misconstrued.

I used to try to do things all the time because it was boring in there – Eugene looking out the window, Makosi's cooking and Derek's cleaning. I used to go into the diary room and say, 'How are you going to edit it tomorrow?' So I'd try to do silly stuff like wear my pants on my head, so they could put it in, and I remember Sharon [a producer] had said to me before I went in, 'Oh, I know you'll be a great housemate, I know you'll get the ratings up,' so I'd do more random stuff and I did get the ratings up by 1,300,000.

ANTHONY HUTTON, Winner, *Big Brother Six*

She did stick it up herself, Craig saw it and I was like, 'Kinga, don't do it.' She was just always trying to create situations for the camera. Then she went into the garden to fuck herself with the bottle and I was like, this lass is crazy. She was pissed, but then again she was acting pissed a couple days later on non-alcoholic wine! It was all for the cameras. I kept thinking, your mother's gonna be watching this.

EMMA GREENWOOD, *Big Brother Five*

The producer took us into a secret bed-sit and Michelle was just frantic, 'Chick, Chick we're not being evicted. We're still in the show!' She was crying, I was crying, the feeling was amazing. One minute you think it's all over and then you realise it's only just begun.

So we live in this bed-sit; it was claustrophobic but we just sat watching them in the main house slagging us off and I used to feel my blood boil, especially when Victor was trying to say I was racist. I started having a panic attack – he was trying to destroy me and then Michelle kept crying because all they showed her was bits of Stu with Shell. She kept analysing every detail and I had to keep reassuring her, 'Come on love, stop looking at it too much.' We had no fresh air or fresh fruit and veg, just tinned food. Honestly it was really crap.

When Big Brother told us we were going back in, we were jumping up and down like lunatics and Michelle kept saying, 'Do not say anything about where we have been and what we've seen . . . We have to play this, Emma . . . We have to play this.' And me being me lost all my senses, and now I think, I'm a clever bitch but why wasn't I then?

I just got so excited and when I got in the house we was jumping about and laughing and Victor's and Jason's reactions were the funniest faces I've ever seen because I knew they were thinking, God, thought I'd got rid of those two, two down two to go, and I was sticking my finger up at them. Then I grabbed Nadia and Marco and told them everything.

I kept saying, 'Don't tell them I told you, but . . .' and I told Nadia that Victor had been taking the piss out of her laugh and her job and all this lot. So then we had a food fight and I was chasing Victor with a hosepipe and you know what? To start with we had a laugh, we were all having fun . . . For once we were all having fun! But then we had a food fight and the House was trashed! Water in the house, food everywhere, maggots, flies would have started coming in. It was vile.

You know what, I can understand . . . Everyone has to live there at the end of the day. Then Victor and Jason started shouting, 'You better fucking clean this up!' then all of a sudden Nadia lost it – 'Who do you think you are?' – then Marco starts dancing in Victor's face and then Nadia chucks the table up.

Then it all kicks off ... I chucked a plate at Victor's head ... I was angry but I fucked up, I really fucked up. But because I've been bullied at school as soon as I feel intimidated by anyone I'm like a dog with hairs at the back of my neck to make me look bigger.

Jason had kicked down one of the doors and started packing – 'You're all a bunch of monkeys.' Then the bouncers came in and Victor was like, 'It wasn't me,' and I'm thinking, you fucking pussy. So then they took me out the House and left me in the secret bed-sit and I was just crying and crying. All I could think was of all the hell ... Big Jason kicking down doors, Nadia slapping Vanessa, tables being chucked, I chucked a plate and I'm like, what the fuck? What the fuck just happened? So I'm crying ... It was war ... It was just war.

VICTOR EBUWA, *Big Brother Five*

So one day we're all having fun and I'm dressed like a clown and there's the table, when the tops came off and I saw Emma it was like seeing someone you murdered a long time ago come back from the dead and spit in your face. Yes, my face said it all. I thought I'd killed the two of them off and now it was back to square one, and not only that, but they were dancing in my face. They may as well have been dancing on my grave, that's how it felt.

I thought right, these guys [the producers] have put twelve maniacs in this house including myself – they never needed to manufacture beef. They should have just left us be, but they deliberately created a situation by taking two people out and showing them the rest of us only saying bad things about them and then sending them back in the house. Absolutely zero good can come of that, can it? They gave stupid people power and what happens if you give stupid people power? Anarchy. And anarchy broke out. I'm a bad character, I can't be anything but what I am, if you show me love I'll show you love back. Come at me looking for war and I'm a soldier.

If they had sent me and Jason into the bed-sit and brought us back, we would have played it differently and pretended we didn't see the footage. Look at the dynamics – for a start you're out of your comfort zone, no matter who the hell you are, you could be Jonny Horizontal* for all I care but out of your comfort zone and away from loved ones and with pent up frustration 24/7, if you have no release valve then it's only a matter of time before you crack up.

I saw people cracking up all over the place. Hence why Emma and Michelle started whispering to the other two [Stuart and Nadia], then they started a food fight and before you know all hell breaks out. It's like being in a movie and it goes black and all you can hear is screaming and people getting massacred and I'm thinking, what the fuck is going on? They didn't show the half of what went on that night. If Emma was a man, as God is my witness I would have battered her with the frying pan.

PHIL EDGAR-JONES, Creative Director, Endemol

We didn't want a fight. When we choose the contestants we can't say, 'Yeah, those two people will fight or those two people will have a romance.' We simply can't predict human behaviour. When we came up with the bed-sit idea what we hadn't accounted for was that two different people – Emma and Michelle – would react like that. I was worried that things might get out of hand, so I made a lot of phone calls. I called Emma's mum and asked her how she thought she would react, and remember we had also heard Emma and Michelle hatching a plan that they weren't going to do anything . . . Which broke in minutes. It got very heated, to a level where we sent in security before it actually became a fight. But we certainly created the situation – a melting pot, with the potential to go too far but we stopped it before it did and we learned a big lesson.

VICTOR EBUWA, Big Brother Five

Endemol wanted a ratings sensation. They built it up and the public wanted to watch them [Emma and Michelle] come back

---

* 'Jonny Horizontal' was an alter ego created by Stu in BB5. The character was an extremely laidback cowboy.

into the house. What you can't factor for is ... you can't legislate for how people will react to any given situation, you can only hypothesize. But for Phil to say, 'How could we have known that Emma and Michelle would react like that?' – that's a cop out. Sorry, it's a cop out.

What happened that night had to be one of the possibilities – when you are drawing up an action sheet of what could happen there would be 'a', 'b', 'c' and 'd' would have to have been all-out carnage breaking out. You can't leave that out of the list. Phil is talking horseshit. He knew, he was hoping like that would happen, not that he wanted it to go too far, but certainly out of hand. There's people's lives involved – I could have lost the plot and even knifed Emma! Who knows? I could have snapped, or Emma could have snapped. Anybody could have snapped and just thought they were defending themselves. It's as simple as that.

There is only so much arguing you can do before you have to smack someone. And I was pissed after, I wanted to leave and have it out with the producers. They were having me for a mug, taking me for a prick. How would they like it? People attacking them physically?

NADIA ALMADA, Winner, *Big Brother Five*

We'd had lots of drink and our friends [Emma and Michelle] have been given the opportunity to get back into the House – we had been deprived of them. And so we lost our sense awareness. It was Jungle Cats versus us. Our feelings were so low, then fuelled by drink, we then see them [Emma and Michelle] and all of a sudden this whole adrenaline rush kicks in and then Emma tells us what they have been saying behind our backs and so we are given this insight!

So we were happily playing along, but then Emma was frustrated about the whole issue that Victor had said she was racist and suddenly the alcohol kicks in and I was being thrown over the sofa! My blouse was ripped off and my breasts coming out. We had a huge food fight just before the house was chaos. Jason was banging on about cleaning up the house and I was shouting, 'We'll clean it when we want to clean it!' and I threw the table over.

Yes – it was manufactured by Endemol. They could have handled it better – they knew something would happen, given the circumstances. They knew that we would find out what had been said about us, given the huge amount of alcohol we had been given. And then being reunited again – the adrenaline. They knew what would happen, they must have had a psychologist working behind them. But I don't think they expected it to go to that extent. I will give them the benefit of the doubt.

Emma was taken out. That wasn't fair. If she went then so should another have. She was vulnerable.

PHIL EDGAR-JONES, Creative Director, Endemol

On the one hand viewers say, 'It's too boring,' and then they say, 'It's gone too far.' We had nine million viewers watching so-called 'Fight Night' and that says something weird about the audience – it's a guilty pleasure. So we walk a very fine line and we know we do. We take our responsibilities very seriously. We aren't bad people – we don't want anyone to get hurt physically or mentally. It's only a TV show for Christ's sake, it's not worth it.

EMMA GREENWOOD, *Big Brother Five*

So I'm crying and after a couple of hours I slept but then I'd get up and cry. I just wanted to say sorry to a couple of people and kept thinking, 'Is this my fault? Did I do all the wrong? It's all my fault . . . I shouldn't have told Nadia.' I fell asleep crying.

And then the next day they [the producers] say, 'Oh Emma, we're gonna get the psychologists to speak to you,' and I've got these beaming lights in my eyes. Like show lights.

So I'm waiting at nine o'clock in the morning, then it's two o'clock in the afternoon and I'm still sat there looking at these four walls, and then they ring again. 'Emma, the psychologist will speak to you soon,' and by then I'm like, 'I don't want or need a psychologist, I just want to speak to anyone. I'm stuck in this room all alone!' and then nine o'clock at night comes, then at ten o'clock they send some food through the hatch.

Shitty fucking food. Tesco beans and 1p crisps. I was in this room on my own for four nights and days.

And then the next day comes and someone calls and says, 'Oh Emma, we're gonna put you back in the house now, we'll let you know what's happening.' Then ten hours later I'm still on my own and I'm ringing them saying, 'What's going on?' and I'm still on my own and I'm pleading with them, 'You can't leave me in this room on my own any longer. I've got no fresh air.' And in the ventilators I can hear the rest of the house laughing and joking, making friends and I'm feeling proper shit and down because I couldn't make up with any of them and I'm sat on my own, unable to do anything and no contact.

Then the third day comes and the psychologist phones me up and I'm like, 'All I need is human contact, that's all I need.' Then that's that and by the next day, my God, I'm pacing the room, I've got to get out this room, I've got to get out . . . Another 24 hours in this room . . . No one to talk to and just four walls . . . Then they call me and ask me what DVD I'd like to watch, so I ask for *Bridget Jones' Diary* and they say I can eat what I like so I ask for a Pot Noodle.

I'm sooo pissed off by this point, but they promised me I'd be going back in the house, ringing me telling me I'd be going back in the house, so I just put up with it . . . Then I watch the film.

Then it was about six o'clock . . . the fourth night on my own. And I just had a huge panic attack, I couldn't breathe and I could hardly speak: 'Get (*gasp*) me (*gasp*) out this house now (*gasp*)!' I couldn't breathe. I'm in a room for four days on my own . . . Three nights . . . And fifteen minutes later [a producer] kicks the door down and grabs me and I was gasping, 'Why . . . have . . . you . . . done . . . this . . . to . . . me?' I couldn't breathe . . . [The producer] was stroking my face and saying, 'I'm so sorry, Emma, we are so sorry.'

KAREN, Emma's Mother

When I got to the studio, they sat me with their lawyer and watched the footage back and there were things they never showed and I said, 'I'm not having this, Victor has got a knife out and I want him arrested,' but [the producer] kept saying, 'No, we don't want that to happen,' and I was like, 'Well, why is Emma suffering and taking the brunt of all this?'

At the end of the day I knew they were panicking because the whole thing could have got really, really out of control if I was demanding arrests and courts, so then they'd try to appease me and say, 'Look, we'll help Emma when she comes out, we'll get her singing lessons, on TV shows,' but I still wasn't happy and when Emma came out she wanted to keep the peace with Endemol and thought they'd help her in a big way but they did nothing.

SHARON MARSHALL, TV Critic, *This Morning*

I became more hardened as the series went on and I was a hard-nosed hack and for us to go, 'Oh my God, I can't believe that just happened!' – we were shocked. And although we loved it as well, it made you feel grubby for watching it, because it made us start thinking, is it actually fair what we are doing in the name of cheap entertainment?

8. EVICTION

Hasta la vista, Baby

(Terminator 2: Judgment Day, 1991)

C oming up for eviction didn't surprise me in the slightest. I would never say I was edited badly – I was a mardey cow the last week, but I also pulled it out of the bag and did have loads of fun with Brian, though they never showed it. Well, the producers only had half an hour to fill, so they just showed Paul talking about his granddad all the time . . . They needed Paul for the romance blossoming between him and Helen – they have a story to tell, and I had to go, but I was OK with that.

I was dying to see my husband and family, so it came as something of a relief when I was voted out. I needed to get out. I never went into the House to win – that was never my game plan. My game plan was all about getting the right start when I came out of the House. But then again the bastards had beaten me, which was annoying.

You don't know it yet but that scramble to pack and get ready to leave is truly your last moment of freedom. Yes, I do mean being in the House. Your last moments of knowing your life as it used to be, the last time you'll ever know yourself. Your life didn't change when you entered the House, no siree, but the moment you hear your name announced and Davina says, 'Please leave the *Big Brother* House' – be afraid. Be very afraid.

The actual walk out of the House was probably one of the best experiences of my life. The moment I'd been waiting for all my life – paparazzi going wild, crowds screaming my name, people trying to grab me, banners saying 'Narinder', big posters of my face . . . and I kept thinking, how do they know me? Where did they get my picture? I know that almost sounds ridiculous, I couldn't have been that naïve to it all but truly I was. My moment.

I can't describe it but it was like being in an altered state of consciousness . . . I was there but it was as if I was floating. I could see but not really hear – I was only aware of movement, and everything was in slow motion. For as long as there is time and as long as the world goes round I will never forget my eviction, every moment, every step of that walk of shame, every exhilarated breath I took and every face in that crowd. It was quite simply the stuff of dreams. I was flying and I hadn't even won – I hadn't even come close. But damn, I was made for this.

I didn't think everybody loved me because I remember jumping into the crowds and someone said, 'Fuck off,' and I laughed because it was funny. I saw my family. My mum was crying and all I remember is talking gibberish. They must have thought I was mad and I was, a bit.

I had my Davina interview and I was bonkers. I then saw the psychologist for a while and he talked nicely to me and got my feet back on the ground. He told me something that I'll always remember – that he felt my eviction had something to do with the racism and that because of the Bradford riots it was inevitable I'd go, and that maybe I should think of doing something in race relations.*

He also showed me some of my press and it's bizarre but I remember not being phased at all by the bad stories. It was only paper after all – who cares? I wish that I'd made that my mantra from that point onwards, but unfortunately, as you'll soon read, it began to affect me in a bad way. Then I was taken away to the hotel, but I wanted to see more of my family. They

---

* The filming of BB2 coincided with rioting in Bradford between different ethnic communities in the town and in other parts of the north of England.

Top: 'Young, good-looking, a BAFTA...' Brian enjoys his post-*Big Brother* success. Courtesy of Brian Dowling.

Above: 'You do this, Brian, and I swear you'll lose weight!' Britney Spears keeps Brian entertained on the set of *SMTV.* © Justin Goff/GoffPhotos.com.

Above: Mel, one of the very first *Big Brother* housemates, enjoys life out of the spotlight. Courtesy of Melanie Hill.

Above: 'YES! First girl to win! 70 grand – nice one!' Kate shows off her DJing skills. Courtesy of Kate Lawler.

Left: Life after *Big Brother*? Narinder shows Sissy how *not* to do it! © Rex Features.

All *Heat* magazine covers courtesy of Mark Frith at *Heat*

Ha! Even **Leslie Ash** is embarrassed by her lips!

This week's hottest celebrity news

heat

MAGAZINE OF THE YEAR!

LATEST DEVELOPMENTS!
Zoë takes off
wedding ring

MORE SERIOUS
THAN WE THOUGHT?

EXCLUSIVE!
**Kate
Lawler**
New look!
New men!
"I snogged Duncan – & Gareth gave me his number!"

Golden
Globes
frocks!

PLUS!
Why all these
couples have
split too…

ANNA &
ENRIQUE   HAYLEY
& KEITH   NATASHA
& FRAN

Above: 'Smile, pose, and get outta there in 15 minutes.' Helen, Amma and Josh show how it's done. © Rex Features.

op: Alex accepts his Nobel Peace Prize.) Rex Features.

bove: 'Who needs aftercare when you can ave Sissy's Surgery?' Sissy models some f the clothes from her own fashion label. ourtesy of Sissy Rooney.

Far left: Another item ticked off Emma's 'to do' list – being on the cover of *Heat*.

Left: Nadia was born a diva, a true diva. J-LO eat your heart out!

Left: Pretty at last! Emma makes the most of life outside the bedsit. Courtesy of Emma Greenwood.

Below: The local celebrity – Victor keeps a low profile while enjoying a night out. Courtesy of Victor Ebuwa.

Top: Derek enjoys his welcome into Downing Street. © Rex Features.

Above: The ONLY man in Sam's life – her dad. Courtesy of Samantha Heuston.

Left: Pretty, no cellulite, giggly ... but Davina stole the limelight.
© Rex Features.

Above: Makosi – the one and only. Courtesy of Makosi Musambasi.

Above: Kinga reckons Britney can keep the fame, she'll have the money! Courtesy of Kinga Karolczak.

Below: 'And this is how to pull a lass post-*Big Brother.*' Anthony and friends try to impress the ladies. Courtesy of Anthony Hutton.

Top: Eugene gives a presentation on the history of superstructures. Courtesy of Eugene Sully.

Above left: Richard and Nikki remember the 'Plastics'. Courtesy of Richard Newman.

Above right: Dicky and Dolly get a few drinks down themselves before they head off to Gaydar to do their radio gig. Courtesy of Richard Newman.

Left: Lea – precious cargo number one. © Rex Features.

Top: 'It's a fix! I should have won! You were just edited well you w***ker!' Richard has a quiet word with Pete. Courtesy of Richard Newman.

Above: 'We did it for love, not fame.' Pete, Nikki and fellow housemates from *Big Brother* Seven. © Rex Features.

wouldn't let me but I threw a strop and they eventually relented. I was allowed five minutes and the Endemol people stood outside the door.

My mum, in typical old Indian fashion, only told me months later that she'd felt that my eviction was like attending my wake. She felt a strong premonition that I had died and people were coming to pay their respects. Dramatic or what! But you know it sent shivers down my spine because my mother had in fact hit the nail on the head. The old Narinder had died – my life as I knew it had gone, I had stepped into one unreal situation and been evicted back out, straight into another unreal situation.

What was this new life? Who was this new Narinder? Would I be able to return to my old life? Did I even want to return to my old life – why would I? This was a whole new world, and it was very, very far from the old world I knew and understood.

PHIL EDGAR-JONES, Creative Director, Endemol

The people who are most disappointed are the ones who think they will win and are voted out in the first two weeks – the ones with the highest expectations. I don't think that's necessarily the programme's fault. What we never set out to do is make somebody a star.

MELANIE HILL, *Big Brother One*

In the first *Big Brother* series we were all allowed to jump out of the doors and wave to family whenever someone got evicted, and we were convinced that the crowds we saw at every eviction were just rent-a-crowds hired to make the show look bigger than it actually was, to fool us. We never thought at all that people would become fans and come down especially to see us be evicted – that just seemed ludicrous. Just silly.

I can't even remember who I was up against, but I was out. I knew I was going, I kind of knew. It was fine when Davina said my name. I had about an hour to get ready. I didn't have a clue what I'd wear and these days they have eviction outfits!

We all went into the girls' bedroom and we chose what I'd wear, then Craig produced a packet of cigs that he'd hidden and I shouted at him and Em, and got ready. Went into the diary room for the chat and Big Brother told me that there would be flash photography and dogs and not to be scared. 'Don't worry about it. Davina will guide it all.' Davina was not big then; we didn't really know who she was. *Big Brother* made her and we used to just say every Friday, 'Hi Davina.' We didn't really know who she was.

It was amazing seeing my mum! I saw her and just ran into her arms and she whispered in my ear, 'Smoking and swearing.' That was what she was really upset about. I was crying when I saw my best mate Ruth and she was crying and I just couldn't understand why, but looking back they had been through a lot and had to deal with it all. I didn't realise that at the time.

I had my interview with Davina and it was all nice and pleasant. She didn't say anything about what had been written and no one really said anything to me about what had been going on. I was driven back to the hotel and, blissfully unaware of the furore that would be waiting for me in the morning, went to sleep.

AMMA ANTWI, *Big Brother Two*

I knew I was never going to win – I hadn't shown enough of myself. I always knew it would be Brian, and I knew that as soon as I was up against Paul that I would go – Paul had beaten everyone in every eviction. When Davina said my name I thought, fair enough.

When I walked out of the House, I enjoyed it – I didn't get booed and my interview with Davina was good – it was less nerve-wracking and was very quick. In fact that's the last thing I remember being good.

I was so happy to see my family, they hugged me and told me they were proud of me and that I had done well, and I only found out later that that was what the producers had told them to say and not to tell me anything about the way I'd been perceived.

If they'd had told me I could have put things right in my interview and it would have made the world of difference to me at least. Anyway the interview went fine and I left. I didn't think that I'd just go home and everything would be normal and fine but I never in my wildest dreams imagined it was going to be like it was.

BRIAN DOWLING, Winner, *Big Brother Two*

At about week six I really thought about walking [out of the house] , because all my friends had gone and I had no one and I sort of withdrew and I even read a book! That's how down I was! John Grisham's *Painted House*. I thought I'd rather read it than talk to anyone in the House – I was missing my family, my friends – and it just wasn't fun anymore. But then I snapped out of it.

Then on the final day me and Helen were playing spin tennis and I kept thinking, this is mean, I just want to hit this ball into her gob. She just had kept yapping and yapping for the whole nine weeks.

I wasn't nervous, because I just wanted to leave and go back to my life. I was convinced Dean had won, so when Davina said Dean's name I was shocked – you could see it in my face – and then I thought it must be Helen, because Dean was the first person that had beaten Paul in an earlier eviction, so I thought Helen would win.

Then it came to announcing the winner and Davina says the winner has 4,300,000 votes and the second place 2,000,000, and I thought, shit, that's a huge gap! It could be me. And for a second I thought, who could like Helen that much? and then Davina said, 'Brian,' and I just pushed Helen out the way and jumped on the sofa! I couldn't believe I'd won – it's a popularity contest and I'm last man standing.

I was in the House alone for twenty-five minutes [after Davina announced that I'd won] and I was banging on the windows saying, 'Talk to me!' and I made sure the oven was off and that I left the House tidy. And then the doors opened – it was different in our day, we had to walk over the bridge and then the gates would open to the world, so to speak, but first of all my family greeted me and I was so happy to see them, just hugging and I asked straight away about my sister Tracy, because she was pregnant and I'd worried all the time in the House about her, and she was OK.

Then the fireworks went off and I always, always remember Davina stroking my face really affectionately saying, 'They're all for you, all for you.'

They then opened the door to the gate and it literally went 'Voom!' – there were people crying, screaming, banners saying 'BRIAN TO WIN', 'QUEEN BRIAN' and I just couldn't think. It was like a dream. It was almost like it was a dream. I could feel what was happening, but it wasn't real. This is not real. These things don't happen to people like me. And people were throwing underwear and I kept thinking, I want to see my housemates; I wanted to see Narinder and Penny. Do you know the one thing I can remember thinking is, why is Josh waving at me and being nice?

Then I go backstage, see my family properly and they're just talking so much – all this information, the papers, Josh . . . too much to take in. Too much. Then I got taken away and to be honest I can't remember what happened, it's all a blank. It's blank.

KATE LAWLER, Winner, *Big Brother Three*

I was up for eviction in week five. I was up against Adele, Jade and Jonny. I immediately thought it would be me or Jade, so when they said, 'Adele' it was the biggest shock of my life. Then in week seven Big Brother told us to draw straws as to who would be up for eviction. Looking back, Big Brother did that on purpose because they knew we would all vote for Jade and they didn't want her out. I remember PJ Ellis saying, 'They've done that on purpose.' Me and PJ drew the short straws.

The advantage was that we got video messages of our families – PJ watched his and had a little cry and then I watched mine and as soon as I saw my mum, Karen and Kelly I could see it in their eyes – I'd done well. I could just see in their eyes and faces that I was doing well and that I wasn't hated, so, if I was evicted that week, I didn't mind. I knew I'd done well.

I was so 50-50 and everyone in the House thought I was going, especially Jade. So when Davina said 'PJ' I was like, 'Oh my God. I can win this, I can really win. Seventy grand – I'm that much closer to it.'

Then it was the final night and it was Jonny, Alex, Jade and me and I kept thinking, Jonny has got to win this, and I didn't think Jade had a hope in hell. I thought to myself, people could not honestly like her. In my head I thought, Jade first, then Alex, then Jonny and I win. That's how I wanted it to happen. But I didn't care if Jonny or me won it as long as one of us did. I didn't want Alex or Jade to win because they both had been two-faced, bullying, nasty people throughout their entire stay in the House.

As soon as Jade was evicted I knew Alex was next. We made a big bowl of alcoholic punch, and we just drank. When Alex was evicted next, I thought, fuck, and needed another drink. I was lagging by this point and just me and Jonny were left. I was so glad it was me and Jonny because we were best mates and I couldn't imagine sitting on the sofa with Jade at the end holding hands.

For me the whole *Big Brother* experience was made for me when I was sat at the end with my best mate. I loved Jonny. He was like my brother. So when they said, 'Kate' it was just weird. I thought, I've won seventy grand, I've got my flat. Seventy grand . . . My life had changed, I knew it. I remember just lying there on the sofa thinking, I've won *Big Brother*, I've won. I'm the first girl ever to win *Big Brother*. I was really drunk. My head was spinning, the House was empty and I was just dying to see my family. It was all crazy.

Next thing Davina was in the House showing me clips of me falling over and people were cheering and I couldn't 'get it' and then she showed me a clip of Duncan from Blue and I was like 'Oh my Gawdddd!' – he was my celebrity dream guy. I remember leaving the House and fireworks going off every-where and all these banners with my name on them. I remember seeing a banner with, 'Kate, will you marry me?' and I thought, who the hell is that?

Davina had a necklace with 'Yes' written on it. I thought, that's cool. Then I saw Karen run towards me and my mum and dad – they kept saying, 'Everyone loves you Kate, everyone fucking loves you,' and I just thought, what's the experience been like for you guys? I really wanted to talk to them about it.

SISSY (JOANNE) ROONEY, *Big Brother Four*

I was up against Federico Martone and Jon Tickle and on the Friday eviction show, they showed Federico called girls 'slags' but they didn't show that till the eviction lines were all closed! So yeah, the producers definitely wanted me out that night, because if they'd showed Federico saying that he would have gone and as it was there was only a few per cent between me and him.

They mark who they want in and out, I definitely think so, it's even more obvious these days.

EMMA GREENWOOD, *Big Brother Five*

So I get out of the bed-sit and they want a psychologist to talk to me but that's the last thing I wanted – all I needed was fresh air, to breathe in some fresh air – and human contact. I was so needing just to see people and talk to them. They took me into their offices and sat me down. Then my mum comes in and she's crying and I'm crying, 'Mum, I've been locked in a room on my own,' and my mum's hugging me and crying.

I probably wasn't making much sense but I said, 'Mum, I've been locked up, sat there on my own looking at hallucinating 70s wallpaper, trippin' me backside off . . . The smell, my God the stench from living there for two weeks with no ventilation was just horrendous.' And my mum's just crying. They then make a bed for me and my mum in their offices because we couldn't leave, because Fight Night had been all over the news.

It then occurs to me, 'How come my mum's here?' They didn't know I would have a panic attack and leave, but she was here when I left the bed-sit. She told me that night that they'd called her in the morning to say I would be coming out but they hadn't told me that – they kept telling me to be patient and I'd be going back into the House. The next day I was arrested.

VICTOR EBUWA, *Big Brother Five*

It was looking like I had a good chance to win but I noticed that Michelle and Stu were turning it into their show and taking over with their antics and I thought, nah – it's my show too. I'm not the supporting actor here. So I decided on the wedding task that I'd be the groom and Shell the bride and that's where it all went wrong.* I'm up for eviction and it's the biggest turnaround in the show's history – at the beginning of the week I'm favourite to win and then I'm evicted all in the same week. I still think it was rigged . . . I still think it was fixed for Nadia to win from day one and I was a threat to that. Jason was ahead of me by 200,000 votes and then I had that fight with Shell and I basically pulled my pants down for Endemol to get me out – she loses it and has mascara running down her face like the mad woman she is.

I was livid when Davina said my name. I was pissed. I wanted that £70,000 and I'm still pissed to this day. Put it this way, I can't moan about the fight with Shell because it happened and I surrendered my rights when I agreed to go on the show and it's up to them to show what they want to show for the best TV, so if the best TV is for them to show me being a wanker then that's up to them and I don't mind that because I chose to go on.

Anyway, life outside was nothing like you could ever imagine, I thought, what the fuck is this all about? What the hell is going on? It's like being in prison for a long time and then everyone clapping and cheering you when you get released and you think, why is everyone so happy?

DEREK LAUD, *Big Brother Six*

I made a tactical error – you can more or less work out at that stage who's voting for whom to be evicted, but I genuinely gave my valid reasons and not just, 'Oh, he snores and that's why I'm putting him up,' and I didn't realise that at that stage people would vote tactically and say, 'Oh, he eats all the

---

* Housemates had to stage a mock wedding, with Victor as groom and Shell as bride. The supposed couple later argued spectacularly.

cornflakes.' And Big Brother allowed that reason! And that's one of the perverse things about *Big Brother* – that they apply the rules as strictly or as liberally as pleases them, as to who they want out. They could have said, 'We aren't going to accept that as a reason.'

So as a result I'm up against Eugene and I'm evicted. I was disappointed but I'd done well. I thoroughly enjoyed my eviction, was hugely cheered and had a lovely interview. I was ready to go home back to my apartment but couldn't, and that was my big disappointment when I came out.

EUGENE SULLY, *Big Brother Six*

When I went in, I was scared that they would all be backstabbing evil bastards and they were all actually really nice people, especially Science – all I had seen of him was him shouting all the time but he was so different to that. I remember when I had to go in the diary room and decide whether to take the £50,000.* I took it and yes, it may have cost me winning the show but that was the decision I made in the sixty seconds given.

I was amazed that I'd even made the final week and even more amazed that I was in the last two. When Davina said my name, I didn't mind – I was happy to see Anthony win. But I was dreading leaving because I thought I'd get so booed for taking the fifty grand and I remember standing waiting for the doors to open and the thirty seconds it took seemed like thirty minutes. It was a bloody long time till the doors opened.

The doors then opened and I heard masses of cheering and I thought, that's all right, I'm not hated. It's weird having seven weeks of not very much noise then 2,000 people cheering for you. However there are more important things to deal with than your own ego, like walking down the stairs strategically so as not to fall. Then it comes back to that old execution analogy – you're dragged along the red carpet, photos, crowds, throwing poses and then Davina interviews you – you're processed. You know you have to perform – I made sure the

---

* In the final week of BB6, Eugene was offered the choice of £50,000 guaranteed or the chance to 'gamble' and potentially win £100,000 in the final public vote.

paparazzi all got their shots. When I watched it back I couldn't believe how animated I was – I've really learned to tone it down since.

SAMANTHA HEUSTON, *Big Brother Six*

I was so cocky I was convinced I wasn't going because Roberto Conte and Derek were up and everyone hated them but obviously they hated me more. Roberto did my head in – that boy with his cooking, we had so many arguments in the last week. And then he would come up to me and say, 'I'm really worried about you, I don't think you're coping very well in here. Are you happy? I don't think you're happy.' I think he was trying to knock me, basically, and I would say, 'Don't talk to me.'

Makosi was looking after me; the chaperone was my counsellor before I went in and then Makosi took over in the House. I thought Big Brother had put her in there to look after me, so that's another reason why I thought I was going to win because she seemed to know everything. I'm sure to this day she was a mole.

They were all being wankers and they just sat there. Anthony said, 'You're going to go tonight,' which was so rude. I did go but it's not very nice. Maxwell was being nasty and saying, 'You're going to go.' It got nearer the time and Makosi was doing my hair and I was laughing at how thick everyone was. I thought they would have shown that but I came across as some bimbo. Then I started to think, shit, maybe I am really going, and Makosi was saying, 'You will be OK.'

It suddenly dawned on me how embarrassing it was to be going out third. I hadn't expected it, and it made it worse thinking, all these wankers are going to laugh. I wasn't concerned about the public but I was about that lot. Davina said my name and I pretended I wasn't bothered but I was upset, but then again I don't think I could have coped in there anyway.

I think in a way they get you out when they know you are cracking. I was in the diary room loads. They don't want you to crack and they don't want people like that in the House.

So I'm waiting at the door and I'm shaking – I'm that scared – but thought, be strong Sam, be strong. I believe in God. The doors open and it's a mixture of boos and cheers – I didn't expect that many boos to be honest And as I'm walking down the stairs someone chucks a bucket of water over me, someone right at the front, all over my back – how did they get a bucket of water through security? I think it was a set up, all for the cameras. And then Davina starts making a big fuss and asks me if I'm alright but she didn't care really, drawing even more attention to it. I then had my interview – Davina had a long coat on and underneath she's wearing a bikini, again all for the PR of the show. I was mortified that that was all they thought of me – a bikini!

But at that point I just wanted to see my family and I couldn't see them. It all adds to your mental anxiety – I only got to see them for about five minutes but it was amazing. I then saw the psychologist for about five minutes and then I was whisked away to a cottage. I was on my own in this cottage in the middle of nowhere on my eviction night with no one to talk to, having just come out to the whole press and media and then – boom! – on my own in the middle of nowhere. I was so scared. There were a few biscuits to eat and I put the telly on and watched *Love Island*.

RICHARD NEWMAN, *Big Brother Seven*

I hold the record for being up for eviction the most times in *Big Brother* history – six times! The great British public kept me in but I'm no fool, I didn't sit there and think, gee I'm so popular. I knew it could be, and probably was the case that I was up against the more hated person. The worst was being up for eviction with Lea, my best mate in the House. You really do form bonds for life, she was my true companion and when we realised we were up against each other we both cried. It was so emotional. It was very close.

I knew I would never win, Pete was the obvious winner from day one and as the show progressed it was clear that Glyn had been through this amazing journey in the House and would come second. If you look at the demographics of how people vote in these shows it's 16–25-year-old women who will vote for the quirky, cute misfit, not for the 34-year-old gay man.

I didn't think Pete deserved to win. If I'm going to be honest and put myself on the line here, I think I deserved to win. I put up with the most shit in that House, I put up with some vile, nasty, verbally abusive people – I didn't walk out because I'm not a quitter, plus I wanted to stay true to my dreams. I'd tried so hard to get on *Big Brother* and had to look at it from that point of view – all those people that have auditioned would have killed to have got on. I couldn't just walk out on that dream. So I stuck it out.

Neither Pete nor Glyn needed the money. My whole argument is how can you hand over £100,000 to an 18-year-old? What work ethic is that portraying? I fucked up my life, made mistakes, I have no money and I've struggled. I would have been more inclined to give Lea or Jane the money – people who deserved the money.

I deserved the money, and when I came fourth of course I was disappointed, as I had taken a risk. My only expectation was to win the money and I didn't win the money . . . the risk didn't pay off. But you know what? The British public kept me in for that long and I'm grateful for that. My eviction was great, I got a massive cheer and a great interview with Davina. I have no complaints.

MAKOSI MUSAMBASI, *Big Brother Six*

I began missing home so much, I missed my environment. The week they evicted Vanessa – in such an awful, nasty way* – I heard the crowds massively booing me and I began to worry terribly about the pool incident and what if my mother has disowned me? I didn't care about the public but my family, what had I done? I knew my mum would not love this and by the end I was a bag of nerves.

I was the last woman standing but what was waiting for me outside has affected me and scarred me for life. The booing

---

* For Vanessa's eviction the usual eviction process was reversed and housemates were forced to make the final decision on who should be evicted, rather than the public. Vanessa was voted out by all but one housemate.

was deafening, it was horrible, but I carried on because I thought, well, maybe they have to boo and I've done wrong and I should take it. But then the Davina interview – that was the nail in the coffin, that is what hit me the worst.*

She is the face of *Big Brother*, she could have stopped them but instead she added fuel to the already angry flames and made them higher. She was horrible in my interview and never gave me a chance, she had already made her mind up to hate me. She gave her opinion of me instead of letting people make their own and you have to remember that certain people look up to Davina like God – her opinion matters. She plays a huge role in *Big Brother* and whatever she says is like gospel [to many viewers].

But her interview with me damaged me even further (*starts to cry*) . . . she has never attempted to apologise and I have tried to contact her because it has scarred me. She knows how badly this affected me, yet she has made no contact to say sorry or even explain – doesn't Davina also have a duty of care towards the contestants? We have been locked away from everything we love for three months and she is our first point of contact with the outside world and she has no right to be that nasty, no matter what I had done in that House . . . I have forgiven her but I won't get over it until she explains.

KINGA KAROLCZAK, *Big Brother Six*

I loved my eviction. I lasted till the last night, the finale, and I was happy with that, I got a mixture of boos and cheers but it was wicked. I felt so famous; I felt like Britney Spears.

But then when I saw my family and saw the hell that they'd been through with the whole bottle incident – my mum had been through hell when it was all aired. I was protected in the House but my mum had the brunt of it, the paparazzi outside the door, through the windows, people shouting abuse. My mum began to have panic attacks, it was awful, the hell that she went through – she even started smoking up to sixty

---

* Makosi's eviction interview, conducted by Davina McCall, resulted in several hundred complaints to Ofcom. McCall was accused of racial discrimination by some viewers, but Ofcom cleared her of any wrongdoing.

cigarettes a day. I put them through hell; how could I love myself?

NADIA ALMADA, Winner, *Big Brother Five*

I never thought I'd win. Never. Never. Never. I thought I'd be out instantly. I was always up for eviction and every time I put my eviction outfit on and said, 'I'm out,' and when I wasn't I couldn't understand it. I would always hold my Virgin Mary and say, 'Whatever the decision is tonight, please just be with me.'

I thought everyone was going to win but me. Dan, Jason, Shell. Not me. I was pleased that I had got that far, that I was there at the last night – that was enough for me. But as they got evicted I couldn't think. I'd had lots of differences with Jason all along but we were the last two standing and I think back and think, well, with the hatred there must have been some love there! (*laughs*) Then when Davina said my name I had a heart attack. Literally, they tell me that they had medics waiting for me.

I was screaming, I couldn't breathe and I was in so much shock that I had pains in my body – like needles in my body. I was in shock. Then the medics got ready to get me. Then the doors opened and I felt like Evita Peron on the balcony, 'Thank you thank you thank you' – that's all I could say. I was grateful to people – why would they do this for me? Why? So I kept saying thank you. I had no other words in my vocabulary. If you remember my interview with Davina it was very short because anything she asked me I just kept saying, 'Thank you thank you thank you.' Then my mum pops out behind me and I was like, 'What the fuck!' and I got all the more emotional.

Then they whisked me away and I insisted on seeing my mum but they wouldn't let me and I was saying, 'But I need to see her and my friends. I need some cuddles and love,' and suddenly I was just driven away here, there and everywhere but I insisted I still needed to see my mum and friends, so they relented but even then there were cameras everywhere because they were filming me for Winner's Week!*

---

* 'Winner's Week' – the series winner features in a documentary following what happens to them in the week that they leave the House.

ANTHONY HUTTON, Winner, *Big Brother Six*

When I went into the House I thought I didn't have a chance but then when I saw the same characters being booted out – like Maxwell, for example – I couldn't understand it. I thought my time was up. But when it got down to the last week, it started going through me head all the time. I knew I stood a chance. But I was shitting meself.

The emotions I was feeling were crazy. I knew Kinga would go first, wasn't sure who would go next, then it was Makosi. So then just me and Eugene were left and I was praying, 'Please God.' I wanted to win the show, I wasn't bothered about the money, I just wanted victory.

And when Davina said my name I was like, 'OH MY GOD.' I'd won the show that I was the biggest fan of. I can't really describe it. Pure and utter joy. Then I was behind the door waiting for it to open and it's funny because me mate that kept the video diary for me shows all me mates going, 'Do the 70s pose, do the 70s pose,' and the doors open and I was doing the 70s pose and they were like, 'YEAAAAAAAAHHHHHHH!' I knew I was gonna do the Travolta pose if I won. Only me and me mates find it funny.

The crowds were screaming, it was craziness and I was on another planet. I kind of wish I could step back in time and go back into my body and really absorb it all because it was so surreal.

Then Davina asked me about Makosi and I couldn't believe she had lied just to make money. I'd even saved her from nominations a couple of times so that hurt.

LEA WALKER, *Big Brother Seven*

I was ready to go, I wanted to go the week before. I'd had enough, I was missing my son too much and I was having a breakdown in there and they never showed this. I couldn't stand it anymore. I kept saying, 'I want to go,' and they kept saying, 'No, you will be fine.' They said, 'H is fine and your mum is fine and you had this letter from your family.' And I said, 'If H at any time turns around and says "I want my mum to come home", then I'm off.'

I just knew that something wasn't right in me. I was so sick of all the mind games Big Brother played, it was patronising. I had to leave and I was dreading the boos but you know what – I got cheered. Thank fuck.

9. THE FIRST WEEK

Show me the money!

(*Jerry Maguire*, 1996)

Think about it, won't you? I was Narinder Kaur, a 28-year-old medical rep from Leicester with a detached home and a nice, decent job. I go into the House as that person and I come out of that House as the same person – or so I think. But that life had just vanished, gone, died. Why? How? Because now I'm being ferried around in a Mercedes Benz; Chris Moyles wants me on his show; Neil Morrissey and Hugo Speers want dinner with me and Kylie asks to meet me in her trailer. And I'm being offered huge amounts of money. Clearer?

I was wanted here, there and everywhere. Newspapers wanted to talk to me, reporters were calling me – I was out of my depth. Everyone wanted a piece of me and I don't think I slept at all well for those first two months – maybe a couple of hours a night – but funnily enough I didn't feel tired because the adrenaline kept me going. It's bizarre but I took it all in my stride, as if I was meant to do this always. Although this was only *Big Brother Two*, I knew two things for sure: that the real game had now begun, and that I had one chance to roll double sixes. But what could I do if I didn't have luck on my side?

I remember my first newspaper deal. I just yapped and

yapped and they inevitably ran with AMMA'S A PIG AND BUBBLE IS RACIST, neither of which statements I'd actually made. I was mortified. The first thing I thought of was their parents; yes, I never got on with the pair of them in the House but strangely you do form a very strong bond and I felt desperately sorry for slating them, but the damage was done. I wanted to run back into the House and explain but it was too late. I had caused pain to them. I had a lot of apologising to do to Amma's mum and Bubble's parents.

The fame was astonishing – the public were lovely, so nice. I couldn't believe how supportive they were. I was so touched by the thousands of emails of support, and kids would come up to me and give me teddy bears and presents – all of which I've kept! I have to say, my faith in human nature was restored, after all the racism I'd suffered at school. I swear the people that approached me were amazing. Richard Madeley gave me some great advice. He told me to try not to let what the papers write get to you, because it hardly ever reflects what the public think of you, and he was right.

I wanted to concentrate on work as my agent had lots of offers coming in and had set up lots of meetings. I felt positive. I was running back and forth from Leicester to London and it was costing a bomb, so we thought about moving south permanently. My husband started applying for jobs, and soon enough he got one. Things happened really quickly and before I knew it we had a nice apartment in north London, my husband had a better job too, and though financially it would be a struggle, I was sure I'd get paid work soon.

It's a whirlwind when you step out of that House – and remember *Big Brother* housemates are just ordinary folk. What do we know about press? Media? Interviews? It's hard and it's cruel but, hey, that's showbusiness. Welcome to the devil. In my day, fame lasted a lot longer than 15 seconds: we actually got a good 25 minutes, but these days once you're out you really are out and forgotten within a night. So you make your money and then for a lot of contestants it's a good swift shove out the door – goodbye, have a nice life.

HANNAH PERRY, News Editor, *Heat*

Big Brother is a real big thing for us. Viewing figures are so high and as a magazine we can't deny that we want to buy into that market, because it sells for us. That's the bottom line. We have to invest in some *Big Brother* people and own that person and make people think we have the real deal on this, we know the truth on their story and yes, we can make people.

RACHEL MORRIS, Psychotherapist, *Big Brother*

The success of *Big Brother* made me think that we as an audience still want Christians thrown to the lions for our entertainment. We want to stand in our auditoriums and feel better than the victims we hurl our superior abuse at. Reality TV is interactive entertainment and there seems to be no shortage of folks willing to put themselves up for the challenge of surviving the fickle crowd and the gladiatorial press. It's only human beings who can watch each other fall repeatedly to the same prey and still think they have a chance because they're harder, bigger, better. We just can't leave that gauntlet alone.

KEVIN O'SULLIVAN, TV Critic, *Sunday Mirror*

The disturbing thing about *Big Brother* is that Endemol participate in the newspaper negotiations. It's Endemol doing the deals. And we just weren't gonna do that. The first series almost happened in a vacuum, by the second series we played the game, by the third we went anti-*Big Brother*, but quite rightly everyone accused us of being hypocrites because we still wrote about it. We were having our cake and eating it, but we wrote O.T.T insults – although that was deliberately O.T.T. and wrapped in them were my misgivings for the show itself, my reservations.

I do my best to be a little less cruel but *Big Brother* contestants are our whipping boys, our ultimate whipping boys. If we take the piss out of them we just know the public are agreeing with us, because what *Big Brother* is about is who you hate and why. The point is, it's the ultimate gladiatorial programme. Gladiators were sacrificed for the entertainment of the majority and that's what *Big Brother* is all about.

As far as [the producers] are concerned, if twelve million are getting entertained, then who cares if the twelve in the House get hurt? 'Who gives a shit?' they think. 'We just made £40,000,000.'

I feel for the contestants – chewed up and spat out like yesterday's fish and chips. Not Channel 4 nor Endemol gives a fuck about anyone in that show – they don't give a damn. You're just the Lego bricks of their product.

PHIL EDGAR-JONES, Creative Director, Endemol

Big Brother people are easy targets for the press because you put yourself up for this and you're fresh meat. They're like a pack of vultures; it's frightening. The press often get it wrong about people and there's all this mass hysteria.

GARY THOMPSON, Senior Associate Editor, *News of the World*

Big Brother people are easy targets and the reason for that is that in terms of privacy, when you go on the programme you are doing a deal with the devil. You are saying, 'I'm going on TV, there are cameras everywhere and so every part of me is fair game.' It gives the press the defence that these people have made the decision to go public with their lives and so the press have carte blanche to go a bit further than they normally would. Because of the outrageous nature of the show – people having sex, fighting – it's become very easy to poke a finger at *Big Brother* and make *Big Brother* people the laughing stock. But we don't deliberately set out to destroy people. As long as the story is accurate and it doesn't break the Press Complaints Commission's Code of Practice, then it's fair game.

SHARON MARSHALL, TV Critic, *This Morning*

I have little sympathy for the women who clearly are out for all the instant fame and cash they can get. Those that go on TV determined to have sex on camera, run round naked, or come out and arrange for snappers to be 'accidentally' passing as they take their top off on the beach. If they take the cash for cheap stunts then they're fair game. I do have sympathy for people where you would say, 'That person has been manipulated, they are not emotionally stable and you can see they are clearly being used by the producers.'

MELANIE HILL, *Big Brother One*

The next morning [after leaving the house] I woke up and the press conference was the first thing I did. I clearly remember them asking me how I felt about being compared to a black widow spider, and I just couldn't understand why I was being compared to an insect. I looked at the PR guy they had given me and he answered, 'Mel doesn't know anything about that because she's just come out.' And I started thinking, eh? This is not right.

Then we went back to the hotel and I was shown all the press cuttings and the headlines read, FLIRTY MEL. I am a flirt, but not the brazen hussy they made me out to be. I couldn't understand why they'd written this about me. And I kept thinking, what house were they watching? Were they watching the same house that I was in? So I had to watch all the shows back to back to make sense of it all, and it slowly dawned on me – they had just showed me massaging men all the time.

The editing was amazing. And I know my critics will say, 'Well, that's not editing – you did do that.' But because there hadn't been another *Big Brother* we just thought it would be a fair representation of what we did in the House. We were all totally naïve about the whole thing. It all dawned on me after a few days.

And then a producer of the show called me a few days later and asked me if I was alright and then at the wrap party I said to him, 'What the hell have you done to me? I'm the most hated woman in Britain!' He said something like, 'When Nick went we needed another fall guy.' He kind of admitted that. They were genuinely worried though, I have to admit.

I didn't know what all the *Big Brother* mania was about. I just stayed in my house, with security. I didn't watch the programme after I left. I didn't interact with the world. I was just finding it so hard to adjust to a different environment, smells, noise – my God, the noise. I couldn't be in a room with too many people speaking because I'd got used to just four people's voices, my senses were soooo dulled.

Visually, I couldn't get used to all the colours. I remember coming out and having sensory overload: my ears were hurting from the noise, my eyes were hurting. It was as if my body had shut down in the House and then, whoosh, overload! I couldn't sleep because the noise was different . . . it was all so bizarre. So I never got the mania.

I saw [an agent] the first night and I remember he asked me whether I was interested in talking to the Sunday papers and I said, 'What? What for?' and he said, 'Because there's a six figure sum involved.' But it didn't seem right, taking that money from a paper that had written such bad stuff about me. I wouldn't have been able to live with myself. They had slagged me off, how could I hold my head up high and then sell my story to them? Soon I'd have to face the world and step outside my house

AMMA ANTWI, *Big Brother Two*

From the minute I stepped out for about two weeks afterwards, my life was taken over by somebody else, and I let them. I allowed them to. 'You know better than I do, I know bugger all, so I'm quite happy that I'm gonna take any advice you give me because I don't know anything.' So when I left the studio and asked to see my mum and sisters they said, 'Oh, we think it's best that you speak to the press first and then you're free to see your family.' And I could have said, 'No, I want to see my family.'

But these chief executives and the top producers are looking out for my best interests, surely – that's what I was thinking. So when they said, 'No, don't do this, do that,' I did it. The only point when I saw my family was just before the Davina interview and I find out after that they had been told what to say to me, by the producers.

They were told not to tell me anything of the way I was perceived in the press but just to say that they were proud of me and that I had done well. So that's what my family said to me. I didn't get any chance to speak to them even before my newspaper interview. I was an idiot. I should have insisted and stamped my feet down to see my family, it would have made the world of difference!

They would have told me how I'd been shown and I could have put those things right in my interview and defended myself, but at the time I was so trusting. This is a world that is so alien to you, so you just trust whatever comes out of their mouth. Basically Endemol got what they wanted – an interview where I'm oblivious to all the negativity and I'm just talking in a Sunday paper about how great it all was – so their PR and marketing was successful for the show. But then I watched the footage back – I put it down to how I was portrayed on *Big Brother*. If they had put in fifty per cent of my good and fifty per cent of my bad stuff, I could accept it but they chose to put in what was going to make their programme better. And yes, that's TV but it didn't seem right to me.

People would come up to me and say, 'Why did you do that? Why did you say that?' and I couldn't defend myself because they would always retaliate, 'Yeah, but we read it,' or 'Yeah, but we saw you do it.' I honestly and naïvely thought [they] wouldn't edit badly or manipulate us – a respected, trustworthy company; they're not gonna make me look bad, they'll look after me.

When I watched the tapes back I thought to myself, I know it's me, it obviously happened, but I swear it didn't happen the way I'm seeing it happen. For example, certain conversations I'd watch back and either the beginning or the end would be missing and it totally changed the whole angle. At times I had to suspend belief, and another major thing that affected me was actually watching myself. I studied all my facial expressions – that wasn't the fault of *Big Brother*, but you don't get to normally watch yourself in everyday situations over and over again, so I saw myself repeatedly doing certain things and I'm thinking, you're a nob, you look like a twat, for doing something like nodding a lot, or being grumpy all the time. So I began to change all of that about me.

The reality is your life may suffer as a result of what they show or they may even improve your life but either way they don't care . . .

My first ever photo shoot with a Sunday paper – that was the most demoralising and humiliating experience ever. Again it comes back to, 'You know better than me and I'll just take your word for it.' Stupid, looking back, and so naïve.

I remember they had me in this red sequinned 'bad granny' outfit. I think they wanted me to look like a two dollar hooker personally, but their rubbish perspective of what a two dollar hooker looks like. If they wanted hooker I could have done it much better than that! They put bright red lipstick on me – I looked like a black clown and I did say to them, 'This is looking horrid, I look disgusting.' 'No, no, no, you wait – it'll look great on camera,' they replied in unison! 'It may look odd now but you wait for the pictures.'

Then they told me to hold bingo cards! So there I was in a red sequinned outfit, bright red lipstick on black skin, looking like a black clown holding bingo cards! Ridiculous. The interview itself was taken out of context and slightly twisted. And because this was my first ever tabloid interview I hadn't quite got the gist that they make things up or twist things around. I wasn't happy with it but didn't know better, they knew better than me – what did I know?

SISSY (JOANNE) ROONEY, *Big Brother Four*

It was a ball, it was wicked. A whirlwind. Everyone interviewing you, Nicky Clarke doing my hair, drinking champagne, people doing me makeup and styling me – I'd never ever worn makeup. If anything that's what going on *Big Brother* gave me – this great lifestyle for about six months and the confidence to wear makeup and change the way I looked! Being invited to parties too, and I'm a party girl and so if I'm gonna be invited to nice parties, then of course I'm gonna go! I made £20,000 from selling my story.

BRIAN DOWLING, Winner, *Big Brother Two*

I was offered an obscene amount of money for my story, and I know it sounds stupid but I'd won £70,000 and that seemed enough to me. Looking back I should have taken it because a week later the interview that I did for the *Big Brother* book was sold to the Sundays anyway! And that fucked me off because someone pocketed that money and it wasn't me.

And also I found out the hell my family went through at this point. A kind of positive hell, if that make sense. The amount of pressure my family went through whilst I was in the House was phenomenal. Every day, if you think about it. They find out on the Tuesday that I'm gay, I go into the House on the Friday and they open the papers in Ireland on the Friday morning and there's a picture of me dressed as Posh Spice with the headline, QUEER WE GO AGAIN.

So my mum's thinking, 'Not only is he gay but he's also a drag queen!' You know my mum – she didn't know what gay was. The outfit was for a Halloween party, and I went as Victoria Beckham. I went the whole hog. Legs waxed, armpits, nails on, wig on, full face. So my mum fainted, literally fainted. Her son was called queer on the cover of the paper.

Everyone in the village was talking, and she was thinking, this is it, and queer dressed as a woman, because you don't know, you don't know. And it just goes to show the power of being under such intense scrutiny that a one-off incident like that could be such a powerful picture. My mum thought I was a tranny! Wearing girls underwear!

Even the first show was bad for my family because they showed me naked in the shower screaming and my mum fainted at the pub, because I was running around naked. It was a cold shower, is all I can say in my defence. You just think, they'll never show that because it's just not interesting – what's interesting about me screaming in the shower?

But my parents were hounded every day of the week for 64 days, paparazzi outside the door. My sister was pregnant and that was a personal thing. My mum said they went through hell. About twenty paparazzi outside your gates, every day for nine weeks. Everywhere she went, people called looking for interviews, and then when it really kicked in for me in the second week, my mum felt she was Jennifer Lopez, literally. She could have brought out her own fragrance in Ireland – that's how popular she was.

KATE LAWLER, Winner, *Big Brother Three*

We went to the after party. Then [the PR company] told me about all the offers.* The big deals were with the *Sun* and the *News of the World*, where I'd have to do five days of interviews and photos and I just turned it all down. I just thought, bore off . . . people must be sick of me. They've seen me for nine weeks already. So I turned it all down.

I could have got *News of the World*, the *Sun*, *OK*, *FHM*, a car, a holiday . . . I had just won £70,000 and it was more than I could ever imagine. I just wanted to go home, but if I'd done the deal I would have been cooped up in a hotel for another week. I just wanted to go home and see my grandparents. I'd been away for nine weeks – why would I want to be in a hotel for another week? Last thing ever, and I didn't have anything to say other than that I'd won and I was happy.

We all got offered these seven-day deals when we got out where you had to sell your soul. I didn't do it but Jade did.

EMMA GREENWOOD, *Big Brother Five*

The next day the police arrested me on breach of the peace because I'd threatened to kill Victor. But then nothing came of it . . . [I think] Endemol just did it to show that, 'Yeah, we're caring and taking our responsibilities seriously.' I knew now that I wasn't going back into the House and I'm thinking, you bastards, why have you done this to me? Why me? When you have a grown man chucking Nadia over the table and kicking doors down? But I got the shit for it. Endemol wanted me out because Victor and Jason were playing the game, they needed them two to stay in the House so there would still be this equal division.

I never questioned why Endemol did this to me . . . I didn't want to piss them off because when it came to doing other TV shows they wouldn't have used me. Most shows are made by Endemol. My mum kept saying, 'Look what they've done to you, I'm gonna have them,' and I'd say, 'No Mum, do what

---

* A PR company is contracted by Endemol to provide management and advice to the contestants during their first few weeks out of the House.

I say. I don't want to piss Endemol off.' But then they just left me to do my thing . . . they just left me to cope with all the aftermath.

Then [the PR company] took over but then [sometimes it feels like they] take half your fucking money anyway! For example, I got £25,000 for my story of Fight Night . . . how can that be? One of the biggest *Big Brother* headlines ever, we're all over the news and that's all I got? My mum was saying she knew from reading papers and magazines what others had got, but that's all I got.

To be honest I didn't have a clue . . . Then I decided to milk the press for all I could. I did get offered £50,000 to go topless but I turned it down, that wasn't the route for me . . . I never heard from Endemol again.

VICTOR EBUWA, *Big Brother Five*

I wasn't right mentally when I came out. I'd been away from my family for a quarter of a year and my brain was mushed. I couldn't add up, I couldn't think right, because I didn't have to do anything of any responsibility in that House. I met with [the PR company] and they had two folders of offers for me and twelve agents wanting to sign me but they recommended I go with the best – John Noel.

I met with him and signed with him – my girlfriend did all the talking because my brain was not right when I came out. I watched the tapes back to see how I'd been portrayed; all they showed of me in the first two weeks was me being a dick to people but if I was just being a dick, then how come I wasn't put up for nomination? And in those two weeks the press toed the same line as what the TV was showing, so you had papers like the *Voice* saying I was a disgrace to black people, and I was some stereotypical black guy from some jungle in Zumanda.

I was being turned into a hate figure, then all of a sudden I find out that I get a following in the production gallery and all of a sudden they show my true self, and I'm suddenly the Great Black Hope. I restrained myself in the face of provocation in response to Fight Night; I'm well read and had been to university and *Voice* are stalking me for an interview. That's how this game works, that's the nature of the business and I'm thinking, I'm not Jesus. I can't carry a cross for black people.

When I saw the psychologist he said, 'Steady yourself now,' and showed me press clippings and . . . the *News of the World* had done an article saying I was a drug dealer and at first I almost pissed myself laughing because whilst I was in the House I thought they'd get all sorts of my shit out but that one story they did – it's not even true.

What had happened was that at about week two in the House we had all been talking about drugs. I said I knew some drug dealers and Stu asked me if I was a drug dealer and I said, 'No,' but the papers were having a quiet week and decided to print this story anyway, VICTOR A VIOLENT DRUG DEALER. And the *People* did a story saying that I was a NO PAY DAD, again total fabrication. [The PR company] got me a meeting with one of their lawyers who basically told me not to bother suing them. He was talking shit so I got an independent lawyer, who when I introduced myself to him said, 'Oh, Victor the drug dealer!' and it was then that I thought this isn't no laughing matter and decided to take them on. What did I have to lose?

DEREK LAUD, *Big Brother Six*

There was one thing that was strange about the departure – they try to saddle you up with this [PR] company . . . They came to see me and tell me what they could do for me and I said, 'Thank you very much but I shan't be needing your help.' Something didn't seem right to me about them. I signed a deal with the *Sun* for £15,000 for just one interview. I gathered that I'd come across well because people kept saying, 'You should have won.' The press had been very kind to me. The *Sun* said I was a statesman, the *Mirror* said I was a gentleman. It would have cost millions and millions in advertising budgets to get them to say that about anyone else – such is the power of *Big Brother*! So I was very comfortable with that; I had seldom read a British PM being described as a statesman!

David Cameron immediately rang me up and asked me to join his leadership campaign but I was rather too busy right at that point but said I'd declare for him.

EUGENE SULLY, *Big Brother Six*

Then I got de-processed. Saw the psychologist; [the PR] company met me for ten minutes and then I went to the after-show party. I just stood on the same spot for the entire evening because people just came up to me all night to talk to me. I'd been told by [the PR company] that *Heat* were interested in doing something with me and I kept umming and ahhing because I'd promised interviews to my mates at the radio stations and by the end of the evening the bidding had gone up to £20,000 and I went for it because they said I could do a few radio interviews too.

Then I got taken back to the hotel with my mates, they got their laptops out and started showing me clips of my best bits. I was seen as one of the less charismatic by the media, because I hadn't really been able to show my all. Anyways, I had my first ever photo shoot and interview, I spoke so much that their tape ran out! And the photo shoot was great fun and it's surprisingly difficult being photographed. I had to do a lot of model-type poses, which was hard work. I really appreciated how hard it is for models after this shoot.

MAKOSI MUSAMBASI, *Big Brother Six*

I met with [the PR company] and the first thing they said to me was, 'Immigration want to have a word with you. You need to get a lawyer.' I said, 'Fuck the immigration. I will talk to them after I've seen my family.' I missed my family too much and I wanted to make sense of it all and see what they thought, if they still wanted to know me. I saw my sister and she was jumping around saying, 'Who was that woman in the House?' and laughing and then I saw my dad's sister and I knew everything was OK. If she hadn't come then I'd know my parents didn't want to know. But she was there and gave me a hug.

I was then offered an agent [. . .] who was just waiting to suck me dry and do things like topless shoots that I wouldn't and shouldn't have done on reflection, but when you come out you have no sense of responsibility. When I left the House I lost my mobile eleven times because that's how much you lose responsibility – for three months I had *Big Brother* doing everything for me, do your shopping, wake you up, even switching your lights off – so when you come out to an alien world of press and media and [the PR company] say, 'Yes, go with this agent,' and when that agent says, 'Jump,' you ask, 'How high?' Whatever Big Brother had told me to do I did and so your brain is still programmed that way. They are trying to make as much money from you as possible and they are very much aware that you have not been in this industry before, so what they say is gospel to you.

[The agent] used to say to me, 'This is what you should be doing and where you'll make money. Go on Makosi, you must do this,' and as long as it made £26,000 or more he'd go ahead and say 'yes' and you just feel lost. Endemol just leave you to deal with it and [the PR company] were never contactable. I just followed the agent, my captor. It was like Stockholm syndrome.

SAMANTHA HEUSTON, *Big Brother Six*

The next morning I saw the psychologist for about five minutes. Considering that what I'd just been through was such a traumatic experience, I don't think five minutes cuts it. Then I met with a couple of agents and the agency that look after Abi Titmuss, but my dad didn't want me to go with them. He kept saying, 'We'll lose you as a daughter,' and I was saying, 'But I fucking love Abi Titmuss.' In the end we went with an agent that [the PR company] recommended but I wasn't happy. That was the first mistake I made.

I signed a deal with the *News of the World* for £15,000 and *Nuts* for £10,000. I did lots of photo shoots and I talked about my on-line magazine idea. I did a *Maxim* photo shoot and they wanted me to do things like put my fingers in my knickers and I didn't want to do that because everyone does it. I was driving around doing all my Carphone Warehouse interviews and people were waving, taking photos and it was lovely. I was getting a good reception and that was so touching considering I'd come out after only a few weeks and not with a good portrayal. That meant a lot to me, I was grateful. They would come over and say that they hated Lesley for bullying me and people still say it to this day.

When I went out I would get paparazzi following me. It was funny how envious people got. The hype and attention was out of this world. And I had a few celeb shags . . . I was lesbian for a week . . . A couple of photographers from the photo shoots. This life was like a huge high and I could soon feel it all slipping out my hands.

SOPHIE PRITCHARD, *Big Brother Three*

When I came out of the House and saw all the stuff Jade said behind my back I was shocked and sick to my stomach at how nasty she actually was . . . I hadn't done anything wrong to her. Nothing. And I always remember thinking, what comes around goes around and you'll get what's coming to you one day. That was worse, what she did behind my back. Stuff like, 'Look at her – she's so skinny.'

I don't know why, it was the same reasons as why Jade hated Shilpa – she was slim, attractive and more importantly just 'nice', and Jade doesn't get 'nice'. She thinks if someone is nice, then it has to be fake. But Jade came out of the House then and became so successful and that really made me question everything I thought was right about society. How has someone so nasty been given so much success? Why did the media love her for that? She made so much money from being such a bully – what message does that give kids? It's wrong.

RICHARD NEWMAN, *Big Brother Seven*

To come out of that House after thirteen weeks is difficult. To suddenly realise that thirteen weeks of your life are actually missing. You have all these stories to catch up on. Time had passed and it was like being born again with people having to tell you about your life and fill in the gaps. And giving you your life back, your life is handed back to you.

And then of course, you have no idea how you have been perceived and you need to know. How did your friends take you? That's important. It was like being in prison but worse, because at least in prison you still have contact with the outside world. It was so exciting getting out, almost a relief – my life was back. I missed so much – weddings, births, news events. I constantly thought of these things. I was very disappointed I didn't win the money – that was my house. I made only enough to pay off my debts – £16,000 – and now I'm struggling.

LEA WALKER, *Big Brother Seven*

It was really weird. You do all your press and the Davina interview, go to Sopwell House Hotel to do your tabloid exclusive on Saturday morning. [The PR company] gave you a list of agents. As advised I went with [an agent recommended by the PR company]. They said she was an up-and-coming agent, in it for the long run. Very loyal.

I didn't bother seeing any other agents because they said to go with her, and you're green under the collar. You're locked away from society. The world could have ended. The House is your home. They are your family. So when you come out, you're thrown straight in. You're treated like gold dust when you go into the House and you think you will be when you leave the House too.

Before we went in Endemol used to refer to us as 'precious cargo'. Everybody uses that term, and when we are in the cars driving to the show they say, 'PC1', 'PC2' . . . You do feel very special. You're from a normal everyday life, then you're ferried around in blacked-out cars, you have everything you want. Security is so hard to come to terms with – you have everything done for you – and then it's taken away.

And the term 'precious cargo' has suddenly disappeared. It's done, it's gone. Endemol don't want to know, you have served your purpose. They lose contact with you and [it seems like] they can't be bothered to talk to you. You're with this agent that you don't know, you don't know what you're doing, who do you call? Who do you talk to? . . . I lost out on so much work at the time when I should have been milking it!

I also should have held back on the exclusive and I would have got more money. I was told that that was the only offer on the table and it was good. In my opinion, they are all in it together because at the end of the day they are all making money from it.

Then I saw all the press and what had been written about me – I was a 65-year-old alcoholic! I made one shit porn film years ago and I couldn't believe the fuss about it! They said I was a bad mum and that hurt too much, I cried my eyes out. They called me a stalker, a psycho. But none of that mattered; H, my son, and my mum were all that mattered. They were there for me and that's all I wanted.

ALEX SIBLEY, *Big Brother Three*

When I came out there was the *Big Brother* wrap party that night and I wanted to go but my mother said, 'No, you're not, you've got a £80,000 job in the morning for Domestos,' and I was like, 'What?' The prize money was like £70,000 and then I got £80,000 for *OK* as well – the more I'd slag Kate off, the more they'd pay me – all for a day's work! It's all about marketing. If I'd looked like PJ I would never had made that much money.

NADIA ALMADA, Winner, *Big Brother Five*

I found out that my exes had sold stories on me and worse, my friends had sold stories on me, but I suppose it was easy money for them. The worst was that my choice to go on *Big Brother* affected my family because the papers went and found my dad and we didn't want him found. My mum and brothers found that hard to cope with and I carry a lot of guilt for that, still to this day.

I did a deal with *Heat*, which was fabulous. I felt like a star. I couldn't believe that literally my life had changed overnight. Here I was, little old me, getting pampered and treated like Madonna. It was like I was in a dream and please, no one wake me up.

ANTHONY HUTTON, Winner, *Big Brother Six*

Saw me Mam and mates after – they were all jumping around and crying their eyes out saying, 'We knew you'd do it!' But then I couldn't stay up and party because I had to do a shoot straight afterwards.

I remember when I first got out and someone shouted me name and I looked around, thinking, how do you know me name? I couldn't figure it out. People kept doing 70s poses and I was just overwhelmed at it all – the sheer power and immenseness of it all and one guy was doing me dance (the hand snake one) and I was just blown away. It was crazy.

The best thing that happened was when I went out one night with Maxwell and co. and I bumped into a Newcastle player – Titus Bramble – and he shook me hand and said, 'Mate, you're a fuckin' legend,' and I was like, 'Fuck me!' And then we met all the Chelsea football team and John Terry was shaking me hand . . . I was truly overwhelmed and that was the epitome, when I thought, what the hell has happened to my life?

KINGA KAROLCZAK, *Big Brother Six*

I got loads of offers when I came out but not the ones I expected. I got wine bottle promotions and rude stuff but I turned it all down – it wasn't what I wanted to do, in fact it disgusted me. I had hurt my parents enough and although it was so much money, I couldn't go down that road again. I didn't want to make money out of something that hadn't even happened!

I concentrated on the thing that I'd done *Big Brother* for in the first place and that was my music. I recorded a couple of songs but then the record company kept saying it was too early to release them because there was too much exposure now and to wait. So I'd gone from no exposure, no record to too much exposure, no record. They wanted the bad press to die down.

I got so much bad press, it hurt my mum so much. People don't know but she'd be standing in the newsagents and people would be picking up the paper with me on the cover and slagging me off and my mum had to listen to it all.

I loved the fame, I'd wanted fame all my life and it was handed over to me like a golden ticket – it was amazing. Soon afterwards I was in Brent Cross and Jane Norman was packed and I basically got mobbed by shoppers saying, 'Oh my God, it's Kinga!' I was in my element. I felt like Britney Spears.

10. MAKING YOUR WAY

You've got big dreams? You want fame? Well, fame costs. And right here is where you start paying. With sweat

(*Fame*, 1982)

I'd been invited to the Radio One Summer Road Show and I was standing outside Kylie's trailer with everyone else – journalists trying to get a quote, photographers, fans – and her manager came out and said, 'Kylie would like to meet Narinder,' and I thought, wow, lucky cow whoever that is. Then everyone looked at me and I thought, me? Why would she want to meet me? I was dumbstruck.

I went into the trailer and I just stared and was lost for words. I couldn't stop staring, she must have thought I was ill. She looked like a porcelain doll with those huge, blue almost glass-like eyes. She was totally lovely to me and she told me how she and her then-boyfriend, James Gooding, used to watch Brian and me till late, and how she really wanted to talk to Brian and would I phone him? So I called Brian and said, 'Brian, guess who I'm with? She wants to talk to you,' and he couldn't guess, and I said, 'Kylie Minogue,' and he said, 'Fuck off Narinder, I'm going back to bed,' and put the phone down!

There was Kylie ready to take the phone off me . . . I said, 'Sorry I'll try again, he just hung up.' This time Brian goes, 'Go on then, Narinder, I'll amuse you – pass the phone to Kylie.'

And she chatted with him, then gave me some great advice about agents. It's hard to believe that things like that happened after *Big Brother* – why would Kylie be watching *us*? Did I really meet her? Did that just happen?

These moments happened all the time, and I never ceased to be surprised – Simon Cowell, Ben Elton, Ricky Gervais, Tara Palmer-Tomkinson, Jonathan Ross, Westlife, Britney Spears, James Nesbitt – I could go on and on. They were so nice and giving. I noticed that the bigger the star, the nicer they were; the smaller, the nastier. Some of the more C-list celebrities were so rude and vile to me. They'd turn their back and if I spoke to them they'd just blank me and make me feel like a piece of poo! They seemed so begrudging, as if only they deserved to be famous and on telly! I thought, my God, I'll only be here five minutes and you can't even give me that?

I'd never worked in the industry and an offer came through my agent – Sky One wanted to do a documentary about me. It all sounded good and so I spent a day with them, though I did start to get a bit suspicious when all they wanted to do was show me going out to different parties, but I didn't really have any to go to and didn't particularly want to, so I began to feel as though I was wasting their time.

They seemed agitated and I began to worry that they would never work with me again so I rang a few mates and they urged me to go to a couple of things. I wasn't even dressed, but I felt I couldn't let these TV companies down and a channel like Sky could really help me out and might want to use me again, so I did as they wanted.

To be fair, what they showed in the end wasn't too far from the truth because I was out and about a lot in the early days, but that's not what I'd agreed to do in the first place, and I felt that the way they edited it made me look like such a twat (and that's the only time I've ever complained about editing!). I had been cheeky to the doorman at *Top of the Pops* but I knew him and we always had a laugh and a running joke with me going, 'Don't you know who I am?' because he'd always make me go to the back of the queue, but Sky made it look like I didn't know him and cut out all our banter so all you saw was me going, 'Don't you know who I am?'

It was, I have to say, the nail in the coffin. My agent hadn't seen it before it went out and the damage was irreparable. At about the same time the most powerful agent in London, John Noel – agent to Davina McCall and Dermot O'Leary among others – held a big industry party and the invite had my picture and a circle with a red line across my face: THE NARINDER-FREE ZONE PARTY.

A producer that I was about to make a pilot show with rang to tell me the bad news and it was as if someone had punched me in the stomach and winded me – I'd never met John Noel! The irony was I didn't choose to do *Big Brother* for a celebrity lifestyle. Remember, it was *Big Brother Two* and that kind of thing hadn't been established yet. I'd done it because I wanted to be working in TV, so I contacted a lawyer and was advised against doing anything – Noel was a powerful agent and it would look like I was making a fuss. It was hard to take that invitation, but it was harder still to ignore it, as I was advised time and time again.

My father passed away the following day and I went back home to Newcastle.

RACHEL MORRIS, Psychotherapist, *Big Brother*

Being on *Big Brother* doesn't make you the programme makers' responsibility. I've listened to the warnings and advice about life after *Big Brother* over and over and its message is unequivocal: nobody knows what will happen afterwards. It could be great, it could be awful, it could be nothing at all, but it's the contestants' choice and responsibility both to make the decision and then to live by its consequences.

BOYD HILTON, TV Editor, *Heat*

Only one or two housemates will achieve lasting fame, but maybe for others two weeks is enough – their friends see them on TV, they're in *Heat* and the papers for a week and maybe that's enough life experience. I don't see why that should be seen as a failure. You were the focus of attention for a brief period and that enhanced your life. It's a failure if you think it will be anything more than that.

Our readers are fascinated by all the people in it as long as they're in it but when it's over that's it, we don't want to know anything else about them because it's about their relationships in the House – that's why we're interested. We don't want to see them at premières; it's embarrassing.

You had your moment in the spotlight and that's it now, go back to what you were doing, go back to your life. That's the nature of *Big Brother*. What I'm trying to say is that *Big Brother* has a new cast each year and you are being replaced, you have to realise that.

HANNAH PERRY, News Editor, *Heat*

You had a little taste of fame, you made a bit of money and actually it's not enough money to live on and you're gonna have to go back to your old job and that's a very bitter pill to swallow. It is cruel. It's given these people an opportunity that they wouldn't ordinarily have had and you can make what you want of it but within reason, because some people aren't going to make it because there just isn't a market for them.

PHIL EDGAR-JONES, Creative Director, Endemol

Big Brother is an access for people that otherwise would never have got on telly. What you do with it afterwards is partly up to you and partly not. There's still an element of *Big Brother* people who themselves manipulate the programme for their own ends as well. It's a two-way relationship.

MELANIE HILL, *Big Brother One*

I wanted to go back to work but I couldn't even get on the tube. I had security for a few weeks, which I thought was so silly and just to create hype. So eventually they went and I thought, it's time now and I have to just get on with it, get on a tube. That was the worst thing I could have possibly done. I got on a tube in the middle of the day and had a group of lads shouting, screaming and intimidating me, so I got on the tube for only one stop, got off and they followed me, shouting

'Show us your bum,' and I was so scared. It was horrible. I thought, oh my God, what have I done?

One night I went out with a mate in Soho and people were pissed and suddenly someone said, 'There's Mel from *Big Brother*!' and it was like a ripple effect and suddenly everyone just started grabbing me, so I walked away and literally they started chasing after me. It was the most . . . just mad, mad thing. I was petrified. Petrified and for about two years I just stopped going out to those places.

I tell you what I think it was – we were the new recognisable faces, we were like the cast of *EastEnders*, in that that's how familiar we were and people felt they knew us but we were real, too. And the public didn't know how to deal with us. They would literally stop in their tracks. It was just mental. A period where people just wanted a part of you – to be part of it all.

You see, back then even the public didn't know how to handle it – they thought they knew us, they thought we were their friends, they didn't realise it was just a fiasco and pantomime behind it all. Nowadays it's all different, the public know, 'Oh, it's just that *Big Brother* lot.' But then it was a fiasco.

This is what I have found so upsetting. Caggy and Sada had sold a story about me, saying they hated me and wanted to rip me from limb to limb. They had obviously been set up massively and got pissed, but I was so hurt by that. But what had happened was that they had come out early and got caught up in the whole 'Everybody hates Mel' campaign. I was the most hated woman in Britain for a while, I didn't really let any of it affect me – I didn't believe the bad stuff that was written, but neither did I believe the good stuff.

I'm glad I didn't do the tabloids. Because I kind of disappeared for a bit, I got really positive press and people respected the fact that I'd turned down the obvious route of celebrity and all of a sudden I got lots of offers. I did a travel column for *Marie Claire* for a whole year, I started filming *Chained* [a game show] and a holiday programme. I did lots of stuff and I enjoyed it. It was great. Anna Nolan and I were doing quite a bit of stuff, TV presenting. But I don't think I was very good at it and you never ever get away from the *Big Brother* tag – no one could ever forget about it. It was extraordinary, and eventually it worked against me. People just couldn't take me seriously.

AMMA ANTWI, *Big Brother Two*

First and foremost I was flabbergasted at the notoriety that came as a result of being on the show and that people knew me. They would go, 'Hi Amma!' and I'd be shopping. I just couldn't believe it. I didn't enjoy it, if I have to be honest. I wasn't designed for fame. I tended to get the psychotics who followed me around. And I never knew what to do with myself. Then when they took security off me I felt like they'd taken off my right arm – I didn't know how to deal with it. The security men were like a crutch, I felt safe. But looking back I wished I hadn't had it because it just took me longer to adjust to normality afterwards.

People would feel free to approach you and say, 'I don't like you,' or 'I didn't like you.' They felt free and obliged to give you their honest opinion and you wouldn't do that in real life. You wouldn't go up to someone and say, 'I don't like you, I think you're disgusting.' Abso-bloody-lutley people came up to me and said, 'I hated you.' And what do you do? I'd just stand there and take it.

I got offered a bit part in *Dream Team* [a drama series], magazines, premières, parties. I never expected any of it – I was amazed that *Dream Team* wanted me to have a part. I was amazed at all the interviews. I was utterly surprised that people wanted me at their parties. I was overwhelmed. Before that point I had no expectations; it was *then* that I started developing expectations.

I thought, bloody hell! This could be quite good, I could have a good time here and do some exciting things and make some money. It'll be really cool . . . I was told not to get an agent [and was] told me not to do certain stories. I should have got an agent immediately.

The only reason I got an agent was because [a TV personality] told me to get one and recommended hers. I did get an interview with John Noel but I messed that up myself because I had started listening to all the people around me and all the hype, so when he said, 'I can see you doing a cookery programme,' I was like, 'No, I want to do music.' I now realise what an idiot I was – I thought far too much of myself by then!

There was a period of time when you allowed yourself to buy into it all and your head just expands. It went to my head, it really did. Anyone who says it didn't go to their head is a bloody liar! I've always been down to earth and pragmatic but it still went to my head – here was one of the most powerful agents in the country and I was umming and ahhing. I sat in front of him and was like, 'What can you do for me? Is that all?' I mean, oh my goodness! I had over-inflated ideas as to what my potential was! I wish now somebody had sat me down and said, 'To be completely honest with you, you don't have very long and chances are you're not gonna get the best offers. Do some personal appearances, do some panto and take your money and run. So whatever happens you can at least say it was worthwhile and at the very least you made some money.'

I believed it when people said, 'No, don't do that, you can do better,' and I wish somebody had said, 'No you can't.' These people were the people from [the PR company], people you'd meet from the entertainment industry and who worked for TV companies. But then again, back in our day, even agents didn't know what to expect from *Big Brother*. The thing I regret most, believe it or not, is not doing panto! My agent said, 'Oh no, you don't want to be doing that!' and it's bloody good money!

I know people don't get it. It's not even Stockholm syndrome. These people weren't my captors – these were people I chose to get advice from and trusted. It stopped being funny when I began seeing pictures of myself when I didn't even know there was a camera there and I looked awful. I'd open the paper and see myself coming out of supermarket and think, eh? Where was the camera? I didn't expect there to be paparazzi outside my house or following me – I'm not Madonna.

My family were pestered and called all the time for stories. My mum and all my family – it disgusts me, the lengths that the press go to, to get what they want. They get your phone number, they sent my mum flowers – they were trying to buy my mum basically, and remember my mum is this innocent African woman who didn't know any different and she just thought they were being lovely. They would also ring her and pretend to be different people. 'We are from the government and need to know where Amma is and what's her number?'

It was my decision to go on *Big Brother* and here it was affecting all their lives – I was amazed at how far-reaching it was as well: they contacted my headmaster from ten years ago, you know!

BRIAN DOWLING, Winner, *Big Brother Two*

You think that you can just walk out that House and walk down the street and go for a pizza, because you've just been in a house for nine weeks and you just want your normal life. I just wanted to take my microphone off and have a shit or piss without thinking I was being watched! I have won £70,000, fantastic, thank you. I just wanted to walk away, if that makes sense. That was my mentality.

You don't think but even getting into a car was madness – people would start rocking the car. You can't walk down the street. I went out of the hotel and walked down the street and literally within five minutes it was just UNBELIEVABLE. Cars had stopped, people had got out of cars, people were beeping. I just couldn't believe it. I was completely shocked. From then on I said to the security guard, 'Right let's play it your way.' And then I cried and I was shocked that people could come up to you and grab you and touch you.

People want to talk to you and they know so much about you and you're thinking, how do they know? Oh my God. When I shaved half my head in the House and was messing around in front of the mirror, going 'Oh, Mr Nasty Guy' and 'Oh, Mr Nice Guy' . . . people *liked* it and people *believed* it and, 'Oh, demons, Brian, woah.' And I was like, 'Yeah, what the fuck is going on?' 'Oh I watched you sleeping,' they'd say, and you're like, 'OK, thank you.' 'We know what you and Narinder were rolling.' 'We hate Josh too.'

People believed it – the characteristics I had in the House, catchphrases I said. And then I was thinking, oh my God. Autographs, how do you do autographs? You're doing it and don't believe in it but of course people had camera phones back in those days. But I was so grateful people had voted and I still say it to this day, 'Thank you.' That's a shock.

KATE LAWLER, Winner, *Big Brother Three*

I couldn't get over the fame. Honestly, I loved *Big Brother* but I never ever thought that it would be the way it was; I never imagined it. I get embarrassed if people ask me for my autograph, embarrassed if I'm recognised. It's sweet though . . . People were so nice to me and I got so much fan mail, no hate mail. I wrote back to everyone who wrote to me and I still do reply to people. What I get the most today is, 'You well look like Kate Lawler,' and some days I will go unrecognised, but when I did *Love Island* [another reality TV show], it all became intense again.

I'm a friendly approachable person and after *Big Brother* I'd see celebrities out but just be too shy to say 'Hi' because it's like you know who they are, but you don't actually know them! The night I presented *Backstage at the Brits 2003* with Foxy for Capital Radio we went to the after-party at the Sanderson Hotel and Mel C came up to me and said, 'Hi Kate, I voted for you in *Big Brother*,' and I literally stood there not knowing what to say! I was really starstruck and I was a major fan of the Spice Girls when I was younger. That was a really cool thing to happen, actually.

ALEX SIBLEY, *Big Brother Three*

It's one of those things: you just don't realise how much fame there will actually be, and it was huge! Even my mum and dad were famous, they sent my mum to the front of the cheese counter queue in Tesco because they recognised her. People even recognised my friends and asked them for autographs – that's how far-reaching the fame was. People were coming to my house from dawn till dusk asking for autographs and if you gave one then they all wanted one, so I'd be standing at my front door all day!

I remember one mate and I went to the airport to pick up his girlfriend and the whole of Heathrow just came to a standstill and security had to actually ask us to leave because me being there was causing a commotion! And even driving down the motorway was dangerous because people would spot you and start chasing you down the motorway!

If I went out to clubs with my mates we'd just get into so many fights with drunk men and so after a while you just stop going out. I just couldn't understand the fuss, I just couldn't handle the fame. I suppose I took myself far too seriously when I came out. I even grew a beard and kept my hair long and people still recognised me!

I did a pilot show for Channel 4 called *At Home with the Sibleys* but we were hardly the Osbournes. It was never gonna get commissioned. I'm glad it didn't because it would have been such an invasion of privacy and that's exactly what I couldn't handle. Yeah, I loved doing the work and being paid stupid money to do it but if I wasn't working I preferred to be left alone.

I got paid £2,000 a pop for silly jobs like going on some TV show. I didn't do any personal appearances because I remember Tim told me how he was doing them for like £2,000 a night but he'd turn up at a club and the host would shout to the audience, 'Did you watch *Big Brother*?' and the crowd would reply, 'YES!' and then he'd ask, 'Did you love it?' and they'd shout 'YES!' and then he'd ask, 'Do you want to meet Kate?' and they screamed 'YES!' and 'Do you want to meet Alex?' 'YES!' and then, 'Well, hard cheese, we've got Tim,' 'BOO!'

EMMA GREENWOOD, *Big Brother Five*

I was living this amazing life, one that I'd always dreamed of. I knew what to expect from watching other *Big Brother* people from previous years – you're just running around and doing photo shoots. I'd always felt like the ugly duckling and when they wanted to do photo shoots and make me look all beautiful, of course I'd do it. I lost weight, learned how to do my makeup and then a magazine editor said to me once, 'Emma you are looking really good these days,' and I was like, woooh, finally! I've been accepted as a pretty girl – do you know what I mean? That was my main aim. I wanted to go to all these parties and when I did, I networked like mad . . .

I remember I went to my first première with Marco – the film was *King Arthur*. Walking down the red carpet, everyone shouting our names and asking for photos. I was like, 'Hiya!' – proper on one . . . First time papped . . . It was a great feeling being the centre of attention but it also goes very quickly and that's the curse of *Big Brother*.

My first fame experience. I went home after two weeks and I went to Primark with my mum and all of a sudden I was just surrounded by a mob of people with their camera phones out taking pictures, and I'm like, what the fuck? What the fuck? I just couldn't deal with it and I felt really stupid signing autographs. 'Why would you want my autograph? I'm no one,' and people were saying, 'Why are you shopping in Primark?' and I was like, 'Because I like Primark.' Stupid question. The best thing that ever happened was sitting next to Madonna at a party. I went into the VIP area and I didn't even know I was sat next to Madonna and I turned around and started talking and thought, shit!

VICTOR EBUWA, *Big Brother Five*

You think you can just pop out and get a paper and that's what I did soon after I came out – left me family at home making breakfast, thought I'd sneak out and go get my paper as I normally would. So I go to the supermarket and I'm thinking, where the fuck is everyone? And I look behind me and everyone is behind me: 'Oh my God, it's Victor!' and before I knew it a big crowd had gathered taking pictures and asking for autographs and I'm thinking, why do you want my autograph?

People were literally going bonkers and they showed me a lot of love. I loved it. I'm not gonna lie – it was magic. High fives in every club I went to. It still happens today, especially if I go out of London somewhere where the local celebrity's the postman.

Personal appearances were chaotic. Chicks baying for my blood: 'Ahh Victor, Victor.' One PA that I went to with my three mates, the chicks found out what hotel I was staying at and I came back from the PA and opened my hotel bedroom door and there was this girl lying naked in my bed. I had a bottle of champagne in my hand and it was like a James Bond moment, so I said, 'Fancy a nightcap?' I passed her a glass of champagne and called my mates. She wanted me but settled for my mate. I didn't because I didn't want no chick selling a story saying VICTOR AND HIS MATES PORKED ME UP THE ARSE.

NADIA ALMADA, Winner, *Big Brother Five*

Oh my God – I couldn't window shop anymore. I was just running from one shop to another, then getting mobbed, running into the car. I couldn't and still can't just stop in the street and have a look around because people will stop and start talking. I get paranoia and I think I must suffer from agoraphobia. If I came off a flight and my car wasn't waiting for me, I'd kick up such a fuss, I'd be ringing them shouting, 'Where the fuck are you?' because they had left me open and vulnerable.

I think it affected my relationships with loved ones because I was always stressed and it was intense. I wanted to feel safe. Looking back I wished I'd appreciated it all more and taken it more slowly. I almost became a diva – I didn't want to feel invaded. I wanted to just get in the car and get out instead of hanging about.

It does die down though, it becomes more gossipy fame and whispering fame, because before that point I had just come out of the House and I was public property, people had voted me and had a right to touch me, have a piece of me – 'I voted for you so you have to give me a picture.' After that it calms down and you become a celebrity. Therefore, you are less touchable.

What always amazed me was the age difference of fans – little kids to old ladies. It was so touching. When I did my panto people came all over to see me. Some people can be quite silly. I remember being in Guernsey one weekend and this man came up to me and said, 'You freak,' and I ignored him and then next moment I realise that he's taking pictures of me! So I grabbed his phone and chucked it. How fucking dare he? He insulted me. Then he threw a glass at me! All this in Guernsey! Yes, people have been nasty but hand on my heart people have showed me so much love.

The money was amazing – I've got two houses, a car and I've travelled the world – Bali, Singapore, Vietnam, Grand Canaria, Australia, Milan. Life was great.

DEREK LAUD, *Big Brother Six*

I wanted to do some serious TV and I got to do that – *Test the Nation*, *Question Time*, a documentary for Channel 4. What was striking was how very quickly they dropped the *Big Brother* tag with me, instead introducing me as a 'Tory speechwriter' because I had something to say other than relying on my *Big Brother* experience.

I didn't do panto or want to, and I had no desire to go on some kids' show and get gunk thrown in my face. Neil and Christine Hamilton, who were by then looking after me, used to get terribly frustrated because I wouldn't do absurdly ridiculous things.

I was cycling on my bike one day and I had a cap on and these three young lads were crossing the road and one of them suddenly said, 'God – it's Derek!' and another said, 'No, it's not,' and 'Yes it is!' and I didn't flinch. Then the other one said, 'Yes it is because he's wearing the same tracksuit bottoms that he did in the *Big Brother* House.' (*laughs*) It was amazing and they were the same! I found that very touching!

EUGENE SULLY, *Big Brother Six*

The first time that I was papped, I'd gone into a hotel and went back to the van to get my luggage and as I opened the van door a guy photographed me and he was quite aggressive. I closed the door and he kicked it open and got some more shots and I was actually scared because at the time I didn't know what it was or why he was taking photos, and so I rang [the PR company] and they told me not to worry and that it was normal. So then after that, every time I was photographed I always played up to it and gave them what they wanted.

After about two weeks I got an agent. I thought because I had worked in radio before that I was quite media savvy but it showed just how much I wasn't, because I'd never had to deal with things like agents before. What happened was that I had to interview a handful of agents and I'd ask questions but I didn't really know what answers I was looking for, I didn't know what the best path was for me to take. So I thought I'd best let [the PR company] help me choose. It's such a complex and highly pressurised situation – you know that you only have a certain amount of shelf life. So you believe anything they say. It's like when a double-glazing salesman tells you your house is gonna fall down unless you get double glazing and you buy it. So I just went with the agent that seemed the most trustworthy but I didn't do much. They got me lots of PAs but not very much else. On reflection I probably should have gone with the agents that said I reminded them of Fred Dinenage.

I thought I'd just go as far as I could with it all and milk it for all I could. I've always liked the idea of working in TV and going on TV, but I never thought that it would happen and suddenly I'm in this situation where I'm incredibly popular and there is an awful amount of interest in me, and I'm thinking, I'm gonna try and pull this off.

SAMANTHA HEUSTON, *Big Brother Six*

It all started to go into freefall when the bad press began. This bitch, who I thought was being a friend, rang me and said she was writing an article on me saying that she'd heard that I did prostitution. I said no, I was offered £2,000 for a snog with a girl and more for a threesome, which was arranged by my agent. This was three agents down the line . . .

My agent had said, 'Come and meet some girls for a drink,' and there were a couple of girls there with a boyfriend who was Asian. They said, 'A grand for a snog,' and talked about it casually, about how they get paid a grand for a snog. I thought, I don't need to be doing this, why is my agent introducing me to these people? I thought, I'm not at the point where I am that desperate, and they would say to me, 'There's more money for a threesome.' So my parents were right about all the sleazeballs.

So this bitch sold the story to the papers saying I did prostitution and there was this big thing about me being a £1,000-a-night hooker on the front of the *News of the World*. They rang me the day before and I said it's not true and it's libel, and they said, 'We are going to print it anyway and we have it on tape,' and I was like, do what you want, it's all good publicity anyway, so in the end I didn't mind.

My parents knew it was nothing to do with me but my brother has wondered because I do sleep around a bit! (*laughs*).

ANTHONY HUTTON, Winner, *Big Brother Six*

I met a few agents the day afterwards, and [the PR company] helped me decide to go to John Noel. He told me to go with him and he seemed a sound bloke. I did get the impression at that stage that this was only gonna last a year, but I wasn't bothered about that. It was one amazing ride to me, and I just wanted to enjoy it for however long it lasted. I did a deal with *OK* magazine for £200,000. I was like, 'WHAT? Two hundred grand just to talk to me?' I thought it was ridiculous. I just rang all me mates and told them, 'This is crazy!'

I'm not gonna say how much I made – me grandma told me not to – it's just wrong.

I've bought a few properties – three flats – and a Range Rover. Me mate's a property developer and he said, 'A word of advice Anthony, you don't know how long this'll last, so be clever and put your money into property.' I've been dead sensible, like.

The first thing I was asked when I got out of the House was, 'Do you want to be a TV presenter?' and I just answered, 'Well, I'm not that good a reader and I don't think I'd be that good actually.' Reading from an autocue wouldn't be me strong point. And then I did get the chance to do *CD:UK* and I was alright. I enjoyed it but you are thrown in at the deep end – they told me I was going to be on *CD:UK* and I thought, wicked, because I thought I was going on as a guest. Then they told me I'd be presenting the show and I nearly shat me pants. That was a big ordeal for us like. I was so nervous.

I didn't go on *Big Brother* to become a TV presenter – I was uncomfortable with it. What I really wanted to do was the musical *Saturday Night Fever* because of me 70s dancing background but I couldn't sing, that was a real shame – I really wanted to do that. I did have a few singing lessons but still couldn't get to that standard.

I was gutted but realistic. I ticked all the boxes but not the singing one. *Chicago* also wanted me to do something but again the singing was a problem.

The PAs was where I made all me money. I could not and still can't get my head round the fact that people were paying me money to just turn up and say, 'Hi!' I've done about . . . well, the most ever by a *Big Brother* contestant – £3,000 a pop. I made loads of money.

MAKOSI MUSAMBASI, *Big Brother Six*

I knew one or two people would recognise me, but I didn't know that I would stimulate love and hate within people's innermost hearts. Because I do have people who see me and they cry, and do you know what, if I saw *Michael Jackson*, I would cry. Why are you crying for me?

There was a little girl who gave me a little purple flower, a plastic flower and she was crying. I was like, 'Baby, why are you crying?' 'Oh Makosi, I love you so much!' I was like, oh my God. I mean, it's me here, do you understand me? With the rash on my face, my big bum, my big tits. I'm like, why are you crying?

So I was actually surprised that I could stimulate some people into wanting to bash my head in . . . This woman [in a shop] was going to bust my head! It will always haunt me, because I have never felt so vulnerable. I have never felt so vulnerable. The manager had to close the entire floor I was shopping on.

See here's the thing, now when I hear people saying Victoria Beckham had to get the shop closed to buy trainers, I don't judge her. Because, I was nearly attacked to the point where the manager asked people to leave the floor while I was trying jeans on. To finish buying my stuff and leave. Because this woman was going for me. She was going to attack me. I have never in my whole entire life – I have been in a car crash when I was three and you know, enough things have happened to me – but I have never felt so vulnerable.

I soon dropped my agent. In three months he had changed my contract so his commission started at twenty per cent and went up to twenty-five per cent. He kept telling me to take my clothes off and in the end I decided I didn't want to take my clothes off anymore and he dropped me. Just when I felt relieved there were even more newspaper allegations waiting for me around the corner.

KINGA KAROLCZAK, *Big Brother Six*

I hit the party scene because I could. I was young and I loved it, the magazines constantly took pictures of me. I was always in the magazines, they had stopped writing about the rest but I was still out there and that probably is because of the bottle incident, because of that one mistake I'll always be remembered. That's the way I look at it at this point. So I carried on partying and that's when I fell in love with Kemal.

RICHARD NEWMAN, *Big Brother Seven*

People stop me all the time because they want to re-live the whole experience. They want to know all sorts . . . were Pete and Nikki real? Grace? The letter I got from home? The troll dance I did? They want to tell you what they enjoyed about the show and what they didn't like.

Autographs are fine, mobile phones are evil. Someone stops you and then it takes them five minutes to work the thing and you're waiting for ever . . . but I love it. People have been very kind to me.

The best famous person I met was Sir Ian McKellen and he came up to me and talked to me about my experience. Pete and I were just stood shocked – to have Ian McKellen, one of

Britain's finest actors, saying he enjoyed you on *Big Brother*! That's WOW. Honestly, that's worth it all (*laughs*).

LEA WALKER, *Big Brother Seven*

The first night I got home it was so surreal, because nobody explains that this is what is going to happen. Millions and millions of people watch it and it really doesn't sink in. We stopped off at the service station and someone called my name and within seconds there were around two hundred people around me and I was like, oh my God.

The money I got offered was brilliant. All of a sudden I didn't have to worry about getting clothes for my son or putting petrol in the car – I was getting PAs left, right and centre, and after I went back into the House and back out again,* my money went up again.

It was really deflating when I got back home. It was normal and I was not in the House anymore. I heard the *Big Brother* music, my mother had the TV on and I hadn't seen it. I came into the lounge and saw my friends on the TV and do you know what? You miss them because they were your life for three months.

I went to parties, yes I did. Why wouldn't I? I was invited! I didn't go to loads, only if I was invited. I don't go to these do's and say, 'Hey, I'm here, take a pic!' How silly is that? I go because a friend has asked me to. It's part of the experience.

---

* Lea had been evicted from the main House but the public voted her and four others, including Nikki, into 'The House Next Door' – a suite connected to the House by the diary room. Nikki was later voted back into the main House, but the others in the House Next Door were knocked out of the game.

11. BACK TO NORMAL?

Snap out of it

(Moonstruck, 1987)

At my father's funeral many members of my mum's extended family blanked me and didn't pay their respects to me in front of everyone. It was cruel beyond belief, and it broke my mum's heart. There we were trying to lay Dad to rest and *Big Brother* gatecrashed. There was no escaping it, but my husband put it into perspective: 'You were the first Indian girl to go into that House, you wore a bikini, you got drunk. What did you expect them to do? Give you a pat on the back? That generation are of the old-fashioned view,' and he was right. Again, I picked myself up, wiped away my tears and dusted myself down.

I kept my head down the following month and my agent and I were careful with everything I did. People kept asking me, 'What are you doing now?' and my husband couldn't do his job properly because everyone was constantly asking, 'What is she doing now? Not got a TV show?' I had had so many meetings, but it had been a year and still nothing had come to fruition, but then out of the blue I had a call to go for a screen test and a month later I had landed my first presenting job for a show on Trouble Channel, called *Undercover Lovers*, which I'm dead proud about.

They took a chance on me and I'll always be grateful. Always. I had my own show, at least I got that. I worked hard and professionally and learned a lot about presenting. But the icing on the cake was that my husband and I could finally say, 'Yes, I've landed my first TV job.' All that people replied was 'Trouble? Is that it, not ITV?' and we'd be knocked for six! Never mind my own expectations – I was perfectly happy with Trouble – it was other people who expected more. I never felt that anything I did was good enough.

The thing is, I was given so much advice, but I didn't really have a clue because it's an alien world and looking back, people were too free with their tips, 'Oh, don't do this, do that,' 'Oh, don't go there, go there,' and 'Oh, don't see him, see them,' and I was just running blindly in every direction.

I realised about a year later that there wasn't really a big market for a strong Asian woman in the mainstream, so I focused on Asian media in the UK. The BBC Asian Network were the gatekeepers: if they weren't on your side you had no chance. I bent over backwards to please programme makers, turning up at short notice, or working late into the night and only getting home at two o'clock in the morning, before leaping out of bed a few hours later and trekking back to the studio.

I still kept quiet but then the crunch came when one vile presenter asked me to be a guest on his show and went on to describe me as 'desperate' and said I 'would do anything for fame'. Another invited me onto his show to talk about Tom Cruise and went on to put me down by saying I was 'the Asian Pete Doherty' and that I'd turn up to the opening of an envelope. That was my limit. I'd been humiliated and they were never going to give me a job, so I drew a line under the BBC Asian Network. Sheer hard work and networking weren't enough once the media had decided they were out to get me.

The British press is one of the most cut-throat industries in the world. I thought being called a 'Paki' at school was the worst thing I'd been through in my life, but at least that made me stronger. The newspapers set out to destroy me systematically: I was called a 'ligger', a 'desperado', a 'wannabe', a 'has-been'. One journalist went so far as to wish I'd die in a car crash. *Heat* called me an 'industry laughing stock' and one paper decided to split the female *Big Brother* housemates into 'pretty' and 'ugly' categories – Nadia, Alison and I were apparently 'ugly'.

How much more could I take? I'm strong but I'm not made of steel. I cried so much that my heart actually ached. It didn't stop. One paper invited me to a party then wrote that I was a gatecrasher when I turned up. My agent dropped me after that; I couldn't blame her. She'd tried so hard for me and we had some good projects in the pipeline, but the press were ruining that.

What is it to anyone if I went out and partied? I wanted to scream, 'If I'm only going to have five seconds of fame, then, God damn, let me enjoy it!' For the record, all the *Big Brother Two* people were invited to masses of premières when we first got out and I didn't go to any of them. I stayed at home. I only went to a première ten months after I left the *Big Brother* House, the following April.

Maybe it was my fault for going out, but if I'd done the sensible thing and kept myself to myself, do you really think anyone would have given me work? It was a vicious circle – you had to be a 'personality' and get press coverage to attract the programme makers, but the media had decided that I was going to be trashed, so it did more harm than good.

I knew the game was over when I was having my photo taken at another première and one of the paparazzi shouted, 'Oh, fuck off Narinder! You're blocking Emma Noble!' I was mortified at first but then I just started to laugh and it broke the spell. The dream I'd started out with didn't include this hell. You play the game or you walk away – I gave back the hand I'd been dealt and turned away.

Besides, we were struggling financially. For the first – and last – time I actually began to regret doing *Big Brother*. My mother, who was already in bad health, began to decline, and certain members of her own family still cut her out of their lives. What could I do? I couldn't put things right. I'd done *Big Brother* now, how could I go back in time? I tried to get a normal job but was told that I wouldn't be taken seriously in the pharmaceutical industry any more.

If I was down, my husband was down too, and it was destructive. My marriage was really suffering, and that was the most precious thing I had in my life. In the end we split up and I was devastated. I was now bottom of the pit. I couldn't fall any further.

HANNAH PERRY, News Editor, *Heat*

There are some *Big Brother* people that don't know where they sit anymore – are they famous? Aren't they? And the press are cruel about everyone, so why should *Big Brother* people be any different? You put yourself up for this with your eyes open. And don't forget, any publicity is good publicity – if they hadn't written about you then you would never have been written about, and the time to start worrying is when they stop writing about you.

RACHEL MORRIS, Psychotherapist, *Big Brother*

If I was really miserable and had to look for a reason for that misery, it would be very human of me to look outside of myself. If my misery is somebody else's fault then it must also be someone else's responsibility to 'fix it'. Making a decision that later backfires is a part of everyone's life, it's just that most of us don't have to suffer such public consequences.

It's this humiliation I think that makes ex-housemates rage against 'the programme makers'. They're actually saying, 'It's not my fault. They should have warned me. How could I have known? I'm a victim and deserve sympathy and an apology.' The victim role is very like a child's role in relation to a parent, in this case *Big Brother*. *Big Brother* was supposed to take care of them and provide them with access to a life of fame, glamour, parties and wealth. It hasn't coughed up the goods, so hopes and aspirations have been thwarted, disappointment overwhelms and the blame and resentment set in.

BOYD HILTON, TV Editor *Heat*

You know, you sold your soul to the devil; you can't then say, 'I thought the devil was a nice benevolent guy' – you know it's the devil.

KEVIN O'SULLIVAN, TV Critic, *Sunday Mirror*

Well that's like taking a nine-year-old kid who wants to drive a car and taking him to the M4, putting him in a sports car and saying, 'Off you go then.' Then after the inevitable, saying, 'Well, you wanted to drive, you deserve it.' It's not good enough. None of these people know what they are getting themselves in for, even by whatever series – they have no idea what the experience will be like, even if they are the lucky ones that do survive the nine weeks and have an alright time afterwards and do quite well, when they come out they think, 'Right, I'm famous now,' and this is what they aren't, and can't be prepared for.

SHARON MARSHALL, TV Critic, *This Morning*

I think people try to play the game and they don't understand the rules. They try to play the press and think they're being clever by saying, 'Let's pretend we're lesbians or lovers' – the whole thing where they just happened to be walking down a street kissing and there just happened to be a photographer there! Yes, of course other celebrities do it all the time and orchestrate events and stagemanage photos. But they'll do it with a bit of class and a bit of discretion and – more importantly – a bit of common sense. At least they get someone else to ring so it doesn't look like they're involved. We had *Big Brother* contestants ringing the papers direct to see how much they'd get for a photo of them kissing in the street!

PHIL EDGAR-JONES, Creative Director, Endemol

All I can say is that we do warn people. At that stage in their life they wanted to do *Big Brother* and they wanted a change in their life. It takes a lot of effort to do *Big Brother* – applications, auditions. It's an intense process. So if life goes wrong afterwards, I think the *Big Brother* problem is a contributing factor but there's lots of things that have nothing to do with *Big Brother* and it's dangerous to blame just one thing.

MELANIE HILL, *Big Brother One*

The transition to normal life was very hard. Because people just couldn't see beyond *Big Brother* and I had to start thinking about other stuff. That's why I started studying law – I couldn't get a normal job for ages, but then I was lucky that the people that I'd worked for before gave me another job. There was no way that I could just ring an agency and say, 'I want a job.' I tried and they almost laughed down the phone. It is very hard to get back to normal living – it's a hard transition . . . I did TV for three years, bought a house. It took a year after that to get back to normal and I still don't feel it's back to what it was – it's been seven years!

AMMA ANTWI, *Big Brother Two*

The point when it started to affect my life in a really negative way was when I did a story with [a newspaper] – it was a complete and utter fabrication and they made me look like such a slapper. They made me look like I went out every night with my skirt around my waist. They said awful things, as though I'd said so much salacious rubbish. I cried about it for days and then what upset me even more was how the public reacted to it – people would call me a slapper as I walked down the road and shout things like, 'You wearing knickers today? Show us them!' Just stupid stuff like that.

I went through a very bad time, I had someone throw stuff at me once – people would throw their shit out their cars at me, it was horrible. I felt I had no right to reply. You're judging me on things that I had no control over, and on somebody that isn't me. After that article, it just started going down hill. I wasn't enjoying it anymore.

It wasn't nice. I've blocked a lot of it out now, but it was a wake up call that this wasn't going to be all roses, this isn't going to be all great and everything started drying up at about that time and people weren't remotely interested in me anymore. But I made excuses for why the phone stopped ringing – oh, it's probably because they're busy, or they'll be in touch next week. I was in denial.

Coupled with that – and I'm sure other *Big Brother* contestants would never admit this – when you see other people from the same *Big Brother* as you do not only better than you, but miles and miles better, it's difficult. Take, for example, Helen. When she told me what she had earned from the papers compared to what I did, I thought, fucking hell, mine was a piece of shit amount! She was living in this fairyland world compared to the reality of my world. And we were from the same show.

Just when I thought things couldn't get any worse they brought out the *Big Brother Uncut* DVD and showed footage of me doing my bikini line. Honestly, honestly, I'd thought that if I did my bikini line out in the open it would be too bad to ever show on TV anyway. Because it was too explicit. They didn't show it on Channel 4 but they did put it on the DVD, which is bad enough because at least with TV it's shown and it's gone!

That was another wanky moment – the producers actually called me and said, 'Is there anything you don't want to go in?' and I said, 'Please don't put that in, I only did it to make it as bad as possible so that it would never be shown,' and [I was led to believe by our conversation that it wouldn't be used in the DVD]. The next thing I know it's gone in. Worse than that, but they actually used that clip to promote the DVD! So that clip went into all the papers as well! I was beyond mortified. That was horrible. I was sat there looking awful.

It was horrid – why would you want to put that in? And again, it started all the public backlash again – 'You're disgusting,' 'You're this, you're that,' and I would just take it all. I was being judged by people who just don't know me and they don't know why things happened. And I cried for days and days after. I know it sounds silly. But I did.

I soon hit rock bottom. I didn't leave my house for months, I lived off the money that I had earned and just stayed at home. I didn't want to go back to a normal job because I thought people would say, 'She's a failure,' and I would be mocked. That I was a loser (*laughs*). The fact of the matter is, people do mock if you go back to your normal job. But I don't care anymore.

When I hit rock bottom, I wanted to kill myself. I wanted to kill myself. I would look at the bar on the mezzanine in my flat and think, I could hang myself now. I didn't want to live. I felt like a failure. I blamed myself for not doing enough with my opportunity, this chance I'd been given. And the whole experience had made me look at myself so much and criticise every part of me. It made me hate myself, I didn't like myself. I started believing the criticism.

I never smoked before *Big Brother* apart from the odd joint – maybe two or three times – but then I started smoking heavily, because you just want to numb everything. It was painful. The press were so punishing. I couldn't defend myself or have any right to reply. It was so long ago and I made a concerted effort to block it out. I became a recluse – I was too frightened to go back to life because of what the repercussions would be. And I realised that I actually gave a shit about what people thought of me – a lot more than I thought I did.

I got to talk to the psychologist on the phone. I didn't get a face to face and I was feeling really unwell and desperately needed help. I couldn't cope and I swear to God all he said to me was, 'I think you're being silly, pull yourself together and get over it.' And that was it. I think I still have the letter. That was the help I got. And at that moment I realized I really was alone.

ALEX SIBLEY *Big Brother Three*

In the beginning it's all enjoyable but after a while I couldn't even pick my nose in public. Soon the new breed of wannabes was out and I had got to the point where I wanted to be left alone. It had changed my personality too much; I used to actually be louder but I'd become quiet. I remember I went to Paris with Melanie and I felt free – I could walk up the street with my head up and make eye contact with people. I'd made money and my agent didn't want me to do any more Domestos adverts because they didn't want me to become known as the 'bleach boy'.

Then I had the car accident where I hit a man and he died, and it basically ruined everything – the press had a field day and I could just imagine what I'd be known as now: ALEX THE *BIG BROTHER* MURDERER. I was obviously found not guilty but

I broke up with my girlfriend, I lost a ton of work and I got really low. The papers were running incorrect stories and people would ask me about it all the time. I knew in my heart of hearts that I wasn't guilty and that's why I eventually got over it. It was more annoying than anything – I lost £20,000 worth of work.

MAKOSI MUSAMBASI, *Big Brother Six*

A Sunday newspaper printed a story saying that I was a prostitute, which I swear is untrue. I never sold my body for money, may God strike me down dead if I'm lying. Just because they have pictures – and lots of girls wear afro wigs like me. But regardless, the damage was done. People would scream at me, 'You whore, you slag,' and I thought, even if I was – how does it affect your life? I lost so many friends as a result because they were scared to be associated with me. Where I come from you are judged by who you hang out with.

I'm a Christian and I was asked to stop going to church but I didn't stop – that's God's house – but they would point at me and said I had a bad spirit in me, a demon. All because I wore a bikini and because I had sex in the jacuzzi. People want to hold onto the pool incident because they want to justify the feelings they have towards me. If that helps people sleep at night then so be it.

There are celebrities on drugs and they lie about it but people are still vicious towards me. If I could change the whole incident, I would wish I was white, with blonde hair and blue eyes and the same personality to see if I would have been treated differently. There are much worse people out there than me . . . [people] who take the hardest drug there is. People from the third world swallow these drugs to smuggle them into this country and die as a result. Such a cruel habit, but the press absolutely love their English roses. But because I am black and an ex-*Big Brother* contestant that's as bad as taking those drugs.

This world is a very racist world. *Heat* magazine has never put a black girl on the cover. Racism is real, it's more real than *Big Brother*.

I look back to my audition and think how could the Talk of Doom have prepared me for what has happened to me? They didn't tell us that you have got the potential scenario that people will hate you to the point of sending you death threats. I have received death threats from Zimbabwe. People have written in because of my culture. They sent a picture of me in a bikini with stabs all over it.

I was thinking to myself, you know, how weird is this? That's when I think it dawned on me that I might never be able to return to Zimbabwe again. You see, so many things have happened, so many people may look at me and think that Makosi is so proud. But behind this so many things have happened in the last year. Things that I couldn't even start to comprehend.

If they'd told me in the Talk of Doom that this would happen, then that would have stopped me. But how were they to know? I am the only person from my culture that has ever gone on *Big Brother*. To be honest if I was told I would never be able to go back to Zimbabwe it would have stopped me, because Zimbabwe is a very beautiful country. I grew up there and all my childhood memories are there. My grandma is in Zimbabwe and she can't travel – she is about 102 now. I have not seen her in two years.

When I went to court over my deportation even the barrister said, '*You* knew you were from a country like Zimbabwe, and they don't like things like that.' Everyone keeps saying to me that I should have known that people in my country don't wear bikinis. I look at myself as a global citizen. Which is really mad. Everybody has a base. I should be able to wear a hijab if I want to wear a hijab, I should be able to wear a sari if I want to wear a sari, I should be able to wear a bikini if I want to wear a bikini. And then my barrister carried on and said, 'With all the tricks that you did in the House you should have known that this was putting you at risk with your country, where you come from.' 'You know what?' I said, 'I should be allowed to do that, this is a free country. I should be allowed to do what I wanna do because otherwise what's the difference between here and Afghanistan – where they don't allow girls to go to school – if you're telling me that because I am from a particular country I should act a certain way. This is a free country, I should be allowed to do what I want to do.' I have won the case but they have appealed. There must be something about me that they need to boot me out of the country.

In a year I have just learned you can't trust anyone, which is the saddest thing because in life you have to trust people around you. Sometimes you could be talking to someone you don't know is a journalist, they can ask you an innocent question, you can *think* it is an innocent conversation and the next thing you know you are reading about it in the next day's newspaper. You think to yourself I couldn't have told them so and so.

You know one woman from the *Sun* took me out for drinks, and I thought she was just being nice. I didn't know that journalists go around with secret tape recorders. I didn't know journalists try and get information out of you and then they put you on the front page talking about this and that.

After coming out of the House you lose so many friends anyway. I have lost so many friends and someone was trying to be friendly. I'm like, here comes a friend, and she betrayed me and that happens a lot. If I go out now and somebody is nice to me, the first thing I think is, why you being nice? Who do you work for, which paper? I'm always careful about what I say and who I talk to.

To me it feels like I am in a prison; I don't want to be careful, I don't want to look around thinking who is listening. That defence thing again makes me feel very snappy. I never used to swear, I used to hate swearing and if you look at my audition tape I said I hate people who swear. Now 'fuck off' is my favourite phrase. I went to a party two days ago at West Ham United and this girl was really funny, she said, 'You are still wearing an afro!' I just poured my champagne over her and walked off. Is that the right way to deal with it? I don't know what is the right way to deal with it.

I am not going to play up to the cameras, if you piss me off I will piss you off right back regardless of who is there. If I am holding a drink I will pour it over your head. I have not let fame get to my head but I have become very venomous and defensive and my experiences after *Big Brother* made me that way.

With what I've been through in the past year, anybody else would have ended up in the Priory. Now I am taking a newspaper to court because they said I was an actress when I went on *Big Brother*, and that Endemol paid a certain agency to have me on the show, so I've had to go to court twice in one year.

EMMA GREENWOOD, *Big Brother Five*

I made stupid mistakes – going to too many parties and coming out drunk and going 'fuck off' and showing me arse to all the paparazzi, hanging out with Page Three girls ... I did it all wrong, I was drunk and pissed, got wasted. Fucked up. It was just not the way to do things if I wanted to be taken seriously in my career and I threw away amazing opportunities – like once when I met Simon Cowell at a party. My exact reason for going to parties was to meet people like him and he was kind enough to give me time. He said, 'Emma, send me a demo tape and I'll have a listen.' I mean, how fucking amazing was that? But guess what? I didn't do it – I was just getting pissed and not concentrating.

I've never had any money all my life and all of a sudden here's £70,000 in my hand and I wanted to spend it and buy Gucci handbags and Parade [Prada] shoes. I could never afford these things in my life before, I'd never had this lifestyle and I was more interested in shopping than concentrating on why I had done all this in the first place. I lost my purpose and I chucked all these opportunities down the pan – I should have had someone guiding me, a proper agent.

I had a great two years ... Then the money started running down and I couldn't find a normal job, like admin work, secretarial work. They'd say, 'Sorry, but you've been on *Big Brother*. You'd be a distraction in the company and bad publicity.' And people thought I was being brave by trying to get back to normality. They'd say, 'God, you're so brave,' and I was like, 'Why is it brave? I've got no money – I've got to get back to normality and live.' How can I carry on with this showbiz life if I ain't got the money? I knew it would die off one day.

VICTOR EBUWA, *Big Brother Five*

It did all really affect my family's life. They were getting followed by the press, phone calls at work – it was hard for them to leave the house as there were always journalists outside and yeah, I carried some guilt for some time over that. My mates were having punch ups all the time, especially in the first couple of weeks, where they'd hear someone saying, 'Victor's a dick.' You know, it's not all sweet.

And you know what? Masses of offers had come through – MTV, a pilot for my own show on E4. You know it all looked so promising but nothing came from none of it. I don't know why. I'm a media whore but even whores get to name their price.

I'd be in [my agent's] office and if Jade ever called crying that she had a tax bill, the whole office would go into meltdown trying to get Jade work and shoving her down people's throats in magazines, but you know I can't complain. They made me money. Yeah, they may not have pushed me and worked for me but I did OK. I won the newspaper case and I got good money – £100,000. I'm thinking, you can print shit about me anytime if that's the kind of money I'll get as compensation – it's a nice little living.

NADIA ALMADA, Winner, *Big Brother Five*

I wasn't doing as well as I would like to, and I'd get upset that although the British public had showed me so much love and acceptance by voting for me, the media industry was very different. It's like they didn't know quite where to place me and I'd get so upset that the TV offers weren't coming in.

I think the reason probably is because my market is a different market. I've always been known as 'Nadia the transsexual', and it used to upset me but I accept it now. If that's my niche then I embrace it now. I have suffered because of that, trying to overcome it. I have to accept it. I can't beat it, I tried. Society can't accept me – I want to fit in but I don't think society is ready to fit me in. I would love society to see me as just Nadia and nothing else. You know, I hurt just like anybody else, I pick my nose just like anybody else, I have my fatty lumps just like any other person and bad hair days in the morning!

EUGENE SULLY, *Big Brother Six*

I noticed that my agents weren't really being proactive. Things weren't coming up but then I'd ask myself, what is proactiveness? Is it that they are asking lots of people and that they just aren't interested? Or is it that they just don't have the right contacts? It's all about knowing what you're about and selling the client to the right contacts, but what actually happened was, 'Oh yeah, we spoke to Men and Motors channel and we mentioned you,' and that was about it.

And you think well, it's going alright, I'm still doing lots of PAs which pays well, and months go by and then more months where you still think, it's OK, and then it comes to a point where you think, I'm not anything. And I should have pressed a bit more. But I didn't want to offend anyone and more importantly, I didn't know how to ask.

I'd never done this before, how do I find out what the market out there is like for me? Should I just be content with my lot and shut up? Or is it worth pursuing? It seemed so arrogant to dump an agent and I did it, but by then it was all so late in the day. Time was running out to try to recapture what it was that people loved and it's very hard to put yourself back out there.

But I'm lucky in that I do have lots of unusual interests – technology, cars and cameras. The problem is they want you to open the local fête, which is fine and I'm charitable but I'm not interested in being in the local paper or any paper for that matter. I'm more interested in for example the *History of Modern Superstructures* on Discovery 6.

I found the fame easy, to be honest. The only thing that annoyed me was when people would notice me and then completely ignore whoever I was with and put their back to them – I found that really rude. And once I was part of the procession in switching on the lights in Bognor and someone threw a coin at me, but I laughed it off. Oh, and once this guy said, 'Aren't you Michael Barrymore?' and I thought, wanker.

DEREK LAUD, *Big Brother Six*

It's difficult to judge when all the furore died down because actually it didn't change my life all that much – I'm still doing what I was doing before I went on *Big Brother*, I still get invitations, I still write, still appear on TV and I'm taking ideas to producers. I'm not waiting for producers to knock at my door.

I think it's important to remind oneself to take something positive from the experience and I do, in that Trevor Phillips said that my stay in the House had done more for race relations in this country in breaking down black stereotypes than any other thing, so I'm very proud of that.

The thing that people get wrong is that idea that just because you are getting media exposure you're also getting lots of money, as if it equates, but it couldn't be further from the truth. And that's the misleading notion that my fellow contestants went into the House with. The earnings of ex-contestants appear in the papers ... So there's a bit of institutionalisation – lying about earnings, to make people feel that this is the way to change your life.

SAMANTHA HEUSTON, *Big Brother Six*

I could start to feel myself come down, because I didn't want the high to come down, I didn't want the high to go. I was in the shower and could feel the high coming down and all those bad thoughts coming in like they did before. It lasted about a month and a half. I started to feel really down and lonely. My friends were working and I felt really depressed, and you start listening to the wrong people and those that don't know you that well. You know you should be listening to your family but I started to lose the plot.

My Nan kept on telling me I was depressed. I wasn't being a nice person and they kept saying that that was depression, so everything was depression. I didn't feel I had my own head. You just don't know who you are anymore, you feel you have lost your own voice and it's someone else's voice telling you what to do. There were so many options, everyone was saying, 'Get a new agent.' I had these different camps going on. I had my family who I should have listened to, who had my best interests – like my sensible side. And then I had my friends that encouraged me to be completely erratic – change your agent, change your accountant, do this, move out, do this, do that. It wasn't the stuff they would have done themselves.

I wanted to keep that hype, stay at that level. I was trying to get that high back. My family were like, 'You can't do it, it's over – get a normal job.' My brother said he'd seen loads of ex-*Big Brother* contestants on *GMTV* saying they have normal jobs and are paying the mortgages. But that's easier said than done because I did try.

I got a job in the accounts department at this real dive and all I'd hear day in, day out was, 'What's she doing working in a place like this? What's Sam doing here?' and then they'd bring their kids in to have their picture taken with me. So I soon left that job and got a job in accounts for ITV. They didn't know who I was when I applied but then when I started all the whispers began again and my boss said at the weekly meeting that I should have said who I was and why I was there – just to stop people talking. I mean, can you imagine how excruciatingly embarrassing that was for me? It was hard, too hard and then I'd start phoning in sick because I was depressed again until finally they sacked me, and again I was at home, alone and very down.

Endemol always said, 'If you ever feel like talking, call the psychologists. We are always here to help.' So I did ring up when I was feeling particularly down and said, 'I keep having negative thoughts, like my dad's gonna die' – I'd been so horrible to my parents since coming out, I was sending his blood pressure through the roof. I was really shitting myself about things, I don't know why, just this massive down after this huge high.

I was beginning to have panic attacks and all the psychologist could say was, 'Well, I could die tomorrow, you could die tomorrow.' And that's hardly what you want to hear from the psychologist is it? I asked if I could see him and he said, 'Well, it has to be all arranged through Endemol but don't worry, I won't charge you for this phone call.' My mum wasn't happy about me using them anyway and just wanted me to see a normal GP. The producers always used to say, 'You can always talk to us' – it was just so untrue.

At one point I tried to slit my wrists – there was lots of blood and my parents called an ambulance. I went to A&E. It was all stupid. I just lost it after *Big Brother* – people were telling me do to this, do that. I ended up stripping for a couple of nights, in Spearmint Rhino. I went on this whole bandwagon thing of 'I'll do want I want to do', but I didn't even know what I was doing.

I was sick of conflicting advice. I wasn't being logical. I had money problems, had no guidance, lost friends, had to choose between my parents' advice and my agent's advice. I had so much shit with agents – not knowing who to go with. Just absolutely no guidance. And I just got so down and so upset. I had [depression] when I first came out and then a year after. The *Big Brother* psychologists were awful – 'Just pull yourself together,' they said.

I slit my wrists in front of my dad. I was hysterical – it was a huge cry for help. I was so angry with all of it – having the wrong agents, getting the wrong advice. It was overload. I just felt I'd wasted so much time getting depressed. If I'd had proper psychological help after *Big Brother* then it wouldn't have got as far as it did in terms of trying to commit suicide. It would never have got to that. I took it out on my parents and I shouldn't have, because they are my rocks.

And the worst thing is, after I had spoken to the psychologists a couple of times on the phone, they said, 'Oh, we will have to start charging you after this,' and I said, 'But I can't afford it.' They asked to see a statement of my accounts to see whether I could afford the help or not . . . So basically, I had to prove I had no money before they would give me help and even then they only gave me an hour. Only an hour and that was a month later! All of the depression could have been prevented if I'd had adequate help after the show.

KINGA KAROLCZAK, *Big Brother Six*

Kemal is bisexual. Everyone thinks that just because he dressed as a woman that he was gay but that's not true, he's had loads of girlfriends.* We went out together in Portsmouth and we had been flirting all evening, had drunk loads of wine and then before we knew it we were kissing, it was all very sweet and then we'd slept together. The sex was amazing, you'd never think he was gay! The next morning we looked at each other so embarrassed.

So we embarked on a relationship but people just thought it was a publicity stunt and they were making a joke of us. It was hurtful because I had feelings for him and I would never use my love life as a stepping stone for gaining more press. We both took stick for it, me more than him and I suppose that it was that as well as other factors that caused too much pressure and we split up several months later. We are still best mates though and will always be in each other's lives.

ANTHONY HUTTON, Winner, *Big Brother Six*

Once I had me nose broken in a club. I was in a nightclub in Chester. I was stood at the end at leaving time and was stood on this slightly raised area and this bloke just randomly punched us and I was on the floor. It was blatantly because I'd been on *Big Brother*, because when the bouncers got him he kept saying, 'Just because he's been on the telly, he thinks he's mint! Rah rah!' The doorman offered to take him round the corner and beat the shit out of him but I said no, and to just do it properly and call the police. Me nose is changed for life – I can tell. There is a slight difference.

It's standard procedure to get the odd pissed bloke shouting abuse but ninety nine per cent of it's all good, and the amount of girls I get! Mind you I fucked a lot before *Big Brother* (*laughs*). Girls love a bloke off the telly – it's so shallow but I love it. My mates have even got laid on the back of me, if I'm not interested they get them. And there's one mate who hasn't missed a PA yet, he's been to them all because of the girls!

---

* After leaving the BB House, Kinga struck up a widely publicised romance with fellow contestant Kemal. Many observers cast doubt on the veracity of this, as Kemal's persona was so flamboyantly camp.

LEA WALKER, *Big Brother Seven*

Later I did confront the producer about why they edited me so badly. I said to her, 'Why did you do that to me?' And she said, 'Because we knew you were a strong character and we knew you could deal with that.' She did say that you sign away your life and I thought, yeah, I suppose. She said this at the wrap party when we were going on about it. She said you sell your soul to the devil.

And I thought, OK, I suppose I did surrender my rights . . . What can you do? I care in the sense that it was wrong what they did, but I don't care if Joe Bloggs says, 'You did this on *Big Brother*.' I don't care because they don't really know what happened on *Big Brother*. They only saw what they saw on TV. They don't know exactly what happened and if they can't speak to me as a person then I don't care.

12. TODAY

Nobody puts Baby in a corner

(Dirty Dancing, 1987)

I f there was a wrong way to do it all, I did it. I played the game wrong. I couldn't even get Z-list celebrity right. If the critics love to laugh at us *Big Brother* people when we fall flat on our faces, and say, 'We told you so,' then I did exactly what they wanted. I tried to play a part, and looking back on the things I've done ... rolled on dwarfs, got locked in a boot, made a pilot show with a monkey ... I took a gamble on my life.

I got back with my husband a month after we split up – we're Indian at the end of the day and we couldn't just give up on our marriage, and besides, I never give up on anything I believe in. We decided we had to stop feasting on the negative, we had to stop listening to other people's opinions and we would have to start taking what they said with a pinch of salt instead of following it blindly: people's feedback to everything I did and said had to start being qualified. What it was all about was managing it all better, not getting so upset about things and simply enjoying them.

Looking back I should have relished the whole palaver. I wish I'd thought like that when I first came out of the House but it's so hard to do that with people constantly putting you down and saying, 'Oh, did you see page 34 of the *Sun?*'

because they'd written something negative. But you know what? So what? The press write awful things about everyone and the old saying is right – the time to start worrying is when they stop writing about you. At least they were writing about me!

It's simple and it's plain. I wish, I wish, *I wish* I'd enjoyed all that nonsense – like *Heat* voting me the worst dressed woman. I remember I was gutted at the time, I could have died of embarrassment, because I believed what they said, that I was this awfully dressed joke of a girl, but I look at that piece today and it was fab! I was alongside the likes of Christina Aguilera and pictured next to Kylie, who was the 'best dressed'. And they were great photographs! I should have laughed and thanked *Heat*.

The trouble is that others are jealous and have a way of making you feel that it's all bad news. It happened all the time, and I was weak enough to listen. My husband and I wasted all that time thinking we were in hell but we were living a life that most people only dream about. It was definitely a life that we wouldn't have been living if I'd carried on being a medical rep in Leicester.

I'd do it all again – with bells on. My mother protected me like a lioness does her cubs – I hadn't done any wrong in her eyes. As far as she is concerned, the war escalated when another Indian woman entered the House – Shilpa Shetty – and the same Asian community that criticised me loved her. My mother's still on the warpath.

Without wanting to sound too much like a Tupac record, I'm glad I was slated so badly in the beginning because it meant that my expectations weren't built up then allowed to come crashing down. I had nothing to fall from because I was already at the bottom rung of the ladder. In fact, it was a huge advantage because I had everything to gain and nothing to lose. And I'm doing OK now.

Sometimes you dream about something and in the end it doesn't turn out how you expected it to. You made a mistake. These things happen, and that's how life is. I can't complain – I got my own TV show, did radio, did my acting, wrote, met people I would never have come across otherwise, went to places that I would never have experienced, moved to London, bought a property and, most of all, the best thing, I've made some amazing friends out of it all.

I've lived a very full and amazing life since *Big Brother*, and that show gave me all of that. And yes, there was so much shit that came with it, but I survived – I didn't die and I certainly didn't go away. I have masses of respect for *Big Brother* housemates who do go back to their lives – they are the courageous ones, they did their thing and they thought, you know what? No thanks. And I love that. It wasn't for me because I did do *Big Brother* to change my life and it did – I don't want or need to be out and about any more, and I don't want to be on TV, unless it's something I feel passionately about.

Yes, I'd love to do radio but I always did from day one. I don't want to be in papers or magazines, because quite frankly I'm not strong enough for that. In the light of the *Celebrity Big Brother* scandal, I did a BBC documentary on race relations in Newcastle, where I grew up, and ended up on the receiving end of a massive backlash from the local papers. It was a reminder that, just as Nasty Nick put it, if you play by the sword you die by the sword. That could be the *Big Brother* motto.

I'm a mother now and all I want to do is to pay my mortgage and look after my family. I won't give up though, never – sorry, but I'm a wannabe, unashamedly so. I'm dancing again, just singing a new song this time. I've been very blessed and I thank the producers for choosing me.

PHIL EDGAR-JONES, Creative Director, Endemol

Big Brother has this halo effect – it increases audience figures for shows around it and pays for dramas and documentaries. I do try to help *Big Brother* people after the show is over with follow-up programmes, and I'm all for it, but then I have to sell these programmes to the media elite who run the channel, and they have this middle-aged view. I can only do so much.

BOYD HILTON, TV Editor, *Heat*

The mantras for all past, present and future contestants should be: 'Your fame will finish after twelve weeks', 'You won't be a success', and 'You will never have long lasting fame.'

MELANIE HILL, *Big Brother One*

Do I regret it? Yes, on balance I do. I've done some amazing things, all because of *Big Brother* and I'm grateful for that, I can't complain. It's opened doors and I've met some amazing people, and I would never have got that if it wasn't for *Big Brother*. But the thing that's priceless is your anonymity. It somehow dampens you. Before *Big Brother* I was so sociable and I'd interact with the world, but if I do that now they say, 'Oh, look at that cow off *Big Brother* – who does she think she is?' You have to become smaller, you make yourself small. I mean, I spent a year wearing baggy clothes and a hat, just not wanting to be noticed.

It's not healthy, it's not good and also I strongly believe that someone from Endemol should have come and stayed with me for a bit and helped me adapt. I mean, I became a bloody recluse . . . We only got one session with the psychologist and that was it. The production team should have given us much more help. Someone should have lived with us for a week afterwards and helped us and I don't care how much it would cost because they make enough money. They should talk to you about agents and press attention. More sessions with the psychologist. Endemol should also help you try to get a normal job afterwards. It's just not good enough to wash your hands of us. And the new contestants should have a chat with old contestants to really hear it from the horse's mouth.

I still get recognised to this day, I don't know whether it is the hair or what, and people still ask me, 'Are you Mel from *Big Brother*?' and I get tired and just say, 'No, I just look like her.'

I would say to anyone who wants to do *Big Brother* now: don't do it. There's too much going wrong now, and horrible things happen to the contestants afterwards – rapes, prostitution, people getting beaten up . . . The show is just getting progressively worse and I do seriously think that it will not end till we have a suicide on our hands.

If someone had said, 'Seven years later you will still not have your life back,' then I would never have done it.

Today – Melanie is studying to be a barrister.

AMMA ANTWI, *Big Brother Two*

It took two years, if not more. It was when I went back to work, that's when life went back up for me. Definitely. I went back to work because I was broke and needed the money. I'd been sat at home spending the money I'd earned. I was afraid to go out and I thought, you're pathetic, Amma, you need to go out and live your life, go back to work, get your tits out and earn some money. And your problems will be solved very easily. I dreaded going back to work because I thought it was going to be the worst thing ever but it was a piece of piss.

I regretted saying to my mum that I would never go back to table dancing. I regretted it because actually going back to work is what got me my life back, without a doubt. The first day back, I was terrified for being seen as a failure, and I was letting my mum and family down, but it was better than everything else they'd seen me go through.

Looking back, maybe I was just being silly about it all – maybe I blew certain things out of proportion – because you know what? I would do it all again, I experienced so many things that I would never have done if I hadn't done *Big Brother* and I do have to look at the two per cent good that happened to me because otherwise I'd go bonkers. It sounds so silly and pathetic but one of my best moments was when I was at *Top of the Pops* and Cher was sat there in the stars' bar and she looked over and went, 'Oh my God, it's Amma! I've been watching you whilst I've been here and I saw you being chucked out – you are so cool!' and I nearly fell off my seat. I mean, how many people can say Cher thinks they're cool?

My advice to future contestants would be: one – in my opinion Endemol don't look after anybody. They look after themselves only and if you think they are looking after you, then they're looking after you to protect themselves. Two – they don't prepare you enough for the media. Any other person on the TV would have been given even the most basic of guidelines in how to deal with the media – for example you don't have to do anything that you don't feel right about just because they keep telling you that it's a good thing to do. That was how convincing they were, how smiley they all were telling you, 'You're just the best.' I saw it happen sooooo many times.

Three – Endemol should compensate all the contestants financially because of the amount of money they [Endemol] make. I'm not suggesting big money, but the fact of the matter is that they made something like £30,000,000 including merchandise, books, T-shirts, calendars, board games, DVDs – which we all contributed to. Even a token gesture. I don't mind if you don't pay me for being on *Big Brother* but I mind the merchandising where my image is being used.

What made me laugh the most is that they didn't even say thank you, not once. Not once. The only person who has thanked us [*Big Brother Two* housemates] publicly was Ben Elton in his book, *Dead Famous*. He thanked us all, but Endemol couldn't, Channel 4 couldn't. I thought, how nice – it made me happy, that finally someone said 'thank you'. But Ben Elton did and all he did was use us as subject matter for his book.

Today – Amma is working for a casting agency in London.

ALEX SIBLEY, *Big Brother Three*

Big Brother people always get slated for wanting to be on TV but all people who go on TV whether it be actors, presenters, whatever – they're all wannabes and desperados. I wouldn't do TV again unless the money was too good to turn down and I'd say to people who want to go on *Big Brother*, 'Don't do it – you won't make anything from it, unless you're a slapper and get your tits out.'

Today – Alex is working for his dad's business.

VICTOR EBUWA, *Big Brother Five*

The offers stopped rolling in about a year ago – you know in this game you have a certain amount of shelf life and you just have to pull your socks up and kick ass somewhere else, as I'm doing, or you go and commit suicide. Suicide isn't an option for me. In my own field I'm still the man, and it shows how bad the TV industry is for ethnic minorities that me, that ME who's done fuck all since *Big Brother* – is still signing autographs and people are still going mad – I'm still huge.

And it sounds like bullshit but I'm adjusting to normality, I don't give a shit about much apart from money. My advice to future contestants is: be prepared for the worst, be savvy – don't think going on this show will be a laugh because if you do then you'll be crucified, and if you're ignorant enough to think they won't show the bad stuff you do, well then, you're just an idiot.

And at the end of the day remember one thing only – you either do the humping or get humped. That's the game.

Today – Victor is doing club promotions and party planning.

EMMA GREENWOOD, *Big Brother Five*

I actually got a job offer just last week . . . Eighteen grand a year, commission as well, and when they said I'd got the job I ran to my mate's house and was crying: 'Oh my God, I've finally got a job, finally I can get back to normality.' And then the director decided, 'No, she's been on *Big Brother*.' I'd been sacked before I'd even started. All because of *Big Brother*, and this is what people don't realise, they think going on *Big Brother* is a laugh.

What they have to understand is that it's fucking difficult if you can't even get a secretarial job for fifteen grand! I went for a job in a shop, selling clothes, taking clothes from the stock room and hanging them up and I couldn't even get that job, and I'm thinking, before *Big Brother* I used to be a supervisor and now I can't even get this . . . I was sooo embarrassed. It's a fact that I can't even get a job as a sales assistant. I went to the job centre the other day to sign on and these blokes spotted me and shouted, 'Oi, what you doing here? You were in *Big Brother*!' I nearly died, everyone was looking at me.

It's scary, if I'm honest – you've been put on this pedestal, you've been going to parties, been in magazines, sat next to Madonna and then it all ends. Just like that. And you're back at home. I mean, it was just like a dream – did it really happen? I loved being in the limelight, who wouldn't? But you have to get back to normality and I did know that at the beginning.

But I won't give up on my dream and stop going to auditions, I still will because that's what I was doing before *Big Brother* and sometimes you have to go backwards to go forward. I was recently approached by a music producer to record some songs and I'm really excited about that.

I told him I was in *Big Brother* before he would find out and kick me out, but thankfully he was OK about it, but he did say the record company may have a problem with it . . . but there is no way that I would tell a record company that I was in *Big Brother* – I look totally different now, they might not even recognise me, and I'm not gonna use my real name till I'm offered a deal, if I was offered a deal! I'd lose the deal before I'd even begun! I'm really excited about it, I really hope this happens for me. I won't make the same mistakes I made with my opportunities before!

Today – Emma is signing on but also has recently been in the studio recording some songs for a potential new girl band.

EUGENE SULLY, *Big Brother Six*

A lot of it is self-inflicted. I wasn't afraid of making myself well known and you know what you're getting into, ultimately. My only gripe is that Endemol should give you some media training about how the press works, agents and TV. All I ask for is a day's media training, it could and would have made all the difference.

My advice to future contestants is don't go in with a game plan, you're not a bloody psychologist unless you're paid a hundred grand to be one. And get an agent before you go into the House. I will persevere in broadcasting – I like TV – either behind the scenes or better still in front of the camera.

Today – Eugene is working as a radio DJ and for BBC Scotland.

SISSY (JOANNE) ROONEY, *Big Brother Four*

I was 27 and so naïve. I hate the way I was edited but that's just the way it is. What I realised and the way I see it is – if you are a nasty person then expect that to be shown, but what I never expected was that if you put an extra dollop of sauce on your plate that you'd be labelled a fatty like someone was in my series. You wouldn't expect that! And that kind of editing really affects someone's life and that's harsh. But if you are conniving or walking around with your tits out all day then the show is justified putting that on telly, and it's fair game. It's a double-edged sword but you have to be strong enough to take it.

I wouldn't say certainly, up until *Big Brother Four*, that *Big Brother* people are 'attention seeking' – if that's what the critics say we are then all people on TV are attention seeking. However to be on *Big Brother* you do have to be extrovert and not a Billy-no-mates. You would have to have come from a background and group of siblings that made you what you are, and that would give you the confidence to go for *Big Brother*, because you know you have the support network behind you.

When people say, 'Go away *Big Brother* people,' I do think, yeah they're right. Unless you really do have a career of your own doing something, don't just drag it out and pretend you're a celebrity. You're not a celebrity, you're just 'known'. I'm still recognised to this day and I always get asked, 'What was it like?' 'Who did you like?'

My advice to future contestants is to be prepared to be owned by *Big Brother* producers, and to be edited however they want to edit you and, more importantly, whatever situation you are trying to get away from *now*, be prepared to be back in that situation a few months after you're evicted.

Today – Sissy has her own dress label, Sissy's Surgery, and is working on a project to combine fashion and social outreach programmes.

DEREK LAUD, *Big Brother Six*

I think what is clear to me is that *Big Brother* is a deep exploitation of very young, very uneducated, very naïve people. That they don't know what they are letting themselves in for. I don't buy that argument that by *Big Brother Four*, *Five*, *Six* and *Seven* they should know what they are getting into. They are too young and all they see are the magazines with all these celebrities and glamour stories.

For example in my House there were three people there and I was old enough to be their father! In many cases they hadn't been to London before and in this cult of celebrity they'd do anything for fame, and Channel 4 exploit that for their own pockets. There is something hugely perverse about *Big Brother*, that in effect really adapts slavery principles – they shackle people and don't pay them a proper wage. TV shouldn't be immune from the law and from the government's rhetoric of minimum wage.

My advice to future contestants would be, think hard about doing this, and don't expect it to change your life because it won't really.

Today – Derek has been asked by David Cameron to be the Tory candidate for Mayor of London.

SAMANTHA HEUSTON, *Big Brother Six*

Yes, I have got myself back together because I've realised that I can be both people – sensible, normal and have a normal job, and also crazy and still enjoy the life. Now there's more of a balance. I don't just try to live the 'fame' life anymore, to live too hard and fast. I'm trying to get a normal job and do whatever else that might come up. Also, I'm not going to feel sorry for myself anymore, there are people much worse off than me. I'm grateful for my life.

I'm also doing my website – Sam Heuston's Hunks – where I went around the country and took pictures of men naked in clubs or whatever. And that was getting 7,000 hits a month, and I'm supposed to be doing Sam Heuston's Sex Diaries, talk all about the celebrity shags! I was trying to give up that kind of life but there will always be a part of me that will want to enjoy it, liking the attention. My sexual experiences have gone to another level since *Big Brother*, for sure.

All I would say more psychological help is needed. Future contestants should have media training and just listen to your loved ones and no one else.

Today – Samantha has done numerous lads mag photo shoots since leaving the House. She is currently setting up Britain's first male glamour model agency and an online magazine. Her first film, *Clubbing to Death*, is due out in 2007.

RICHARD NEWMAN, *Big Brother Seven*

I coped very well with adjusting back to normality. It's only been a few months and I can already walk out looking a mess now, compared to how it was at the beginning when it was so very intense that I couldn't even go shopping! Normal life is all but back. It's been quick. I'm one of the very few that's mentally stable – I'm happy to go back to working in a bar. I didn't expect to come out and be famous or earn loads of money. I'm not famous and I never was – I was a contestant on a reality TV programme and that's it. I'm very proud I was part of a great British institution for a little while.

My advice to future contestants is have only one expectation – to win the money and nothing else. If you expect any more then you will be the one doing your *Big Brother* ruined my life line. Please don't go in there thinking you will be famous at the end of it. It's also slightly disgusting being famous just for being on *Big Brother* – people should be famous for having a talent. It's worrying that so many kids aspire to be Chantelle Houghton or Kate.* It's disgusting – be a lawyer, be a doctor.

My last thought on it all – I'm glad it's only fifteen minutes of fame.

Today – Richard is writing for on-line magazines. He and Lea have their own radio slot, *The Dicky and Dolly Show* on Gaydar digital radio.

KINGA KAROLCZAK, *Big Brother Six*

I haven't given up on showbiz. I did try the music thing and I've seriously thought about going to the States to pursue it if nothing works out here, but I don't have my head in the clouds anymore. There is no way a record company would sign an

---

* Chantelle Houghton was an ordinary member of the public who competed in, and won, *Celebrity Big Brother* in 2006.

ex-*Big Brother* contestant. I don't think a *Big Brother* person can ever get away from the *Big Brother* tag and I'll always be known as '*Big Brother* Kinga' but all I can do is try my best.

I'm concentrating on my acting now – I'm going to Cannes in April for this film that I've just done – *Cash and Curry*. I've got theatre work coming up, I'm filming a pilot show for a comedy. I'm doing bits and bobs. I don't see why I should go back to a normal job, I did *Big Brother* to change my life. I will see how things go over the next couple of years.

After a while, although I loved the fame, it started becoming a hindrance and I couldn't even go out for a coffee with my mates because of the constant attention and people coming up to me, but I don't get recognised at all anymore because I look so different. People do take the piss sometimes – that I'm not that famous anymore – and someone sent me a horrible email one day to my MySpace page. This band wrote, 'This website is for wannabes not has-beens and I'm looking at my watch and it says your time is up,' and I replied, 'At least I can say I made it – you never will' (*laughs*).

Big Brother has changed me totally. I'd had enough of the press constantly talking about the way I looked in a negative fashion and I've just spent three months losing over three stone. I look completely different now and I have so much more confidence in myself now I've lost weight, I've changed how I look and I take myself more seriously. I actually have my life back now and I get wolf whistled again now, like I used to before *Big Brother*! If someone offered me Britney Spears' fame tomorrow I'd say, 'I'll take the money but you can keep the fame, thanks.' I've stopped being this silly, stupid girl; I learned a lot of harsh lessons. I always say that I went into *Big Brother* a girl and I came out a woman.

My advice to future contestants would be, 'Don't make a prat of yourself like I did.'

Today – Kinga has just starred in her first film, *Cash and Curry*, released in summer 2007, and she has a role in a forthcoming theatre comedy.

ANTHONY HUTTON, Winner, *Big Brother Six*

I say I had the best experience ever, I made a load of money and I'm set up for life. To me that's success. I got on, I won, me dream came true – to play footie at St James' Park. I've got a couple of flats and a car and that's all because of *Big Brother*, so when people say, 'Where's Anthony now? Not doing anything?' I say, 'Bothered!'

My advice to future contestants would be, 'Aye, go for it.'

Today – Anthony is planning to open his own hair salon in Newcastle.

NADIA ALMADA, Winner, *Big Brother Five*

My advice to future contestants would be, on reflection of the last two series, 'Don't do it.' It's exploitative and demoralising. You won't get what you think you will out of it.

Today – Nadia is still working in TV and the media.

LEA WALKER, *Big Brother Seven*

You're sent into a whirlwind, you go in as yourself and you come out as yourself but to the rest of the nation you're this character that's been highly edited and been judged. You're pushed out into society, not having a clue what the hell's been going on in the outside world and it's like, 'Bye bye, there you go,' and people will never understand that unless they have been in that House.

They always say, 'It's only *Big Brother*, it's only a game show,' but that's my life – you have no respect. Your whole life is them four walls and your life is in the hands of Big Brother, and they play mind games with you all the time. I always wanted to leave because of the mind games.

My advice to future contestants would be, be thick-skinned, don't keep any skeletons in the closet. Know who your friends are as they can sell stories on you. Be thick-skinned as there are a lot of nasty journalists who will try and upset you, try to put you down. You have to realise that there are thousands upon thousands of other reality stars who don't get upset about making a career of it, it's not a one-off. Don't expect to be the next Tom Cruise when you come out. You have to milk it for whatever it is. People are so right about this fifteen minutes of fame and some people can make it last a lot longer but if you make as much money as you can out of it then fine. I accept fifteen minutes of fame.

Today – Lea is now co-hosting *The Dicky and Dolly Show* with Richard on Gaydar digital radio.

SOPHIE PRITCHARD, *Big Brother Three*

I didn't actually watch this year's *Celebrity Big Brother* at the beginning because I knew Jade was going in and it made me sick. Then my mum was watching it one night and I was ready to walk out of the room when I heard Jade say to Shilpa, 'I don't understand you, I find you very false and fake,' and I thought, oh my God! It's déjà-fucking-vous! Have you not learned? You have been given a chance to put right what you did wrong with me, you could have become an even bigger star if you put it all right!

But of course she hadn't learned because in *Big Brother Three* after she came out the House, no one asked her about her treatment towards me and the media decided to make a star out of [her]. She had no backlash. Nothing. I couldn't believe what I saw when she went mental on Shilpa.

What I couldn't understand was some people – especially magazines – commenting, 'We can't believe Jade is like this, can't believe she's a bully, it's not like our Jade.' And I was furious, I was burning, thinking, what? YOU ARE JOKING! Please tell me that people haven't forgotten what that girl put me through for a month in that House. And people had forgotten . . . The Oxo cube fight was evil.* She's a mother, does she really want her kids seeing and growing up with that?

And then she gets all this special treatment when she was evicted – she should have been booed, had to face a press conference and she escapes all of that, and I'm sorry but it's pretty obvious she was briefed about what was going on. People ask me, 'Do you wish you'd made the money Jade has?'

---

* One of the most notorious arguments between Jade Goody and Shilpa Shetty in *Celebrity Big Brother* 2007 was triggered by a row over cooking and Oxo cubes.

and I say, 'Hell no, if it means making money on the back of bullying people, no, no. I'm happy with who I am and what I have thank you.' She may have all this supposed money but she still has to live with how she treats people.

Her career was selling her stories to magazines! That's it. And as far as I can see the magazines – especially *Heat* – are still giving [her] a career by putting her on the cover every week with headlines like POOR JADE. It astonishes me. I'm not baying for blood but just what's right is right and what's wrong is so wrong.

Today – Sophie now runs her own mobile tanning business.

MAKOSI MUSAMBASI, *Big Brother Six*

To be honest I don't blame anyone, it was my choice. I don't have anything against Endemol. At the end of the day they are a company that is out to make money and they are making money. If I was in Endemol's shoes I would employ the same editors who work on it now. I have got nothing on them. It's the media that created that picture of me. I still don't have anything against the Endemol staff because they need to get paid. See I am very weird like that. I am one person who doesn't say, 'Any news is good news', or 'Any news is publicity' – that is bollocks.

Of course people still come up to me, every day. Sometimes it's lovely, sometimes not. That's how it is. I do think, what right does anybody have to come up to me and say, 'Oh, have you lost weight? Are you gaining weight?' Or people say, 'You are so small, you know *Big Brother* made you look really big. Oh my gosh, you're quite big.' What right do you have? At least say, 'Hello Makosi' first (*laughs*). And that's the advice I would give to any future contestant – expect to be loved and hated.

I have to look at the good that has come out of it – I have been blessed to do *Big Brother*. I am starting a charity called The Big Five. I am a co-founder. The *Sun* are playing a big role, but there is a catch. If I hadn't have done *Big Brother* these people would not have come to me. There has been a lot of good and there has been some bad stuff.

I have just finished recording a film – *Cash and Curry* – and God knows which way that is going to go, and if it goes well, then God knows where I will end up. I want to go into presenting and I've got a show, and I've designed dresses since I was thirteen that I need to put into life now. I want to go into bikinis, I want to go into so many things. I won't give up.

I think media training should be given to housemates. I made so many mistakes because I had no idea what to do . . .

I don't regret *Big Brother*, to regret is to be embarrassed. It brought many tears to my life for sure, and I lost friends, but it helped me to get to know me better. You know, before *Big Brother* I was perfect, I was this cardiac nurse that everyone loved, it was like, 'Hail Makosi!' everywhere I went. I thought I was this princess and you know what? *Big Brother* brought me down a peg or two – I needed that. But I'm on my way back up to being a princess again (*laughs*). The sky is the limit for me, but my life is not a PR circus, it's a passion-driven one.'

Today – Makosi's first film, *Cash and Curry*, will be out in 2007 and she's working for her charity, The Big Five, in aid of African girls.

13. THE SUCCESS STORIES

I'm king of the world!

(*Titanic*, 1997)

There have been over a hundred housemates in and out of the *Big Brother* House's doors, but only a handful have been successful. But how do you define success? As Boyd Hilton said, who says going back to your normal job isn't a success – why is that seen as a failure? Mark Frith counts 'success' as 'anyone who is happy with their experience of *Big Brother*' – not a lot of people can say that!

However, when I began researching this book and asked all the people I interviewed – some of whom appear in this book and some of whom don't – who they thought was the most successful, two names always came out on top: Brian Dowling and Kate Lawler. Before the events of the 2007 *Celebrity Big Brother* series, lots of people also mentioned Jade, but added her success was more financial than anything else, in that she didn't really have a job in TV or radio. After *Celebrity Big Brother* many people took back their support for Jade.

I did approach Jade for an interview both before *Celebrity Big Brother* and again after the series, and on both occasions she declined. Before *Celebrity Big Brother* I thought, well I'll just have to write about her anyway because it would be weird not to have her as a success story, even though my heart and head were against it.

Many former *Big Brother* housemates felt Jade had always been a bully and, quite frankly, lots of *Big Brother* housemates have had colourful lives – maybe not one-armed lesbian mums – but ignorance should never have been celebrated in the first place by the British media. To be fair to Jade, she should never have been called 'pig' either. But then again, lots of *Big Brother* contestants have been called worse.

But that's why I do believe that Brian and Kate really are the success stories of *Big Brother*. Let's look at the evidence: they didn't sell out as soon as they came out of the house; they didn't do every reality TV programme going, and they actually got 'jobs'. Thus they are still around today; they have worked and learned their trade; they have had their own TV shows – which they have actually presented – and had their own radio shows; they have hosted big events and now have real careers.

Maybe in the beginning it was down to luck – they did win – but luck alone couldn't have lasted the distance and in fact, when luck did run out, they both proved themselves, knuckled down and forged careers . . . all without sitting in front of cosy fires in glossy magazines.

Brian Dowling won *Big Brother* by the biggest margin ever: 2,300,000 votes. In a recent survey he was voted the most popular housemate of all time. The nation fell in love with him in 2001 after his displays of self-mockery and vulnerability. And I know that you're all aware by now that he is my best mate (the best thing to come out of *Big Brother* for me), although this is the one time I wish we weren't mates because it sounds so corny for me to write about how well he's done! But I have to do it, because the truth of the matter is Brian is a success, whichever way you look at it. No other housemate has achieved so much, and all without having to sell out. When I interviewed Gary Thompson of the *News of the World* he summed it up: 'If you were to ask me which *Big Brother* person will still be around in ten years time I'd say Brian Dowling.'

So why Brian? How did he land a job on the BAFTA-award winning *SMTV*? Or host the *Elle* Style Awards and go on to have his own show on ITV? He's fond of saying himself that he was 'just an air steward' before *Big Brother*. Here's Brian's take on his success.

BRIAN DOWLING, Winner, *Big Brother Two*

I was always going to go back to flying when I came out of the House – I didn't expect anything other than that. Before I'd gone in the House I'd spoken to my boss to keep my job open and it was. So when I came out, it was obviously all a whirlwind and I laugh looking back, because in interviews they kept asking me, 'So what will you do now?' and I always thought that was weird – I'm an air steward, I'll go back to that as planned.

My intention was to go back in September and enjoy a bit of time off, enjoy this new experience and that was that. So when I got this agent, it was mainly to look after this and that and personal appearances, but one day she called and said, 'How would you like to guest present on *SMTV*?' and I thought, eh? Why? Why would they want me to? But I thought this is part of my experience – and I was shit, I thought, I was so, so nervous standing next to Ant and Dec . . . I kept thinking, God's having a huge laugh here! But astonishingly they asked me back again! I wasn't as nervous that time and as a result more natural. I was supposed to start work but then *SMTV* offered me a deal and I thought, I have to take this opportunity. It was all very bizarre and surreal – a year ago I was an air steward and here I was presenting with Tess Daly! And presenting a children's TV programme, as the first openly gay presenter – I had to keep pinching myself all the time in breaks. Arm full of bruises!

Narinder: So it was that easy?

No, you see that's the thing, I think all *Big Brother* people think it was easy and I was lucky to get offered such a great show. But don't forget, I had never done any TV in my life, let alone live TV! I was thrown in at the deep end and worked harder than the next person to prove myself – learning scripts, how to use an ear piece, someone talking in your ear, telly terms (camera left actually is right hand, VT . . .). It was all alien to me, all I'd known before that was 'tea or coffee?' It was the best job in the world I have to admit – one week interviewing J-Lo, then Britney, Beyoncé. I did *SMTV* for two years.

Then what?

Soon after I left *SMTV* it ended anyway and I went on to present my own TV show on ITV called *Brian's Boyfriends*, a makeover programme. Then I did voiceover for *The Salon* and I know people thought, 'Oh that's a step down,' but it wasn't – I was lucky with *SMTV* but I still hadn't proved myself as an all-round presenter! Nowhere near, doing voiceovers was another string to my bow and it was about proving to people that I wanted to work hard and that not everything was handed to me on a plate.

And don't forget I was offered a lot of reality shows but I felt that if I wanted to be taken seriously then I had to turn these shows down because saying 'yes' to everything just seemed so desperate, and it's not what you do if you want a long-lasting career. And then as a result I got more work. It wasn't always going to be as easy as *SMTV*. I went to Living TV where I was lucky enough to present shows such as *Celebrity Extra*, *I'm Famous and Frightened* and to narrate *Trolly Dollies*. I then landed a late night quiz show on ITV1 – *The Mint* – that was four hours of live TV! A great learning curve.

Best moments?

Without a shadow of doubt – the *Elle* Style Awards. I hosted with Jo Whiley and there were all these amazing people there like Stella McCartney, Danni and Kylie Minogue. A-Listers!

So why are you successful and other Big Brother *people didn't quite achieve what you have?*

You know I always say luck played a big part but also I played it right. I did *Big Brother* at the right time – if I'd done *Big Brother* now, I'd never get a job in TV. More significantly, I didn't sell out as soon as I came out and I continued not to sell out. Having said that if they offered me a five-star holiday with the man of my dreams – who knows? (*laughs*).

Others are so desperate for it that it shows, and it's too much – it's unattractive. That's if they want a media career, that is. Jade Goody said 'yes' to every reality TV show going and every day she was in papers and magazines for just farting, and it's overexposure. Look what happened. It's not good.

I never hated my old life so much that fame would be the be all and end all. I don't need to be in magazines to feel good about myself, I don't want to live my life like that, my life is private. And you know what? I'm not sure what 'successful' is but all I know is that I've always worked.

I wouldn't say I've got to where I want to be yet, I still have lots to learn and I'm working hard. I won't ever play the gay card, that only blue-eyed males get all the jobs; if I don't get a job it's down to presenting skills and that's it.

I don't have any sympathy for BIG BROTHER RUINED MY LIFE people, especially now that it's series eight! I mean, give it all back – the fame, the money, the parties. Give it all back and remember when you wanted it so much.

Kate Lawler is one of the very few *Big Brother* people to have managed to stay in the limelight without resorting to staged paparazzi shots. Pretty, fun and a grafter for sure, she's the kind of girl you think you love to hate, but actually when you meet her, you realise that she's that rare combination of tomboy and girly girl, and if you were her best mate, she'd kill for you.

When I met Kate, I wasn't sure what to expect, but I was surprised at how down-to-earth and sweet she was. I could see exactly why she won *Big Brother* – she's not offensive in the slightest. It's clear that her family mean the world to her, and the other thing that surprised me was what a hard worker she is – she wants to work for her goals and is extremely ambitious. She presented *RI:SE* for two years, hosted *Party in the Park* and had her own show on Capital Radio. More recently she's done modelling campaigns for Ann Summers, columns for papers and magazines, and her own best-selling fitness DVD that she's 'well proud of'. Here's Kate's own answer to the question, 'Why are you a success?'

KATE LAWLER, Winner, *Big Brother Three*

I don't know how you would define success. For example, if you come out of the House and you do go back to your old job and life then why isn't that a success? Why is that a failure? I don't know why I'm a success but I've worked damn hard and went back to basics and learned the ropes. I came out and wanted to work, I was never bothered about going to any of the parties – only if I really wanted to. I just wanted to work.

The only premieres that I've ever been to are *Gangs of New York* because I wanted to go, *Charlie's Angels* because we filmed it for *RI:SE* and one other thing with my nephew. And as for selling out to magazines, I don't know, only if it's in relation to promoting any work I'm doing – even when I was dating Jonathan Woodgate [a footballer who plays for Middlesborough FC] we never did the whole *OK* magazine thing, it just wasn't me.

But anyway, the first job I ever did was working on *Celebrity Extra*, pre-recording a show about the latest celebrity gossip, movies and music across the UK and abroad. I nearly peed my pants when I was told Matt Damon would be my first ever celebrity interview! MATT DAMON! He was so lovely. I only had five minutes to ask him questions about his film, *The Bourne Identity*, and he was so friendly and charming that he made the whole process go from really nervewracking to fun and enjoyable. My fave celeb ever!

I was over the moon when I landed the job presenting Channel 4's breakfast show *RI:SE* with the lovely Iain Lee. Even though the show had previously been slated I was confident that Iain and I would pull back the viewers – which we did, hooray! It was only a year but it was live every morning for two hours – I couldn't have asked for better TV presenting experience. The most fun of jobs I've ever done, loved everything about the show, loved Iain and was gutted when it ended. But one door closes, another opens!

Capital FM was a great radio station to work for. I got to meet some wonderful people – Chris Tarrant, Margarita Taylor (lovely lady), the legend that is Foxy and of course Andi Peters. I presented the *Late Night Steve Penk Show* a few times when he was on holiday – that was my favourite as you can get away with more on radio at night and all the nutcases used to call up! Then I got my own weekend show called *Hit Music Sunday* with Andi Peters and he taught me a lot about the industry and that you have to work hard to stay where you are!

And I have worked hard – my interest in DJing began from the age of sixteen when I just used to go round my mate's house and have a go on his Technic 1210s. I'd always thought, I'd love to DJ at some point in my life, and before *Big Brother* I was saving for a flat so couldn't afford to buy my own decks. After *Big Brother* I was so busy with work I just didn't even have time to think about even doing it as a hobby.

But after I filmed *Celebrity Wrestling* in early 2005 we had a few months before the show went on TV so I took those months off work and finally bought my decks in May. Through the summer of 2005 till Christmas I'd be on my decks every day learning to mix by myself and practising until my mixing was perfect and I felt confident enough to DJ in public.

I've now been DJing for a year and two months and enjoy it so much. I make mixed CDs all the time and spend a lot of my time downloading and searching for new cutting-edge house music. I want to take my DJing abroad a lot more. Having played in Wales, Scotland, Ireland, Ibiza, Norway, Dubai and Tokyo already, it'd be my dream to build up my DJ career outside the UK where people do not have any idea who I am.

I'm currently working on my first house track which I hope will be signed in the summer. And I'm also going to be starting a monthly podcast. Having a residency at my favourite club in the UK – Sankeys, Manchester – is my ultimate dream and I hope to be a success as a DJ, following in the footsteps of other female DJs.

I know I've done a few reality TV programmes like *Love Island*, but seriously, would you turn down two weeks in Fiji? And the possibility of meeting a new bloke? Besides, it wouldn't interfere with my DJing. That's what swung it for me.

I do get compared to Jade as we are from the same series. I am really happy that I've always kept a low profile, however. It keeps me out of trouble! I'm also very proud of where I am today and that I'm not in Jade's situation.

Although I don't get too bothered about what papers and magazines say, to have the whole country turn against you and see the papers write stuff like they did [about Jade] must be horrible. I'd want to leave the country and never come back!

CONCLUSION

So now you've read everyone's thoughts, their opinions and the answers to the whys and the hows. Lea admits she did it for fame, Richard for the money, Anthony because he was *Big Brother*'s biggest fan and Derek to prove a political point.

You've read how the housemates felt when they got that call, how it was entering the House and what life was like inside. I found it hard, Lea hated the mind games, but for Derek the juvenile tricks played by Big Brother were just plain tedious, and Victor believed he could see how it was all manufactured.

You have also read the other side to the argument – you know that, as Phil Edgar-Jones from Endemol puts it, the producers warn the contestants until they are 'blue in the face'. He argues that everyone has a right to be on TV, and asks why should only talented people have that right? It's true – why should just actors and presenters have a monopoly on TV?

Big Brother is a passport to fame for ordinary folk who don't have a particular talent but who do have larger-than-life personalities that can generate great entertainment, and that is what TV is about – entertainment. And Endemol are just giving Joe Bloggs the opportunity to be on TV, if he should so wish. They 'don't go fishing for these people', it's true – people choose to stand in that queue, nobody forced them or 'handcuffed them to go', as journalist Boyd Hilton points out.

Boyd thinks it's that delusional aspect of the housemates' personalities – desperate for fame – that make them so funny and interesting to watch. Rachel Morris doesn't see why vulnerable people shouldn't be represented on TV. After all, if they weren't then a show like *Big Brother* would only feature well-rounded individuals who'd make for some boring television and wouldn't be representative of society.

So what are the contestants complaining about? They should have known what they were letting themselves in for, shouldn't they?

Some of you may have scoffed at the stories, maybe at Makosi for believing her treatment was racist, or you might have laughed out loud at Eugene and his fig leaf, but some of you may have cried too, like I did many times. Cried at how naïve they were for chasing a dream – Nadia, who wished she would finally be accepted then realised that the media still saw her as 'different'; Kinga, who still wanted her singing career after so many failed auditions.

Maybe you shook your head in disbelief at the courage it took to step into the House, in particular for Brian and Amma, who had to tell their mothers big secrets about themselves before they went in, and for Richard, whose mum was being treated for cancer as the series aired.

Now you also know how editing may or may not be used by the producers and, although it makes great viewing for you at home (and that's what it is all about after all – entertainment), you also know how editing is perceived by some of the people who have actually lived in the House and experienced it firsthand.

Mel was the most hated woman in Britain and needed security – she couldn't even get on the tube for fear of being followed; Amma watched the tapes back and felt so bad that she changed all her mannerisms for life; Makosi can't even go to her local church; Lea is looked on by some as a stalker and Richard as a bully; and Kinga can't ever get away from the bottle incident. Alex virtually became a recluse and only felt free to walk with his head held high when he was in another country. Nadia was called a 'freak' by strangers and Makosi was called much worse.

But many people would argue that they should have known that they couldn't control the way they were edited, right? And do they have a case now that E4 runs a live feed? There's no editing there, and besides, the producers can't fabricate whole conversations or make the housemates do things they didn't do. Phil Edgar-Jones of Endemol gave a compelling argument when he pointed out that everyone edits – the viewer himself edits by choosing the bits he or she watches, and two people might react completely differently to the same bit of footage. Endemol can't control the viewers' reactions, or what the housemates do on live TV.

Besides, a favourite observation of all my media contributors was that 'by *Big Brother Four, Five, Six* and *Seven*, the housemates should know what they're letting themselves in for'. So should we accept that all the housemates from the first and second, and – at a push – third series were 'innocent', but that the rest of them could not possibly have been misled?

Yes, many housemates should have known what might happen.

The housemates have also told you how their lives changed the minute they walked out of the door into this strange new world of paparazzi, press and fame. You may have been happy for them when their dreams were realised – Kinga felt like Britney Spears (pre-breakdown) and Victor loved the love he was shown by hundreds.

Or maybe you just thought, 'Well, you got what you wanted, game over.' But you might have more sympathy if you looked at it like psychotherapist Rachel Morris: '*Big Brother* is in our homes 24/7 and that's a long time, and that's why overnight you become a household name and face, and it's disturbing to become that famous.'

Were housemates wrong to think it'd be anything other than nine weeks in the House, a week or two of being a celebrity and then all the attention dwindling away? The same thing happens to almost all celebrities, after all, not just *Big Brother* people – everyone has their time. It's just that *Big Brother* gives you a shorter shelf life than most.

But the housemates should have known that, right?

You have also been privy to the earnings of *Big Brother* contestants. Some made lots of money and invested wisely and now they're set up for life, namely the winners – Anthony, Kate and Brian. Some made enough money to live off until it was feasible to go back to a normal job, but then found it impossible to get that normal job – Sam tried and was ridiculed, Mel tried and couldn't, and Emma to this day can't get a job and her money has run out. Who'd take a *Big Brother* person seriously?

But they should have known that, right?

But hang on a minute. Let's consider who is there to help the contestants after they leave the House. When it comes to dealing with the media, the housemates are all initially Joe Bloggs off the street, with no training. The PR company paid for by Endemol do offer some support, advising housemates on agents and assisting with the press, but Lea and Richard say they were advised to go with an agent who they felt unhappy with; and Eugene felt he didn't have a clue about agents and as a result made the wrong choice and lost a few of his fifteen minutes of fame. To some ex-housemates, it felt like they were given a week or two of support and then fobbed off with any old agent.

The press are notorious for having no mercy and they certainly don't pull their punches when it comes to the *Big Brother* people. It's fair game – the nature of the show is such that even I have to agree that you should realise you're a target when you go into the House – but thinking that you know what you're getting into, and actually *experiencing* the wrath of Fleet Street is like imagining being beaten up versus actually being beaten up. It's more painful than you could have dreamed and the recovery takes a lot longer – try twelve rounds in the boxing ring as a novice fighting a pro, and then, just when you're within an inch of your life, someone shouts, 'Well, you said you wanted to do it! No one forced you.'

How do you take it when, like Kinga, you are called 'minga' and you lose your confidence overnight? Or if, like Makosi, you are accused of prostitution? Or when the world reads that you're a drug dealer and you know it's a lie, like Victor? You're only a *Big Brother* contestant, you don't have the power of a superstar behind you to keep you protected or advise you how to deal with the press, and so you blindly go running ahead and smash straight into a wall. Everyone keeps reminding you that you're only a game show reject, but you're dealing with the kind of press that a criminal or an Oscar winner faces. Its overwhelming, The amount of fame that Big Brother can bring you is phenomenal, and if you are just an ordinary person, how do you cope? I remember I used to ask my publicist whether I should do this or that. And they'd respond, 'It's up to you.' To be fair, sometimes I'd be too damn scared to ask a thing. I vividly remember sitting with my PR guy and being about to ask him about agents when his phone rang and it was Elton John calling! I nearly fell off my seat! I refrained form asking my silly, mundane question . . . how could I? I'd look stupid. These guys were dealing with people like Elton John: why would they bother with me? Mrs. Fifteen minutes?

Endemol do argue that they provide psychotherapists and psychologists for the housemates before, during and after the show. Nadia agrees: 'I even had an extra interview . . . they just wanted to safeguard, they were worried. Because of who I am, maybe they were worried that I wouldn't be strong enough to handle it.' Phil Edgar-Jones says that mental health charities have investigated what goes on behind the scenes and have 'gone away satisfied'.

But what about Emma, left on her own in the bed-sit? Or Amma, feeling suicidal? Or Sam, slitting her wrists after leaving the house? Or the criminologist Professor David Wilson, whom Endemol hired to 'spice things up' and who walked off the show ten days into series five, refusing to cooperate any more? Should Endemol have known that things like this might happen? Is the help provided to housemates by the official Big Brother psychologists and therapists enough? And what of the fact that contestants are then asked to pay for psychological treatment sessions after Endemol have paid for their quota? That is shocking to me. Out of everything I discovered while researching this book, that has disturbed me the most. It seems to me that this company simply doesn't care enough – why else would ex-contestants have to PAY for psychological sessions for feelings triggered by the programme? By the time the seventh series of Big Brother was over, and producers were busy preparing for the fifth *Celebrity Big Brother*, it might have been fair to assume that the lessons of previous series, and the experiences of former housemates, would be informing the decisions made about the way the programme was produced and the housemates cared for.

Celebrity Big Brother 2007 was a train wreck and resulted, unbelievably, in what was the biggest race row of recent times, played out in headlines all over the world. When Bollywood star Shilpa Shetty was allegedly bullied by fellow housemates Jade Goody, Jo O'Mera and Danielle Lloyd, Indians burned effigies of the *Big Brother* producers in the streets.

Shetty was called 'Shilpa Poppadom' and 'Shilpa Fuckawala' and told to 'go back to where you came from'. No charges were pressed as a result of events in the house, as what occurred wasn't against the law, but many of us who saw what happened would agree that the things that were said and done were unacceptable. I for one don't care what the police say – bullying and racist comments (even if the motivation behind the words cannot be proved to be racial prejudice) are the lowest form of human behaviour, and in my opinion that is just how Shilpa Shetty was treated.

Kevin O'Sullivan commented, 'Channel 4 have not got away with it this time. They did with Fight Night – it was overlooked because they did so well out of it. And Endemol thought that whatever scandal hits the show would be good for [it]. They made the mistake of thinking that the Shilpa race row would do the same thing as the others. But it didn't: they don't understand the nature of the British people – we do not accept certain things, like racism, and by the way it was without a doubt racism.'

Instead of intervening, the *Big Brother* producers allowed the show to go on, only stepping in to tell housemates to think about their behaviour, and to ask Shilpa for her take on events. Presenter Davina McCall announced that *Big Brother* was a democracy and that it was up to the viewer to pick up the phone and evict the wrongdoers, while Peter Bazalgette, the boss of Endemol, defended the series: 'There have been no mistakes in the running of this programme,' he said. He praised the show's history and the earlier series winners, saying it had raised 'incredibly interesting and profound issues.' But as Professor David Wilson argues, 'They present *Big Brother* as a social experiment but I disagree; do we know anything more about transgenders after Nadia was in the House, or Tourette's syndrome because of Pete's involvement? No.'

The producers of the show questioned whether what happened in the House during *Celebrity Big Brother* was racism at all, because the viewer couldn't be sure of the motivation of the housemates. Everyone seemed to have an opinion on the issues, and the most popular opinion seemed to be that these girls were just 'ignorant'. I'm sorry, but I believe ignorance is no excuse, and neither is 'lack of education'. I don't think you need good GCSEs to know that calling someone 'poppadom' is wrong! I am a British Asian woman and it remains my opinion that what I saw on my screen was clear-cut, out-and-out racism, the kind many Britons face in the playground, the workplace or on the street.

To be fair, Shilpa herself said she felt Jade's comments were not racially motivated. While she initially indicated that she did feel race was an issue, she later went to the diary room and said, 'No, actually I take that back. I don't think that is true. You know, people say things in a fit of anger. I stand corrected. I don't want people to think and feel that way . . . I think there are a lot of insecurities from her end but it's definitely not racial.' She went on to say, 'I think it's a sequence of events that created that misunderstanding and made me believe for maybe a fraction of a second that I thought she was being racist.' I have to say, I lived with Jade during the Big Brother Christmas panto for E4 some years ago, and I don't think the girl is racist, but what she said to Shilpa *was* racist, and besides, bullying can be just as bad.

At the time of the race row, *Big Brother* producers pointed out that bullying isn't a crime, but what kind of message does that give to the millions of youngsters watching the show? Anti-bullying campaigns have struggled for years to reduce the bullying that takes place in schools and workplaces throughout the country. The response of producers to the events of this year's Big Brother was hardly what they would have hoped for. As it turned out, the British public did take a stand against what was happening and voted off the perpetrators, making the victim the winner, but Channel 4 came off the biggest winner. The ratings soared and they were still selling adverts. But maybe not for long. As Kevin O'Sullivan says, 'Channel 4 has had its balls chopped off.' Will it be different this year? Will the producers take better care, and if they do will YOU still watch?

Since her eviction from the CBB house, Jade has apologised for her actions. In her interview with Davina after her eviction, she was shown a series of clips of herself arguing with Shilpa. She told Davina, 'I'm disgusted in myself for saying what I have just seen myself saying. I do not approve of any of my actions and I do not approve of the words that came out of my mouth.'

At the time of writing, Jade is in India trying to salvage her career. I don't know what she's doing in India – she offended British Asians, among others, and she did it in this country. Why go to India to apologise?

At least Endemol and the press are still paying attention to her. Jo O'Meara told the *News of the World* in March that she took a cocktail of whisky and prescription drugs in an attempt to kill herself after leaving the *Big Brother* House. She had found her career in tatters after the series, and herself depicted as an ally in the allegedly racist bullying. When Endemol later sent a psychologist to see her, she was told her that she should never have been sent into the House in the first place – she'd only had a ten-minute interview with a psychotherapist before she appeared on the show. Angrily, she told the *News of the World*, 'It's disgraceful that someone can slip through the net on a show that prides itself on its support for people's mental welfare . . .

Jo went on to talk about suffering 'eight panic attacks in one night . . . they see it as entertainment . . . they can tease and torment the contestants. Everything is manipulated in there, they know how to pull the strings, so you can do what they say without realising it.'

Kevin O'Sullivan comments, 'When *Big Brother 8* starts they have got to be seen to really demonstrably not be seen to wind the contestants up or manipulate them . . . The programme has been neutered ... they've had their balls chopped off basically.'

The continual games and the feeling of being manipulated while you are in the house is one of the more sinister sides to the *Big Brother* experience for housemates. My own main memory of *Big Brother* is of feeling starving hungry all the time, while other former contestants remember the games, the noises that Big Brother played to break them down – babies crying, people vomiting – or the way the room temperature rose and fell. At the time it feels like psychological torture.

Peter Bazalgette wrote an article for *Prospect* in which he argued that the way everything unfolded on *Celebrity Big Brother* 2007 was 'unplanned'. It is true that the producers couldn't have seen what was going to happen, but it is my opinion that the situation was manipulated, as are the circumstances in all series of *Big Brother*, and I believe that is the producers' responsibility.

By putting Jade and her mum, Jackiey, into the House together and making them lord it over all as 'masters of the House', then whisking Jackiey out of the diary room in a surprise eviction, it did seem to some viewers that the show's producers were hoping to create a volatile, sensational situation. The show's ratings were poor until the controversy kicked off, and some have suggested that this was part of the reason producers allowed the situation to go as far as it did

Jo has received the sympathy of many since leaving the show. The frenzy whipped up around her and the other girls was something that even the most experienced politicians might have had trouble with, and I do feel sorry for them. They are now casualties of the *Big Brother* experience. Getting a psychologist to phone former contestants who are experiencing problems and telling them to pull themselves together – as Amma and Sam say happened to them – is not 'providing adequate care'. This show may only be reality TV but it does have a real impact on real people's lives. The producers have a duty of care to the contestants, even when they are no longer their 'precious cargo'. In my opinion, if they cannot fulfil that duty – even after seven series of *Big Brother* and five of *Celebrity Big Brother* – then the show should be taken off the air before someone does take their own life. Kevin O'Sullivan agrees: 'As much as I didn't like all three of the girls in the house, I don't accept that "they got what they deserved" – is that what a TV programme has done? It's disgraceful that someone has gone on a TV programme and then tried to kill themself. No one seems to have noticed that.'

But you know what? I actually think that the events of *Celebrity Big Brother*, though disturbing, may have helped past, present and future *Big Brother* contestants, because maybe now, just maybe, the public and media will start to see the *real* effects appearing on the show can have on the *real* people who put themselves forward as contestants. The housemates are not just characters in a panto, as Davina always tells them when they are getting booed on eviction night. They are real and they do have feelings, even if they did 'ask for it' by appearing on the show in the first place. It's unlikely that people will stop saying, 'Oh, they should know what they are getting themselves in for,' or, 'It's only a game show,' but perhaps some of us will now be a bit more aware of just what *Big Brother* can give to – and take away from – contestants. *Celebrity Big Brother* 2007 has done something, as Gary Thompson told me: 'The Shilpa racism row has been a big watershed and it is going to change the way the papers report *Big Brother* from now on. We've had two people in rehab, the sponsor has pulled out, it has taught everyone that the people in *Big Brother* are real people and there are serious consequences if the show gets it wrong. The Shilpa row has certainly made the public more wise to the way things can be edited.'

When *Big Brother* first appeared on our screens in 1999 it was described as a social experiment, and many viewers tuned in to the first series for that reason – to see just what would happen when a group of complete strangers were thrown together and locked away from the rest of the world for several months. Initially at least, viewers weren't watching simply to get to know and laugh at the latest batch of 'wannabes'. As Mel has explained, in those days contestants grew some of their own food, and had no idea what to expect from the series. The

'Nasty Nick' controversy, and press reports of Mel's flirting and other events ensured the first series captured the public's attention. And so the tone began to sink . . . In later series the show became increasingly known for the instant fame it could give to housemates – and the daily dose of gossip it could provide to the public. The idea of 'social experiment' largely disappeared from descriptions of the programme, to be replaced by words more along the lines of 'freak show'. While the programme has undeniably been career-making for some former contestants, it has also been life-changing in a less positive way for others. The days of gladiators fighting to the death as a justifiable form of entertainment may be long gone but, as Kevin O'Sullivan has argued, in recent years there has been a distinct gladiatorial air to the way several *Big Brother* series have unfolded. Just where the line between acceptable entertainment and the abuse of vulnerable people for the amusement of others lies is a debatable point, especially when those people have voluntarily put themselves forward for the experience. The show's producers may be right when they argue that they try to select contestants who will be able to cope with the pressures both inside the house and outside when it's all over, but the question remains: what does it say about our society that we take such pleasure in watching a new group of strangers fight with, bitch at and bond with each other every summer? What does the pleasure we take in reading about their exploits after they leave the house say about us?

Most of us will probably admit we love a good gossip or bitch on the odd occasion, and we are all probably big enough to accept that at one point or another we will have been on the receiving end of bitchiness and gossip ourselves. It doesn't feel nice, but it's usually forgotten quickly enough. But what happens when it's the whole nation bitching and gossiping about you? When contestants enter the house with the express goal of becoming stars, glamour models or just plain rich, can we really argue that they have given proper thought to the type of treatment they are opening themselves up to, that they have really sat back and considered the negatives as well as the positives? Just look at Anthony, one of the housemates who has only positive things to say about his *Big Brother* experience. He was a *Big Brother* fan and it wasn't his intention to become a star. He enjoyed the ride, bought some real estate, and then got on with his life. Compare that to the negative, disturbing experiences of some arguably more fragile housemates who really just wanted to become famous.

We have all read the BIG BROTHER RUINED MY LIFE stories – some former housemates, like Lea, have even admitted they read but didn't believe those stories before entering the house. But the fact remains that season after season ex-housemates have complained about their experiences. And yet, season after season, members of the British public continue to volunteer – to go through a rigorous selection process, in fact – to appear on the programme, and season after season viewers tune in to watch. The show continues to carry the promise of fame and fortune (or at least infamy). The fact that it often delivers much less than expected is a bitter pill for many of us former housemates, but it is what it is. Ultimately *Big Brother* is a TV show. It cannot make housemates feel better about themselves, or give them skills or talents they do not already possess. It cannot guarantee that production companies will want to use them as presenters (I should know!), or that the public will be interested in hearing about them once the initial tell-all stories are published. It is always going to be a risk to expose yourself (both metaphorically and, in the case of some former contestants, literally) on national television.

Phil Edgar-Jones talked about *Big Brother* having a 'halo effect' – damn right it does. Shilpa became a star in this country after *Celebrity Big Brother*, the newspapers are thriving on the 'exclusives' and Endemol have a hit – all they need to ensure they're booked to do another series. Channel 4 makes millions. Great halo! It just seems a great pity that the halo couldn't extend to Emma, Amma, Jo, Makosi, Mel . . . need I go on? What happened to the halo there? It just didn't stretch all that far after all.

This book is for the people who the halo didn't reach. Yes, they chose to do it, and yes, some had good experiences and some bad, but it took courage to take part, to want to change their lives and to actually do something about it. The *Big Brother* housemates took their lives in their own hands, and while they may at times seem ridiculous, self-indulgent, even downright nasty, who are we to criticise them when we take such pleasure in watching it all unfold before our eyes? Many housemates have stumbled and yes, some have fallen hard, but somehow they have all still managed to make it through with what sometimes felt like no help, with none of the protection other TV stars get these days. They did it to a large extent alone, and maybe it didn't work out the way they planned, but that just makes them better, more interesting people to me. They truly are the gladiators of the modern world. The real stars. They went into that house with only a dream and were, perhaps foolishly, prepared to be slaughtered for that dream.

Whether they won or not is hardly the point, because like the old cliché says, it's the taking part that counts, having the guts to get up out of your armchair and try and live your dream. I hope this book has given them a voice.

THE HOUSEMATES INTERVIEWED FOR THIS BOOK

NADIA ALMADA, *Big Brother Five*

Originally from Portugal, Nadia had done stints as a children's bookshop manager, a bank cashier and working at a perfume counter in a department store before signing up to *Big Brother*. She was outed as a transsexual during the course of the series but it had no effect on her popularity – she won with 74 per cent of the public vote. Her single, 'A Little Bit of Action', went to number 27 in the UK charts and she has taken part in many more TV shows.

AMMA ANTWI, *Big Brother Two*

Amma worked as a table dancer before she mailed off her application form to *Big Brother* and found herself in the House. She didn't enjoy her time on the show and believed she hadn't been given a chance to show her best side. After a year or so of media appearances she now works for a casting agency in London.

BRIAN DOWLING, *Big Brother Two*

'The Most Popular *Big Brother* Housemate of All Time' started out as 'just an air steward'. He was the first and only gay winner of the show and went on to score another first: he was the first openly gay children's TV host, on SMTV Live. He's since paid his dues fronting several series and is a much-in-demand TV personality.

VICTOR EBUWA, *Big Brother Five*

Victor was studying politics when he got 'the call' and his dedication to his *Big Brother* 'game plan' made him a tabloid legend. He was second favourite to win until an argument with Shell Jubin cost him votes. He has appeared in various TV shows post-*Big Brother* and is now working in club promotions.

EMMA GREENWOOD, *Big Brother Five*

Emma left a job as an admin assistant to take her chance in *Big Brother*. She was removed from the House as a result of her involvement in the notorious 'Fight Night'. In the last three years she has featured on several TV shows and worked on her singing career.

SAMANTHA HEUSTON, *Big Brother Six*

Sam Heuston left her degree in marketing behind when she entered the *Big Brother* House. She experienced a typical example of media hypocrisy: on the one hand she was mocked for wearing a bikini in the House, and on the other, when she was evicted she was inundated with requests for photo spreads in men's magazines. She's now developing several Internet sites and has a cameo in *Clubbing to Death*, which will be released in 2007.

MELANIE HILL, *Big Brother One*

A contestant in the very first series, Melanie couldn't have known that she would become a tabloid whipping girl after it was decreed that she was a 'flirt'. When the media interest died down a little she tried her hand both as a TV presenter and as a travel writer for *Marie Claire*. She is now studying law.

ANTHONY HUTTON, *Big Brother Six*

Big Brother's biggest fan saw his dream come true when he won the sixth series and relished his fifteen minutes of fame, appearing on numerous TV and radio programmes, posing for magazine photo shoots and hitting the nightclub promotions circuit. He's now returned to his career as a 70s dancer with a nice little nest egg.

KINGA KAROLCZAK, *Big Brother Six*

With a Polish mother and a Kuwaiti father, Kinga was a market researcher with an eye on a career in the music business. She gained notoriety in the House for the infamous 'bottle' incident and has since been riding out the tabloid storm. She continues to pour her passion and energy into her first love, singing.

DEREK LAUD, *Big Brother Six*

A political lobbyist, Master of Fox Hounds, speechwriter and businessman who has worked for two prime ministers, Derek was a popular and controversial member of the House. He has recently said that he would like to stand at the next General Election, and is being mooted as a candidate for Mayor of London.

KATE LAWLER, *Big Brother Three*

For IT helpdesk worker Kate, *Big Brother* was the springboard to an international career as a DJ, TV presenter, model and radio personality. She was the first woman to win the show and has remained a popular figure in the public eye.

MAKOSI MUSAMBASI, *Big Brother Six*

Makosi moved to the UK from Zimbabwe to work as a cardiac nurse, a job she left in order to appear on *Big Brother*. She was the last woman to leave the House, finishing third, and Ofcom received over 450 complaints about her treatment by Davina McCall in her eviction interview. She has appeared in numerous other television shows and has just made her film debut in *Cash and Curry* (2007).

RICHARD NEWMAN, *Big Brother Seven*

Richard was born in London but spent most of his childhood and teenage years in Canada before moving back to the UK, where he was working as a waiter prior to *Big Brother*. He was the 'dad' of the series seven House, intervening in arguments and lending a sympathetic ear. He now works as an on-line journalist and as a DJ for Gaydar Radio.

SOPHIE PRITCHARD, *Big Brother Three*

Sophie swapped work in a recruitment agency for life as a housemate, replacing Sunita Sharma who left after a week. She struck up a romance with fellow contestant Lee Davey and they married and had a child, although they parted ways in 2006.

SISSY (JOANNE) ROONEY, *Big Brother Four*

Having graduated with a degree in fashion, Sissy joined the House for series four. She has since launched her own label, Sissy's Surgery, and is establishing a not-for-profit social enterprise that works with schools, youth clubs and young offenders' institutions to create designs and choreograph fashion shows.

ALEX SIBLEY, *Big Brother Three*

Former male model Alex unwittingly earned himself an advertising campaign for Domestos cleaning products because he spent so much time doing housework during the series. Five years after his eviction, he has now left showbiz in all forms to work in his father's business.

EUGENE SULLY, *Big Brother Six*

Prior to *Big Brother*, Eugene worked as a Spectrum Planning Engineer in the BBC Research and Development department.

He came second in 2005, scooping half the prize money, and has since carved out a career both as a presenter on TV and radio and behind-the-scenes at BBC Scotland.

LEA WALKER, *Big Brother Seven*

Although the show claims to pick a broad range of contestants it wasn't until series seven that it featured someone who was a mother – Lea. She hoped that appearing on the show would boost her career as a model and lead to a better life for herself and her son. She had already featured in several documentaries and chat shows talking about plastic surgery. She's now working as a digital radio DJ with Richard Newman.

ACKNOWLEDGEMENTS

My biggest thanks go to all of the former *Big Brother* housemates who agreed to be interviewed for this book. Without you it just wouldn't have happened – sorry for stalking you all! Thanks to (in order of *Big Brother* series): Melanie, Brian, Amma, Sophie, Alex, Kate, Sissy, Victor, Nadia, Emma, Derek, Eugene, Sam, Makosi, Kinga, Anthony, Richard, and Lea.

A huge thanks also to Ed Faulkner at Virgin Books for taking on my book. In light of recent *Celebrity Big Brother* events you showed you certainly had your finger on the pulse before its time. Thanks for giving me the chance to prove myself – I'm eternally grateful.

Amanda Stocks – you would have to be the greatest agent in the world. You took me on when no one else would, believed in me and made something out of me. That's an agent, not one that has an easy ride with someone who is already successful! Thank you always. Here's to the future.

Diane Banks – thank you for taking my book and believing in it, and for your hard work and professionalism.

Susanna Forrest, for taking my mish mash of words and actually making them into a book! Thanks so much for all your hard work and kindness.

My family. My husband Jatinder – the day you were born was the luckiest day of my life. My baby boy Jeevan, my life – 'I love you too many days' (you know what I'm saying).

My blood family – my brothers and my sister – for never stopping my dreams and putting up with me. I can never repay any of you, ever.

Suk – my brother-in-law, for all the support and for never being judgemental.

My best mate Brian – thank you for saving my marriage before the book, during the book and no doubt in the future. I am the luckiest girl ever to have you as my best mate. We have been through so much – God knows why you put up with me, not forgetting listen to all my BB contestants' stories! Jat and I love you. Thank you for letting me write about you (although, it did kill me to have to write nice things about you!).

HEAT magazine – for all the bad and good stuff. You made me want to never give up. And thanks to Mark, Hannah and Boyd for interviews, and to Dan for all the photos.

Phil Edgar-Jones – for giving me an interview, and showing me that Endemol did care enough to meet me. And a big thank you to Emma Lewis – she was fantastic!

Gary Thompson – gis a job? Thank you.

Big thanks to Kevin O'Sullivan – your interview was music to my ears.

Sharon Marshall – massive thanks for you time.

Rachel Morris – thank you for a great interview. I wish I was as intelligent as you!

Special thanks to all at Virgin for your patience and all round general niceness! What a pleasant surprise to be working for 'nice' people!

Davina Russell – many thanks for helping put it all together at the last minute – phew!

Jane Wood – my neighbour, my friend. Thank God for you and James! For the nappies, the favours, the advice, the help (Boxing Day), I could go on and on . . . You and James are the best neighbours ever. And Libby is far too good for skinny Jeevan!

Big thanks to Frankie (Rehwald) for bringing friendship into my life and never giving up on me. Thank you for all your help, and for actually reading my manuscript.

Nick Ede – for sticking by me and always giving great advice.

Nikki de Metz – you taught me a lot about myself, how to carry myself, good manners, and the art of discretion.

ATul – for being so happy for me when I got a book deal and happy that finally people thought I was clever!! Haha. We don't see enough of each other.

Stuart Hosking – although you didn't do my book! I will never forgive you for that! However, you have been such a good mate for listening to all my whinging! And a massive thanks to your girlfriend – Jo Jordan – my very own Supernanny! I swear Jo, if you hadn't come round that night and sorted out Jeevan's routine this book would NEVER have been written. Thank you both, too too much.

Marco Sabba – for listening to me and laughing with me over the past year, despite your own personal tragedy. I'll always be here for you, and don't forget we'll always have 'Nosh'.

My oldest friend in the world, Fiona Clarke. You reminded me that I loved writing as a kid and encouraged to put pen to paper. You have never minded me, despite everything, and I love you for that.

Rob Tavernier: for all your help, advice, and laughter.

Thanks to Simon and Kris at Hackford Jones.

Christina at braindowling.biz. Thanks so much.

To Amanda Palmer, thanks for all your help.

Joe at the best BB website – bigbrotherwebsite.net

Evening Chronicle – thank you for all your support over the years.

I mustn't forget *ASIANA* magazine – for being the only Asian media that has supported me and for using airbrushing so effectively! Thanks to Shabbs and Poorna.

Finally, thanks to all the BB fans. Never mind editing, press and Endemol – when the chips were down you stood by all the BB contestants through thick and thin. You made the whole ride worthwhile.

INDEX